CHRISTMAS GHOSTS

J.P. DAVIS-SPEER

CHRISTMAS GHOSTS

EDITED BY

KATHRYN CRAMER & DAVID G. HARTWELL

ARBOR HOUSE

NEW YORK

 Published in the United States
of America by Arbor House Publishing Company and in Canada by
Fitzhenry & Whiteside, Ltd.

Designed by Robert Bull Design

Manufactured in the United States of America

10 9 8 7 6 5 4 3 2 1

Library of Congress Cataloging in Publication Data

Christmas ghosts.

1. Christmas stories, English. 2. Christmas stories,
American. 3. Ghost stories, English. 4. Ghost stories,
American. I. Cramer, Kathryn, 1962– . II. Hartwell,
David G.

PR1309.C5C48 1987 823'.01'0833 87-11355
ISBN 0-87795-873-4

PERMISSIONS

"Christmas Night" by Elizabeth Walter. Copyright © 1975 by Elizabeth Walter. Reprinted by permission of the author.

"A New Christmas Carol" by Arthur Machen. Copyright © 1924 by the estate of Arthur Machen. Reprinted by permission of A. M. Heath.

"A Christmas Game" by A.N.L. Munby. Copyright © 1950 by Dobson Books Ltd. First published in *The Alabaster Hand and Other Stories* by A.N.L. Munby. Reprinted by permission of Dobson Books Ltd.

"A Christmas Meeting" by Rosemary Timperly. Copyright © 1952 by Rosemary Timperly. Reprinted by permission of the author.

"Christmas Reunion" by Sir Andrew Caldecott. Copyright © 1947 by Edward Arnold and Company. [Publisher and editors seek copyright claimants to compensate them for use of this story.]

"The Crown Derby Plate" by Marjorie Bowen. Copyright © 1952 by Hilary Long. Reprinted by permission of Hilary Long.

"Calling Card" by Ramsey Campbell. Copyright © 1981 by Ramsey Campbell. Reprinted by permission of the author's agent.

ACKNOWLEDGMENTS

The editors are grateful for the assistance of all the people who contributed suggestions or other aid in the compilation of this anthology, especially including:

L. W. Currey
Jo Fletcher
Ramsey Campbell
Peter D. Pautz
Jack Sullivan
Jessica Amanda Salmonson

TO

Laurence B. Hughes, whose good idea this was,

AND TO

John Jr., Pauline, Karen, and John III, the Cramer family

Patricia, Alison, and Geoffrey, the Hartwell family

TABLE OF CONTENTS

CONTENTS

INTRODUCTION

THE SPIRITS OF CHRISTMAS

WHAT a wonderful idea, we thought, to present an anthology of Christmas ghost stories, by which we mean ghost stories that take place at Christmas, just like, you know, "A Christmas Carol." Christmas and ghosts form a ready association in the minds of contemporary readers through the agency of Charles Dickens's great work, but other stories of Christmas ghosts are not so repeatedly put forward year after year for our Christmas delight.

In fact, other examples of the Christmas ghost story tradition do not spring readily to mind, although one of the things that everyone knows about Christmas is that there is such a tradition. What has happened to Christmas ghosts?

A bit of research has revealed two interesting facts about

Christmas ghosts. First, that the figure of Charles Dickens looms largest and most central, and second, that the tradition is *not,* historically, centered on Christmas but rather on ghosts.

Not only did Dickens write a number of enormously popular Christmas ghost stories in his day (of which "The Chimes" was at the time even more popular than "A Christmas Carol"), he also, as editor of *Household Words,* published a number of Christmas issues of his periodical featuring ghost stories by his contemporaries, thus giving great support and wider popular distribution to the tradition of telling stories of ghosts during the Christmas season (which tradition extended at least into the century before Dickens). So Dickens was the key figure in developing and focusing the tradition for his age, and ours.

Only a very few of the huge number of ghost stories associated with Christmas published in the last 150 years actually take place during the Christmas season; most, even when published in Christmas issues, are set at any and every time of year, with, perhaps, a one-line mention of Christmas somewhere in the text. For more than a hundred years, some of the finest ghost stories have been, originally, tales told at Christmas, but not tales *of* Christmas. And this is the real and enduring Christmas Ghost tradition, a tradition that has fallen into substantial decline in recent decades consequent to the decline of popular fiction periodicals.

So, to fulfill our purpose and present a collection of stories from the Christmas ghost tradition which are *about* Christmas ghosts, we read through many anthologies and collections looking for Christmas stories. In the end we found, embedded in the tradition, a number of fine works, from humor to horror (and occasionally both), that represent the Christmas spirit, in all its varied forms and humors. We were aided by expert acquaintances, in particular Jessica Amanda Salmonson, whose antiquarian researches yielded a number of suggestions, and Peter D. Pautz, whose contemporary reading experience was a valuable help. And we give a special bow to Everett F. Bleiler's wonderful *Guide to Supernatural Literature.*

Here are big ghosts and dear little ghosts, ghosts of love and ghosts of hatred, ghosts moral and amoral, all at Christmas. We have avoided the familiar Dickens in favor of two somewhat shorter pieces, one from earlier and one from later in his career, and included as our longest selection what might be considered the Yankee version of the Dickens classic: William D. O'Conner's "The Ghost." We have mixed, in full measure, English and American stories, for the tradition has been vigorous in both countries, from Dickens's time to the present, seventeen stories spanning fifteen decades. We have chosen pieces whose energy and freshness (many of the stories have never been reprinted in modern times), regardless of age and style, will stimulate and entertain the contemporary reader, especially at Christmas.

These days, we have fallen out of the habit of reading aloud to the family except, perhaps, to the children, and, of course, on the night before Christmas. For a hundred years or more, families did gather to hear ghost stories told and read, for Christmas is a time of mystery, of the supernatural. Perhaps you might attempt a reading during this Christmas season, of one of the works from this collection; for the power of Christmas spirits to reawaken sensitivities deadened by daily life is not lost, we believe, in our generation.

DAVID G. HARTWELL

CHRISTMAS
GHOSTS

ELIA WILKINSON PEATTIE

THEIR DEAR LITTLE GHOST

A good child comes home for Christmas.

THE first time one looked at Elsbeth, one was not prepossessed. She was thin and brown, her nose turned slightly upward, her toes went in just a perceptible degree, and her hair was perfectly straight. But when one looked longer, one perceived that she was a charming little creature. The straight hair was as fine as silk, and hung in funny little braids down her back; there was not a flaw in her soft brown skin; and her mouth was tender and shapely. But her particular charm lay in a look which she habitually had, of seeming to know curious things—such as it is not allotted to ordinary persons to know. One felt tempted to say to her:

"What are these beautiful things which you know, and of

which others are ignorant? What is it you see with those wise and pellucid eyes? Why is it that everybody loves you?"

Elsbeth was my little godchild, and I knew her better than I knew any other child in the world. But still I could not truthfully say that I was familiar with her, for to me her spirit was like a fair and fragrant road in the midst of which I might walk in peace and joy, but where I was continually to discover something new. The last time I saw her quite well and strong was over in the woods where she had gone with her two little brothers and her nurse to pass the hottest weeks of summer. I followed her, foolish old creature that I was, just to be near her, for I needed to dwell where the sweet aroma of her life could reach me.

One morning when I came from my room, limping a little, because I am not so young as I used to be, and the lake wind works havoc with me, my little godchild came dancing to me singing:

"Come with me and I'll show you my places, my places, my places!"

Miriam, when she chanted by the Red Sea might have been more exultant, but she could not have been more bewitching. Of course I knew what "places" were, because I had once been a little girl myself, but unless you are acquainted with the real meaning of "places," it would be useless to try to explain. Either you know "places" or you do not—just as you understand the meaning of poetry or you do not. There are things in the world which cannot be taught.

Elsbeth's two tiny brothers were present, and I took one by each hand and followed her. No sooner had we got out of doors in the woods than a sort of mystery fell upon the world and upon us. We were cautioned to move silently; and we did so, avoiding the crunching of dry twigs.

"The fairies hate noise," whispered my little godchild, her eyes narrowing like a cat's.

"I must get my wand first thing I do," she said in an awed undertone. "It is useless to try to do anything without a wand."

The tiny boys were profoundly impressed, and, indeed, so

was I. I felt that at last, I should, if I behaved properly, see the fairies, which had hitherto avoided my materialistic gaze. It was an enchanting moment, for there appeared, just then, to be nothing commonplace about life.

There was a swale near by, and into this the little girl plunged. I could see her red straw hat bobbing about among the tall rushes, and I wondered if there were snakes.

"Do you think there are snakes?" I asked one of the tiny boys.

"If there are," he said with conviction, "they won't dare hurt her."

He convinced me. I feared no more. Presently Elsbeth came out of the swale. In her hand was a brown "cattail," perfectly full and round. She carried it as queens carry their scepters—the beautiful queens we dream of in our youth.

"Come," she commanded, and waved the scepter in a fine manner. So we followed, each tiny boy gripping my hand tight. We were all three a trifle awed. Elsbeth led us into a dark underbrush. The branches, as they flew back in our faces, left them wet with dew. A wee path, made by the girl's dear feet, guided our footsteps. Perfumes of elderberry and wild cucumber scented the air. A bird, frightened from its nest, made frantic cries above our heads. The underbrush thickened. Presently the gloom of the hemlocks was over us, and in the midst of the shadowy green a tulip tree flaunted its leaves. Waves boomed and broke upon the shore below. There was a growing dampness as we went on, treading very lightly. A little green snake ran coquettishly from us. A fat and glossy squirrel chattered at us from a safe height, stroking his whiskers with a complaisant air.

At length we reached the "place." It was a circle of velvet grass, bright as the first blades of spring, delicate as fine sea-ferns. The sunlight, falling down the shaft between the hemlocks, flooded it with a softened light and made the forest round about look like deep purple velvet. My little godchild stood in the midst and raised her wand impressively.

"This is my place," she said, with a sort of wonderful gladness in her tone. "This is where I come to the fairy balls. Do you see them?"

"See what?" whispered one tiny boy.

"The fairies."

There was a silence. The older boy pulled at my skirt.

"Do *you* see them?" he asked, his voice trembling with expectancy.

"Indeed," I said, "I fear I am too old and wicked to see fairies, and yet—are their hats red?"

"They are," laughed my little girl. "Their hats are red, and as small—as small!" She held up the pearly nail of her wee finger to give us the correct idea.

"And their shoes are very pointed at the toes?"

"Oh, very pointed!"

"And their garments are green?"

"As green as grass."

"And they blow little horns?"

"The sweetest little horns!"

"I think I see them," I cried.

"We think we see them too," said the tiny boys, laughing in perfect glee.

"And you hear their horns, don't you?" my little godchild asked somewhat anxiously.

"Don't we hear their horns?" I asked the tiny boys.

"We think we hear their horns," they cried. "Don't you think we do?"

"It must be we do," I said. "Aren't we very, very happy?"

We all laughed softly. Then we kissed each other and Elsbeth led us out, her wand high in the air.

And so my feet found the lost path to Arcady.

The next day I was called to the Pacific coast, and duty kept me there till well into December. A few days before the date set for my return to my home, a letter came from Elsbeth's mother.

"Our little girl is gone into the Unknown," she wrote—"that Unknown in which she seemed to be forever trying to pry. We knew she was going, and we told her. She was quite brave, but she begged us to try some way to keep her till after Christmas. 'My presents are not finished yet,' she made moan. 'And I did so want to see what I was going to have. You can't have a very happy Christmas without me, I should think. Can you arrange to keep me somehow till after then?' We could not 'arrange' either with God in heaven or science upon earth, and she is gone."

She was only my little godchild, and I am an old maid, with no business fretting over children, but it seemed as if the medium of light and beauty had been taken from me. Through this crystal soul I had perceived whatever was loveliest. However, what was, was! I returned to my home and took up a course of Egyptian history, and determined to concern myself with nothing this side the Ptolemies.

Her mother has told me how, on Christmas eve, as usual, she and Elsbeth's father filled the stockings of the little ones, and hung them, where they had always hung, by the fireplace. They had little heart for the task, but they had been prodigal that year in their expenditures, and had heaped upon the two tiny boys all the treasures they thought would appeal to them. They asked themselves how they could have been so insane previously as to exercise economy at Christmas time, and what they meant by not getting Elsbeth the autoharp she had asked for the year before.

"And now—" began her father, thinking of harps. But he could not complete this sentence, of course, and the two went on passionately and almost angrily with their task. There were two stockings and two piles of toys. Two stockings only, and only two piles of toys! Two is very little!

They went away and left the darkened room, and after a time they slept—after a long time. Perhaps that was about the time the tiny boys awoke, and, putting on their little dressing gowns and bed slippers, made a dash for the room where the Christmas things were always placed. The older one carried a candle which gave out a feeble light. The other followed behind through the silent house. They were very impatient and eager, but when they reached the door of the sitting room they stopped, for they saw that another child was before them.

It was a delicate little creature, sitting in her white night gown, with two rumpled funny braids falling down her back, and she seemed to be weeping. As they watched, she arose, and putting out one slender finger as a child does when she counts, she made sure over and over again—three sad times—that there were only two stockings and two piles of toys! Only those and no more.

The little figure looked so familiar that the boys started toward it, but just then, putting up her arm and bowing her face in it, as Elsbeth had been used to do when she wept or was offended, the little thing glided away and went out. That's what the boys said. It went out as a candle goes out.

They ran and woke their parents with the tale, and all the house was searched in a wonderment, and disbelief, and hope, and tumult! But nothing was found. For nights they watched. But there was only the silent house. Only the empty rooms. They told the boys they must have been mistaken. But the boys shook their heads.

"We know our Elsbeth," said they. "It was our Elsbeth, cryin' 'cause she hadn't no stockin' an' no toys, and we would have given her all ours, only she went out—jus' went out!"

Alack!

The next Christmas I helped with the little festival. It was none of my affair, but I asked to help, and they let me, and when we were all through there were three stockings and three piles of toys, and in the largest one was all the things that I could think of that my dear child would love. I locked the boys' chamber that night, and I slept on the divan in the parlor off the sitting room. I slept but little, and the night was very still—so windless and white and still that I think I must have heard the slightest noise. Yet I heard none. Had I been in my grave I think my ears would not have remained more unsaluted.

Yet when daylight came and I went to unlock the boys' bedchamber door, I saw that the stocking and all the treasures which I had bought for my little godchild were gone. There was not a vestige of them remaining!

Of course we told the boys nothing. As for me, after dinner I went home and buried myself once more in my history, and so interested was I that midnight came without my knowing it. I should not have looked up at all, I suppose, to become aware of the time, had it not been for a faint, sweet sound as of a child striking a stringed instrument. It was so delicate and remote that I hardly heard it, but so joyous and tender that I could not but listen, and when I heard it a second time it seemed as if I caught the echo of a child's laugh. At first I was puzzled. Then I remembered the little autoharp I had placed among the other things in that pile of vanished toys. I said aloud:

"Farewell, dear little ghost. Go rest. Rest in joy, dear little ghost. Farewell, farewell."

That was years ago, but there has been silence since. Elsbeth was always an obedient little thing.

F. Anstey

The Curse of the Catafalques

A cad woos an heiress, but must face a Christmas demon to win her.

Chapter I

Unless I am very much mistaken, until the time when I was subjected to the strange and exceptional experience which I now propose to relate, I had never been brought into close contact with anything of a supernatural description. At least if I ever was, the circumstance can have made no lasting impression upon me, as I am quite unable to recall it. But in the "Curse of the Catafalques" I was confronted with a horror so weird and so altogether unusual, that I doubt whether I shall ever succeed in wholly forgetting it—and I know that I have never felt really well since.

It is difficult for me to tell my story intelligibly without some account of my previous history by way of introduction, although I will try to make it as little diffuse as I may.

I had not been a success at home; I was an orphan, and, in my anxiety to please a wealthy uncle upon whom I was practically dependent, I had consented to submit myself to a series of competitive examinations for quite a variety of professions, but in each successive instance I achieved the same disheartening failure. Some explanation of this may, no doubt, be found in the fact that, with a fatal want of forethought, I had entirely omitted to prepare myself by any particular course of study—which, as I discovered too late, is almost indispensable to success in these intellectual contests.

My uncle himself took this view, and conceiving—not without discernment—that I was by no means likely to retrieve myself by any severe degree of application in the future, he had me shipped out to Australia, where he had correspondents and friends who would put things in my way.

They did put several things in my way—and, as might have been expected, I came to grief over every one of them, until at length, having given a fair trial to each opening that had been provided for me, I began to perceive that my uncle had made a grave mistake in believing me suited for a colonial career.

I resolved to return home and convince him of his error, and give him one more opportunity of repairing it; he had failed to discover the best means of utilizing my undoubted ability, yet I would not reproach him (nor do I reproach him even now), for I too have felt the difficulty.

In pursuance of my resolution, I booked my passage home by one of the Orient liners from Melbourne to London. About an hour before the ship was to leave her moorings, I went on board and made my way at once to the stateroom which I was to share with a fellow passenger, whose acquaintance I then made for the first time.

He was a tall cadaverous young man of about my own age, and my first view of him was not encouraging, for when I came in, I found him rolling restlessly on the cabin floor, and uttering hollow groans.

"This will never do," I said, after I had introduced myself; "if you're like this now, my good sir, what will you be when we're fairly out at sea? You must husband your resources for that. And why trouble to roll? The ship will do all that for you, if you will only have patience."

He explained, somewhat brusquely, that he was suffering from mental agony, not seasickness; and by a little pertinacious questioning (for I would not allow myself to be rebuffed) I was soon in possession of the secret which was troubling my companion, whose name, as I also learned, was Augustus McFadden.

It seemed that his parents had emigrated before his birth, and he had lived all his life in the Colony, where he was contented and fairly prosperous—when an eccentric old aunt of his over in England happened to die.

She left McFadden himself nothing, having given by her will the bulk of her property to the only daughter of a baronet of ancient family, in whom she took a strong interest. But the will was not without its effect upon her existence, for it expressly mentioned the desire of the testatrix that the baronet should receive her nephew Augustus if he presented himself within a certain time, and should afford him every facility for proving his fitness for acceptance as a suitor. The alliance was merely recommended, however, not enjoined, and the gift was unfettered by any conditions.

"I heard of it first," said McFadden, "from Chlorine's father (Chlorine is *her* name, you know). Sir Paul Catafalque wrote to me, informing me of the mention of my name in my aunt's will, enclosing his daughter's photograph, and formally inviting me to come over and do my best, if my affections were not pre-engaged, to carry out the last wishes of the departed. He added that I might expect to receive shortly a packet from my aunt's executors which would explain matters fully, and in which I should find certain directions for my guidance. The photograph decided me; it was so eminently pleasing that I felt at once that my poor aunt's wishes must be sacred to me. I could not wait for the packet to arrive, and so I wrote at once to Sir Paul accepting the invitation. Yes," he added, with another of the hollow groans, "miserable wretch that I am, I pledged my honor to present myself as a suitor, and now—now—here I am, actually embarked upon the desperate errand!"

He seemed inclined to begin to roll again here, but I stopped him. "Really," I said, "I think in your place, with an excellent chance—for I presume the lady's heart is also disengaged—with an excellent chance of winning a baronet's daughter with a considerable fortune and a pleasing appearance, I should bear up better."

"You think so," he rejoined, "but you do not know all! The very day after I had despatched my fatal letter, my aunt's explanatory packet arrived. I tell you that when I read the hideous revelations it contained, and knew to what horrors I had innocently pledged myself, my hair stood on end, and I believe it has remained on end ever since. But it was too late. Here I am, engaged to carry out a task from which my inmost soul recoils. Ah, if I dared but retract!"

"Then why in the name of common sense, *don't* you retract?" I asked. "Write and say that you much regret that a previous engagement, which you had unfortunately overlooked, deprives you of the pleasure of accepting."

"Impossible," he said; "it would be agony to me to feel that I had incurred Chlorine's contempt, even though I only know her through a photograph at present. If I were to back out of it now, she would have reason to despise me, would she not?"

"Perhaps she would," I said.

"You see my dilemma—I cannot retract; on the other hand, I dare not go on. The only thing, as I have thought lately, which could save me and my honor at the same time would be my death on the voyage out, for then my cowardice would remain undiscovered."

"Well," I said, "you can die on the voyage out if you want to—there need be no difficulty about that. All you have to do is just to slip over the side some dark night when no one is looking. I tell you what," I added (for somehow I began to feel a friendly interest in this poor slack-baked creature): "if you don't find your nerves equal to it when it comes to the point, I don't mind giving you a leg over myself."

"I never intended to go as far as that," he said, rather pettishly, and without any sign of gratitude for my offer; "I don't care about actually dying, if she could only be made to believe I had died that would be quite enough for me. I could live on here, happy in the thought that I was saved from her scorn. But how can she be made to believe it?—that's the point."

"Precisely," I said. "You can hardly write yourself and inform her that you died on the voyage. You might do this, though: sail to England as you propose, and go to see her under another name, and break the sad intelligence to her."

"Why, to be sure, I might do that!" he said, with some animation; "I should certainly not be recognized—she can have no photograph of me, for I have never been photographed. And yet—no," he added, with a shudder, "it is useless. I can't do it; I dare not trust myself under that roof! I must find some other way. You have given me an idea. Listen," he said, after a short pause: "you seem to take an interest in me; you are going to London; the Catafalques live there, or near it, at some place called Parson's Green. Can I ask a great favor of you—would you very much mind seeking them out yourself as a fellow-voyager of mine? I could not expect you to tell a positive untruth on my account—but if, in the course of an interview with Chlorine, you *could* contrive to convey the impression that I died on my way to her side, you would be doing me a service I can never repay!"

"I should very much prefer to do you a service that you *could* repay," was my very natural rejoinder.

"She will not require strict proof," he continued eagerly; "I could give you enough papers and things to convince her that you come from me. Say you will do me this kindness!"

I hesitated for some time longer, not so much, perhaps, from scruples of a conscientious kind as from a disinclination to undertake a troublesome commission for an entire stranger—gratuitously. But McFadden pressed me hard, and at length he made an appeal to springs in my nature which are never touched in vain, and I yielded.

When we had settled the question in its financial aspect, I said to McFadden, "The only thing now is—how would you prefer to pass away? Shall I make you fall over and be devoured by a shark? That would be a picturesque end—and I could do myself justice over the shark? I should make the young lady weep considerably."

"That won't do at all!" he said irritably; "I can see from her face that Chlorine is a girl of a delicate sensibility, and would be disgusted by the idea of any suitor of hers spending his last cohesive moments inside such a beastly repulsive thing as a shark. I don't want to be associated in her mind with anything so unpleasant. No, sir; I will die—if you will oblige me by remembering it—of a low fever, of a noninfectious type, at sunset, gazing at her portrait with my fading eyesight and gasping her name with my last breath. She will cry more over that!"

"I might work it up into something effective, certainly," I admitted; "and, by the way, if you are going to expire in my stateroom, I ought to know a little more about you than I do. There is time still before the tender goes; you might do worse than spend it in coaching me in your life's history."

He gave me a few leading facts, and supplied me with several documents for study on the voyage; he even abandoned to me the whole of his traveling arrangements, which proved far more complete and serviceable than my own.

And then the "All-ashore" bell rang, and McFadden, as he bade me farewell, took from his pocket a bulky packet. "You have saved me," he said. "Now I can banish every recollection of this miserable episode. I need no longer preserve my poor aunt's directions; let them go, then."

Before I could say anything, he had fastened something

heavy to the parcel and dropped it through the cabin-light into the sea, after which he went ashore, and I have never seen nor heard of him since.

During the voyage I had leisure to think seriously over the affair, and the more I thought of the task I had undertaken, the less I liked it.

No man with the instincts of a gentleman can feel any satisfaction at finding himself on the way to harrow up a poor young lady's feelings by a perfectly fictitious account of the death of a poor-spirited suitor who could selfishly save his reputation at her expense.

And so strong was my feeling about this from the very first, that I doubt whether, if McFadden's terms had been a shade less liberal, I could ever have brought myself to consent.

But it struck me that, under judiciously sympathetic treatment, the lady might prove not inconsolable, and that I myself might be able to heal the wound I was about to inflict.

I found a subtle pleasure in the thought of this, for, unless McFadden had misinformed me, Chlorine's fortune was considerable, and did not depend upon any marriage she might or might not make. On the other hand, *I* was penniless, and it seemed to me only too likely that her parents might seek to found some objection to me on that ground.

I studied the photograph McFadden had left with me; it was that of a pensive but distinctly pretty face, with an absence of firmness in it that betrayed a plastic nature. I felt certain that if I only had the recommendation, as McFadden had, of an aunt's dying wishes, it would not take me long to effect a complete conquest.

And then, as naturally as possible, came the thought—why should not I procure myself the advantages of this recommendation? Nothing could be easier; I had merely to present myself as Augustus McFadden, who was hitherto a mere name to them; the information I already possessed as to his past life would enable me to support the character, and as it seemed that the baronet lived in great seclusion, I could easily contrive to keep out of the way of the few friends and relations I had in London until my position was secure.

What harm would this innocent deception do to anyone? McFadden, even if he ever knew, would have no right to complain—he had given up all pretentions himself—and if he was merely anxious to preserve his reputation, his wishes would be more than carried out, for I flattered myself that whatever ideal Chlorine might have formed of her destined suitor, I should come much nearer to it than poor McFadden could ever have done. No, he would gain, positively gain, by my assumption. He could not have counted upon arousing more than a mild regret as it was; *now* he would be fondly, it might be madly, loved. By proxy, it is true, but that was far more than he deserved.

Chlorine was not injured—far from it; she would have a suitor to welcome, not weep over, and his mere surname could make no possible difference to her. And lastly, it was a distinct benefit to *me,* for with a new name and an excellent reputation success would be an absolute certainty. What wonder, then, that the scheme, which opened out a far more manly and honorable means of obtaining a livelihood than any I had previously contemplated, should have grown more attractively feasible each day, until I resolved at last to carry it out? Let rigid moralists blame me if they will; I have never pretended to be better than the average run of mankind (though I am certainly no worse), and no one who really knows what human nature is will reproach me very keenly for obeying what was almost an instinct. And I may say this, that if ever an unfortunate man was bitterly punished for a fraud which was harmless, if not actually pious, by a visitation of intense and protracted terror, that person was I!

Chapter II

After arriving in England, and before presenting myself at Parson's Green in my assumed character, I took one precaution against any danger there might be of my throwing away my liberty in a fit of youthful impulsiveness. I went to Somerset House, and carefully examined the probate copy of the late Miss Petronia McFadden's last will and testament.

Nothing could have been more satisfactory; a sum of between forty and fifty thousand pounds was Chlorine's unconditionally, just as McFadden had said. I searched, but could find nothing in the will whatever to prevent her property, under the then existing state of the law, from passing under the entire control of a future husband.

After this, then, I could no longer restrain my ardor, and so, one foggy afternoon about the middle of December, I found myself driving towards the house in which I reckoned upon achieving a comfortable independence.

Parson's Green was reached at last; a small triangular open space bordered on two of its sides by mean and modern erections, but on the third by some ancient mansions, gloomy and neglected-looking indeed, but with traces on them still of their former consequence.

My cab stopped before the gloomiest of them all—a square grim house with dull and small-paned windows, flanked by two narrow and projecting wings, and built of dingy brick, faced with yellow-stone. Some old scrollwork railings, with a corroded frame in the middle for a long departed oil lamp, separated the house from the road; inside was a semicircular patch of rank grass, and a damp gravel sweep led from the heavy gate to a square portico supported by two wasted black wooden pillars.

As I stood there, after pulling the pear-shaped bell-handle, and heard the bell tinkling and jangling fretfully within, and as I glanced up at the dull housefront looming cheerless out of the fog-laden December twilight, I felt my confidence beginning to abandon me for the first time, and I really was almost inclined to give the whole thing up and run away.

Before I could make up my mind, a mouldy and melancholy butler had come slowly down the sweep and opened the gate—and my opportunity had fled. Later I remembered how, as I walked along the gravel, a wild and wailing scream pierced the heavy silence—it seemed at once a lamentation and a warning. But as the District Railway was quite near, I did not attach any particular importance to the sound at the time.

I followed the butler through a dank and chilly hall, where an antique lamp hung glimmering feebly through its panes of dusty stained glass, up a broad carved staircase, and along some tortuous paneled passages, until at length I was ushered into a long and rather low reception room, scantily furnished with the tarnished mirrors and spindle-legged brocaded furniture of a bygone century.

A tall and meager old man, with a long white beard, and haggard, sunken black eyes, was seated at one side of the high chimney-piece, while opposite him sat a little limp old lady with a nervous expression, and dressed in trailing black robes relieved by a little yellow lace about the head and throat. As I saw them, I recognized at once that I was in the presence of Sir Paul Catafalque and his wife.

They both rose slowly, and advanced arm-in-arm in their old-fashioned way, and met me with a stately solemnity. "You are indeed welcome," they said in faint hollow voices. "We thank you for this proof of your chivalry and devotion. It cannot be but that such courage and such self-sacrifice will meet with their reward!"

And although I did not quite understand how they could have discerned, as yet, that I was chivalrous and devoted, I was too glad to have made a good impression to do anything but beg them not to mention it.

And then a slender figure, with a drooping head, a wan face, and large sad eyes, came softly down the dimly-lighted room towards me, and I and my destined bride met for the first time.

As I had expected, after she had once anxiously raised her eyes, and allowed them to rest upon me, her face was lighted up by an evident relief, as she discovered that the fulfillment of my aunt's wishes would not be so distasteful to her, personally, as it might have been.

For myself, I was upon the whole rather disappointed in her;

the portrait had flattered her considerably—the real Chlorine was thinner and paler than I had been led to anticipate, while there was a settled melancholy in her manner which I felt would prevent her from being an exhilarating companion.

And I must say I prefer a touch of archness and animation in womankind, and, if I had been free to consult my own tastes, should have greatly preferred to become a member of a more cheerful family. Under the circumstances, however, I was not entitled to be too particular, and I put up with it.

From the moment of my arrival I fell easily and naturally into the position of an honored guest, who might be expected in time to form nearer and dearer relations with the family, and certainly I was afforded every opportunity of doing so.

I made no mistakes, for the diligence with which I had got up McFadden's antecedents enabled me to give perfectly satisfactory replies to most of the few allusions or questions that were addressed to me, and I drew upon my imagination for the rest.

But those days I spent in the baronet's family were far from lively: the Catafalques went nowhere; they seemed to know nobody; at least no visitors ever called or dined there while I was with them, and the time dragged slowly on in a terrible monotony in that dim tomb of a house, which I was not expected to leave except for very brief periods, for Sir Paul would grow uneasy if I walked out alone—even to Putney.

There was something, indeed, about the attitude of both the old people towards myself which I could only consider as extremely puzzling. They would follow me about with a jealous care, blended with anxious alarm, and their faces as they looked at me wore an expression of tearful admiration, touched with something of pity, as for some youthful martyr; at times, too, they spoke of the gratitude they felt, and professed a determined hopefulness as to my ultimate success.

Now I was well aware that this is not the ordinary bearing of the parents of an heiress to a suitor who, however deserving in other respects, is both obscure and penniless, and the only way in which I could account for it was by the supposition that there was some latent defect in Chlorine's temper or constitution, which entitled the man who won her to commiseration, and which would also explain their evident anxiety to get her off their hands.

But although anything of this kind would be, of course, a drawback, I felt that forty or fifty thousand pounds would be a fair set-off—and I could not expect *everything*.

When the time came at which I felt that I could safely speak to Chlorine of what lay nearest my heart, I found an unforeseen difficulty in bringing her to confess that she reciprocated my passion.

She seemed to shrink unaccountably from speaking the word which gave me the right to claim her, confessing that she dreaded it not for her own sake, but for mine alone, which struck me as an unpleasantly morbid trait in so young a girl.

Again and again I protested that I was willing to run all risks—as I was—and again and again she resisted, though always more faintly, until at last my efforts were successful, and I forced from her lips the assent which was of so much importance to me.

But it cost her a great effort, and I believe she even swooned immediately afterwards; but this is only conjecture, as I lost no time in seeking Sir Paul and clenching the matter before Chlorine had time to retract.

He heard what I had to tell him with a strange light of triumph and relief in his weary eyes. "You have made an old man very happy and hopeful," he said. "I ought, perhaps, even now to deter you, but I am too selfish for that. And you are young and brave and ardent; why need we despair? I suppose," he added, looking keenly at me, "you would prefer as little delay as possible?"

"I should indeed," I replied. I was pleased, for I had not expected to find him so sensible as that.

"Then leave all preliminaries to me; when the day and time have been settled, I will let you know. As you are aware, it will be necessary to have your signature to this document; and here, my boy, I must in conscience warn you solemnly that by signing you make your decision irrevocable—*irrevocable,* you understand?"

When I had heard this, I need scarcely say that I was all eagerness to sign; so great was my haste that I did not even try to decipher the somewhat crabbed and antiquated writing in which the terms of the agreement were set out.

I was anxious to impress the baronet with a sense of my gentlemanly feeling and the confidence I had in him, while I naturally presumed that, since the contract was binding upon me, the baronet would, as a man of honor, hold it equally conclusive on his own side.

As I look back upon it now, it seems simply extraordinary that I should have been so easily satisfied, have taken so little pains to find out the exact position in which I was placing myself; but, with the ingenuous confidence of youth, I fell an easy victim, as I was to realize later with terrible enlightenment.

"Say nothing of this to Chlorine," said Sir Paul, as I handed him the document signed, "until the final arrangements are made; it will only distress her unnecessarily."

I wondered why at the time, but I promised to obey, supposing that he knew best, and for some days after that I made no mention to Chlorine of the approaching day which was to witness our union.

As we were continually together, I began to regard her with an esteem which I had not thought possible at first. Her looks improved considerably under the influence of happiness, and I found she could converse intelligently enough upon several topics, and did not bore me nearly as much as I was fully prepared for.

And so the time passed less heavily, until one afternoon the baronet took me aside mysteriously. "Prepare yourself, Augustus" (they had all learned to call me Augustus), he said; "all is arranged. The event upon which our dearest hopes depend is fixed for tomorrow—in the Gray Chamber of course, and at midnight."

I thought this a curious time and place for the ceremony, but I had divined his eccentric passion for privacy and retirement, and only imagined that he had procured some very special form of license.

"But you do not know the Gray Chamber," he added. "Come with me, and I will show you where it is." And he led me up the broad staircase, and, stopping at the end of a passage before an immense door covered with black baize and studded with brass nails, which gave it a hideous resemblance to a gigantic coffin lid, he pressed a spring, and it fell slowly back.

I saw a long dim gallery, whose very existence nothing in the external appearance of the mansion had led me to suspect; it led to a heavy oaken door with cumbrous plates and fastenings of metal.

"Tomorrow night is Christmas eve, as you are doubtless aware," he said in a hushed voice. "At twelve, then, you will present yourself at yonder door—the door of the Gray Chamber—where you must fulfill the engagement you have made."

I was surprised at his choosing such a place for the ceremony; it would have been more cheerful in the long drawing room; but it was evidently a whim of his, and I was too happy to think of opposing it. I hastened at once to Chlorine, with her father's sanction, and told her that the crowning moment of both our lives was fixed at last.

The effect of my announcement was astonishing: she fainted, for which I remonstrated with her as soon as she came to herself. "Such extreme sensitiveness, my love," I could not help saying, "may be highly creditable to your sense of maidenly propriety, but allow me to say that I can scarcely regard it as a compliment."

"Augustus," she said, "you must not think I doubt you; and yet—and yet—the ordeal will be a severe one for you."

"I will steel my nerves," I said grimly (for I was annoyed with her); "and, after all, Chlorine, the ceremony is not invariably fatal; I have heard of the victim surviving it—occasionally."

"How brave you are!" she said earnestly. "I will imitate you, Augustus; I too will hope."

I really thought her insane, which alarmed me for the validity of the marriage. "Yes, I am weak, foolish, I know," she continued; "but oh, I shudder so when I think of you, away in that gloomy Gray Chamber, going through it all alone!"

This confirmed my worst fears. No wonder her parents felt grateful to me for relieving them of such a responsibility! "May I ask where *you* intend to be at the time?" I inquired very quietly.

"You will not think us unfeeling," she replied, "but dear papa considered that such anxiety as ours would be scarcely endurable did we not seek some distraction from it; and so, as a special favor, he has procured evening orders for Sir John Soane's Museum in Lincoln's Inn Fields, where we shall drive immediately after dinner."

I knew that the proper way to treat the insane was by reasoning with them gently, so as to place their own absurdity clearly before them. "If you are forgetting your anxiety in Sir John Soane's Museum, while I cool my heels in the Gray Chamber," I said, "is it probable that any clergyman will be induced to perform the marriage ceremony? Did you really think two people can be united separately?"

She was astonished this time. "You are joking!" she cried; "you cannot really believe that we are to be married in—in the Gray Chamber?"

"Then will you tell me where we *are* to be married?" I asked. "I think I have the right to know—it can hardly be at the Museum!"

She turned upon me with a sudden misgiving; "I could almost fancy," she said anxiously, "that this is no feigned ignorance. Augustus, your aunt sent you a message—tell me, have you *read* it?"

Now, owing to McFadden's want of consideration, this was my one weak point—I had *not* read it, and thus I felt myself upon delicate ground. The message evidently related to business of importance which was to be transacted in this Gray Chamber, and as the genuine McFadden clearly knew all about it, it would have been simply suicidal to confess my own ignorance.

"Why of course, darling, of course," I said hastily. "You must think no more of my silly joke; there *is* something I have to arrange in the Gray Chamber before I can call you mine. But, tell me, why does it make you so uneasy?" I added, thinking it might be prudent to find out beforehand what formality was expected from me.

"I cannot help it—no, I cannot!" she cried, "the test is so searching—are you sure that you are prepared at all points? I overheard my father say that no precaution could safely be neglected. I have such a terrible foreboding that, after all, this may come between us."

It was clear enough to me now; the baronet was by no means so simple and confiding in his choice of a son-in-law as I had imagined, and had no intention, after all, of accepting me without some inquiry into my past life, my habits, and my prospects. That he should seek to make this examination more impressive by appointing this ridiculous midnight interview for it, was only what might have been expected from an old man of his confirmed eccentricity.

But I knew I could easily contrive to satisfy the baronet, and with the idea of consoling Chlorine, I said as much. "Why will you persist in treating me like a child, Augustus?" she broke out almost petulantly. "They have tried to hide it all from me, but do you suppose I do not know that in the Gray Chamber you will have to encounter one far more formidable, far more difficult to satisfy, than poor dear papa?"

"I see you know more than I—more than I thought you did," I said. "Let us understand one another, Chlorine—tell me exactly how much you know."

"I have told you all I know," she said; "it is your turn to confide in me."

"Not even for your sweet sake, my dearest," I was obliged to say, "can I break the seal that is set upon my tongue. You must not press me. Come, let us talk of other things."

But I now saw that matters were worse than I had thought; instead of the feeble old baronet I should have to deal with a stranger, some exacting and officious friend or relation perhaps, or, more probably, a keen family solicitor who would put questions I should not care about answering, and even be capable of insisting upon strict settlements.

It was that, of course; they would try to tie my hands by a strict settlement, with a brace of cautious trustees; unless I was very careful, all I should get by my marriage would be a paltry life-interest, contingent upon my surviving my wife.

This revolted me; it seems to me that when law comes in with its offensively suspicious restraints upon the husband and its indelicately premature provisions for the offspring, all the poetry of love is gone at once. By allowing the wife to receive the income "for her separate use and free from the control of her husband," as the phrase runs, you infallibly brush the bloom from the peach, and implant the "little speck within the fruit" which, as Tennyson beautifully says, will widen by and by and make the music mute.

This may be overstrained on my part, but it represents my honest conviction; I was determined to have nothing to do with law. If it was necessary, I felt quite sure enough of Chlorine to defy Sir Paul. I would refuse to meet a family solicitor anywhere, and I intended to say so plainly at the first convenient opportunity.

Chapter III

The opportunity came after dinner that evening when we were all in the drawing-room, Lady Catafalque dozing uneasily in her armchair behind a fire screen, and Chlorine, in the further room, playing funereal dirges in the darkness, and pressing the stiff keys of the old piano with a languid uncertain touch.

Drawing a chair up to Sir Paul's, I began to broach the subject calmly and temperately. "I find," I said, "that we have not quite understood one another over this affair in the Gray Chamber. When I agreed to an appointment there, I thought—well, it doesn't matter *what* I thought, I was a little too premature. What I want to say now is, that while I have no objection to you, as Chlorine's father, asking me any questions (in reason) about myself, I feel a delicacy in discussing my private affairs with a perfect stranger."

His burning eyes looked me through and through; "I don't understand," he said. "Tell me what you are talking about."

I began all over again, telling him exactly what I felt about solicitors and settlements. "Are you well?" he asked sternly. "What have I ever said about settlements or solicitors?"

I saw that I was wrong again, and could only stammer something to the effect that a remark of Chlorine's had given me this impression.

"What she could have said to convey such an idea passes my comprehension," he said gravely; "but she knows nothing—she's a mere child. I have felt from the first, my boy, that your aunt's intention was to benefit you quite as much as my own daughter. Believe me, I shall not attempt to restrict you in any way; I shall be too rejoiced to see you come forth in safety from the Gray Chamber."

All the relief I had begun to feel respecting the settlements was poisoned by these last words. *Why* did he talk of that confounded Gray Chamber as if it were a fiery furnace, or a cage of lions? What mystery was there concealed beneath all this, and how, since I was obviously supposed to be thoroughly acquainted with it, could I manage to penetrate the secret of this perplexing appointment?

While he had been speaking, the faint, mournful music died away, and, looking up, I saw Chlorine, a pale, slight form, standing framed in the archway which connected the two rooms.

"Go back to your piano, my child," said the baronet; "Augustus and I have much to talk about which is not for your ears."

"But why not?" she said; "oh, why not? Papa! dearest

mother! Augustus! I can bear it no longer! I have often felt of late that we are living this strange life under the shadow of some fearful Thing, which would chase all cheerfulness from any home. More than this I did not seek to know; I dared not ask. But now, when I know that Augustus, whom I love with my whole heart, must shortly face this ghastly presence, you cannot wonder if I seek to learn the real extent of the danger that awaits him! Tell me all. I can bear the worst—for it cannot be more horrible than my own fears!"

Lady Catafalque had roused herself and was wringing her long mittened hands and moaning feebly. "Paul," she said, "you must not tell her; it will kill her; she is not strong!" Her husband seemed undecided, and I myself began to feel exquisitely uncomfortable. Chlorine's words pointed to something infinitely more terrible than a mere solicitor.

"Poor girl," said Sir Paul at last, "it was for your own good that the whole truth has been thus concealed from you; but now, perhaps, the time has come when the truest kindness will be to reveal all. What do *you* say, Augustus?"

"I—I agree with you," I replied faintly; "she ought to be told."

"Precisely!" he said. "Break to her, then, the nature of the ordeal which lies before you."

It was the very thing which I wanted to be broken to *me!* I would have given the world to know all about it myself, and so I stared at his gloomy old face with eyes that must have betrayed my helpless dismay. At last I saved myself by suggesting that such a story would come less harshly from a parent's lips.

"Well, so be it," he said. "Chlorine, compose yourself, dearest one; sit down there, and summon up all your fortitude to hear what I am about to tell you. You must know, then—I think you had better let your mother give you a cup of tea before I begin; it will steady your nerves."

During the delay which followed—for Sir Paul did not consider his daughter sufficiently fortified until she had taken at least three cups—I suffered tortures of suspense, which I dared not betray.

They never thought of offering *me* any tea, though the merest observer might have noticed how very badly I wanted it.

At last the baronet was satisfied, and not without a sort of gloomy enjoyment and a proud relish of the distinction implied in his exceptional affliction, he began his weird and almost incredible tale.

"It is now," said he, "some centuries since our ill-fated house was first afflicted with the family curse which still attends it. A certain Humfrey de Catafalque, by his acquaintance with the black art, as it was said, had procured the services of a species of familiar, a dread and supernatural being. For some reason he had conceived a bitter enmity towards his nearest relations, whom he hated with a virulence that not even death could soften. For, by a refinement of malice, he bequeathed this baleful thing to his descendants forever, as an inalienable heirloom! And to this day it follows the title—and the head of the family for the time being is bound to provide it with a secret apartment under his own roof. But that is not the worst: as each member of our house succeeds to the ancestral rank and honors, he must seek an interview with "The Curse," as it has been styled for generations. And, in that interview, it is decided whether the spell is to be broken and the Curse depart from us forever—or whether it is to continue its blighting influence, and hold yet another life in miserable thraldom."

"And are you one of its thralls then, papa?" faltered Chlorine.

"I am, indeed," he said. "I failed to quell it, as every Catafalque, however brave and resolute, has failed yet. It checks all my accounts, and woe to me if that cold, withering eye discovers the slightest error—even in the pence column! I could not describe the extent of my bondage to you, my daughter, or the humiliation of having to go and tremble monthly before that awful presence. Not even yet, old as I am, have I grown quite accustomed to it!"

Never, in my wildest imaginings, had I anticipated anything one quarter so dreadful as *this;* but still I clung to the hope that it was impossible to bring *me* into the affair.

"But, Sir Paul," I said—"Sir Paul, you—you mustn't stop there, or you'll alarm Chlorine more than there's any need to do. She—ha, ha!—don't you see, she has got some idea into her head that *I* have to go through much the same sort of thing. Just explain that to her. *I'm* not a Catafalque, Chlorine, so it—it can't interfere with me. That is so, *isn't* it, Sir Paul? Good heavens, sir, don't torture her like this!" I cried, as he was silent. "Speak out!"

"You mean well, Augustus," he said, "but the time for deceiving her has gone by; she must know the worst. Yes, my poor child," he continued to Chlorine, whose eyes were wide with terror—though I fancy mine were even wider—"unhappily, though our beloved Augustus is not a Catafalque himself, he has of his own free will brought himself within the influence of the Curse, and he, too, at the appointed hour, must keep the awful assignation, and brave all that the most fiendish malevolence can do to shake his resolution."

I could not say a single word; the horror of the idea was altogether too much for me, and I fell back on my chair in a state of speechless collapse.

"You see," Sir Paul went on explaining, "it is not only all new baronets, but every one who would seek an alliance with the females of our race, who must, by the terms of that strange bequest, also undergo this trial. It may be in some degree owing to this necessity that, ever since Humfrey de Catafalque's diabolical testament first took effect, every maiden of our House has died a spinster." (Here Chlorine hid her face with a low wail.) "In 1770, it is true, one solitary suitor was emboldened by love and daring to face the ordeal. He went calmly and resolutely to the chamber where the Curse was then lodged, and the next morning they found him outside the door—a gibbering maniac!"

I writhed on my chair. "Augustus!" cried Chlorine wildly,

"promise me you will not permit the Curse to turn you into a gibbering maniac. I think if I saw you gibber I should die!"

I was on the verge of gibbering then; I dared not trust myself to speak.

"Nay, Chlorine," said Sir Paul more cheerfully "there is no cause for alarm; all has been made smooth for Augustus." (I began to brighten a little at this.) "His Aunt Petronia had made a special study of the old-world science of incantation, and had undoubtedly succeeded at last in discovering the master-word which, employed according to her directions, would almost certainly break the unhallowed spell. In her compassionate attachment to us, she formed the design of persuading a youth of blameless life and antecedents to present himself as our champion, and the reports she had been given of our dear Augustus's irreproachable character led her to select him as a likely instrument. And her confidence in his generosity and courage was indeed well-founded, for he responded at once to the appeal of his departed aunt, and, with her instructions for his safeguard, and the consciousness of his virtue as an additional protection, there is hope, my child, strong hope, that, though the struggle may be a long and bitter one, yet Augustus will emerge a victor!"

I saw very little ground for expecting to emerge as anything of the kind, or for that matter to emerge at all, except in installments—for the master-word which was to abash the demon was probably inside the packet of instructions, and that was certainly somewhere at the bottom of the sea, outside Melbourne, fathoms below the surface.

I could bear no more. "It's simply astonishing to me," I said, "that in the nineteenth century, hardly six miles from Charing Cross, you can calmly allow this hideous 'Curse,' or whatever you call it, to have things all its own way like this."

"What can I do, Augustus?" he asked helplessly.

"Do? *Anything*!" I retorted wildly (for I scarcely knew what I said). "Take it out for an airing (it must want an airing by this time); take it out—and lose it! Or get both the archbishops to step in and lay it for you. Sell the house, and make the purchaser take it at a valuation, with the other fixtures. I certainly would not live under the same roof with it. And I want you to understand one thing—I was never told all this; I have been kept in the dark about it. Of course I knew there was some kind of a curse in the family—but I never dreamed of anything so bad as this, and I never had any intention of being boxed up alone with it either. I shall not go *near* the Gray Chamber!"

"Not go near it!" they all cried aghast.

"Not on any account," I said, for I felt firmer and easier now that I had taken up this position. "If the Curse has any business with me, let it come down and settle it here before you all in a plain straightforward manner. Let us go about it in a business-like way. On second thoughts," I added, fearing lest they should find means of carrying out this suggestion, "I won't meet it anywhere!"

"And why—*why* won't you meet it?" they asked breathlessly.

"Because," I explained desperately, "because I'm—I'm a materialist." (I had not been previously aware that I had any decided opinions on the question, but I could not stay then to consider the point.) "How can I have any dealings with a preposterous supernatural something which my reason forbids me to believe in? You see my difficulty? It would be inconsistent, to begin with, and—and extremely painful to both sides."

"No more of this ribaldry," said Sir Paul sternly. "It may be terribly remembered against you when the hour comes. Keep a guard over your tongue, for all our sakes, and more especially your own. Recollect that the Curse knows all that passes beneath this roof. And do not forget, too, that you are pledged—irrevocably pledged. You *must* confront the Curse!"

Only a short hour ago, and I had counted Chlorine's fortune and Chlorine as virtually mine; and now I saw my golden dreams roughly shattered forever! And, oh, what a wrench it was to tear myself from them! What it cost me to speak the words that barred my Paradise to me forever!

But if I wished to avoid confronting the Curse—and I *did* wish this very much—I had no other course. "I had no right to pledge myself," I said, with quivering lips, "under all the circumstances."

"Why not," they demanded again; "what circumstances?"

"Well, in the first place," I assured them earnestly, "I'm a base impostor. I am indeed. I'm not Augustus McFadden at all. My real name is of no consequence—but it's a prettier one than that. As for McFadden, he, I regret to say, is now no more."

Why on earth I could not have told the plain truth here has always been a mystery to me. I suppose I had been lying so long that it was difficult to break myself of this occasionally inconvenient trick at so short a notice, but I certainly mixed things up to a hopeless extent.

"Yes," I continued mournfully, "McFadden is dead; I will tell you how he died if you would care to know. During his voyage here he fell overboard, and was almost instantly appropriated by a gigantic shark, when, as I happened to be present, I enjoyed the melancholy privilege of seeing him pass away. For one brief moment I beheld him between the jaws of the creature, so pale but so composed (I refer to McFadden, you understand—not the shark), he threw just one glance up at me, and with a smile, the sad sweetness of which I shall never forget (it was McFadden's smile, I mean, of course—not the shark's), he, courteous and considerate to the last, requested me to break the news and remember him very kindly to you all. And, in the same instant, he abruptly vanished within the monster—and I saw neither of them again!"

Of course in bringing the shark in at all I was acting directly contrary to my instructions, but I quite forgot them in my anxiety to escape the acquaintance of the Curse of the Catafalques.

"If this is true, sir," said the baronet haughtily when I had finished, "you have indeed deceived us basely."

"That," I replied, "is what I was endeavoring to bring out. You see, it puts it quite out of my power to meet your family Curse. I should not feel justified in intruding upon it. So, if you will kindly let some one fetch a fly or a cab in half an hour—"

"Stop!" cried Chlorine. "Augustus, as I will call you still, you must not go like this. If you have stooped to deceit, it was for love of me, and—and Mr. McFadden is dead. If he had been alive, I should have felt it my duty to allow him an opportunity of winning my affection, but he is lying in his silent tomb, and—and I have learnt to love *you.* Stay, then; stay and brave the Curse; we may yet be happy!"

I saw how foolish I had been not to tell the truth at first, and I hastened to repair this error. "When I described McFadden as dead," I said hoarsely, "it was a loose way of putting the facts—because, to be quite accurate, he isn't dead. We found out afterwards that it was another fellow the shark had swallowed, and, in fact, another shark altogether. So he is alive and well now, at Melbourne, but when he came to know about the Curse, he was too much frightened to come across, and he asked me to call and make his excuses. I have now done so, and will trespass no further on your kindness—if you will tell somebody to bring a vehicle of any sort in a quarter of an hour."

"Pardon me," said the baronet, "but we cannot part in this way. I feared when first I saw you that your resolution might give way under the strain; it is only natural, I admit. But you deceive yourself if you think we cannot see that these extraordinary and utterly contradictory stories are prompted by sudden panic. I quite understand it, Augustus; I cannot blame you; but to allow you to withdraw now would be worse than weakness on my part. The panic will pass, you will forget these fears tomorrow, you *must* forget them; remember, you have promised. For your own sake, I shall take care that you do not forfeit that solemn bond, for I dare not let you run the danger of exciting the Curse by a deliberate insult."

I saw clearly that his conduct was dictated by a deliberate and most repulsive selfishness; he did not entirely believe me, but he was determined that if there was any chance that I, whoever I might be, could free him from his present thraldom, he would not let it escape him.

I raved, I protested, I implored—all in vain; they would not believe a single word I said, they positively refused to release me, and insisted upon my performing my engagement.

And at last Chlorine and her mother left the room, with a little contempt for my unworthiness mingled with their evident compassion; and a little later Sir Paul conducted me to my room, and locked me in "till," as he said, "I had returned to my senses.

CHAPTER IV

What a night I passed, as I tossed sleeplessly from side to side under the canopy of my old-fashioned bedstead, torturing my fevered brain with vain speculations as to the fate the morrow was to bring me.

I felt myself perfectly helpless; I saw no way out of it; they seemed bent upon offering me up as a sacrifice to this private Moloch of theirs. The baronet was quite capable of keeping me locked up all the next day and pushing me into the Gray Chamber to take my chance when the hour came.

If I had only some idea what the Curse was like to look at, I thought I might not feel quite so afraid of it; the vague and impalpable awfulness of the thing was intolerable, and the very thought of it caused me to fling myself about in an ecstasy of horror.

By degrees, however, as daybreak came near, I grew calmer—until at length I arrived at a decision. It seemed evident to me that, as I could not avoid my fate, the wisest course was to go forth to meet it with as good a grace as possible. Then, should I by some fortunate accident come well out of it, my fortune was ensured.

But if I went on repudiating my assumed self to the very last, I should surely arouse a suspicion which the most signal rout of the Curse would not serve to dispel.

And after all, as I began to think, the whole thing had probably been much exaggerated; if I could only keep my head, and exercise all my powers of cool impudence, I might contrive to hoodwink this formidable relic of medieval days, which must have fallen rather behind the age by this time. It might even turn out to be (although I was hardly sanguine as to this) as big a humbug as I was myself, and we should meet with confidential winks, like the two augurs.

But, at all events, I resolved to see this mysterious affair out, and trust to my customary good luck to bring me safely through, and so, having found the door unlocked, I came down to breakfast something like my usual self, and set myself to remove the unfavorable impression I had made on the previous night.

They did it from consideration for me, but still it *was* mistaken kindness for them all to leave me entirely to my own thoughts during the whole of the day, for I was driven to mope alone about the gloom-laden building, until by dinnertime I was very low indeed from nervous depression.

We dined in almost unbroken silence; now and then, as Sir Paul saw my hand approaching a decanter, he would open his lips to observe that I should need the clearest head and the firmest nerve ere long, and warn me solemnly against the brown sherry; from time to time, too, Chlorine and her mother stole apprehensive glances at me, and sighed heavily between every course. I never remember eating a dinner with so little enjoyment.

The meal came to an end at last; the ladies rose, and Sir Paul and I were left to brood over the dessert. I fancy both of us felt a delicacy in starting a conversation, and before I could hit upon a safe remark, Lady Catafalque and her daughter returned, dressed, to my unspeakable horror, in readiness to go out. Worse than that even, Sir Paul apparently intended to accompany them, for he rose at their entrance.

"It is now time for us to bid you a solemn farewell, Augustus," he said, in his hollow old voice. "You have three hours before you yet, and if you are wise, you will spend them in earnest self-preparation. At midnight, punctually, for you must not dare to delay, you will go to the Gray Chamber—the way thither you know, and you will find the Curse prepared for you. Good-bye, then, brave and devoted boy; stand firm, and no harm can befall you!"

"You are going away, all of you!" I cried. They were not what you might call a gay family to sit up with, but even their society was better than my own.

"Upon these dread occasions," he explained, "it is absolutely forbidden for any human being but one to remain in the house. All the servants have already left, and we are about to take our departure for a private hotel near the Strand. We shall just have time, if we start at once, to inspect the Soane Museum on our way thither, which will serve as some distraction from the terrible anxiety we shall be feeling."

At this I believe I positively howled with terror; all my old panic came back with a rush. "Don't leave me all alone with *It!*" I cried; "I shall go mad if you do!"

Sir Paul simply turned on his heel in silent contempt, and his wife followed him; but Chlorine remained behind for one instant, and somehow, as she gazed at me with a yearning pity in her sad eyes, I thought I had never seen her looking so pretty before.

"Augustus," she said, "get up." (I suppose I must have been on the floor somewhere.) "Be a man; show us we were not mistaken in you. You know I would spare you this if I could; but we are powerless. Oh, be brave, or I shall lose you forever!"

Her appeal did seem to put a little courage into me; I staggered up and kissed her slender hand and vowed sincerely to be worthy of her.

And then she too passed out, and the heavy hall door slammed behind the three, and the rusty old gate screeched like a banshee as it swung back and closed with a clang.

I heard the carriage-wheels grind the slush, and the next moment I knew that I was shut up on Christmas eve in that somber mansion—with the Curse of the Catafalques as my sole companion.

I don't think the generous ardor with which Chlorine's last words had inspired me lasted very long, for I caught myself shivering before the clock struck nine, and, drawing up a clumsy leathern armchair close to the fire, I piled on the logs and tried to get rid of a certain horrible sensation of internal vacancy which was beginning to afflict me.

I tried to look my situation fairly in the face; whatever reason and common sense had to say about it, there seemed no possible doubt that *something* of a supernatural order was shut up in that great chamber down the corridor, and also that, if I meant to win Chlorine, I must go up and have some kind of an interview with it. Once more I wished I had some definite idea to go upon; what description of being should I find this Curse? Would it be aggressively ugly, like the bogie of my infancy, or should I see a lank and unsubstantial shape, draped in clinging black, with nothing visible beneath it but a pair of burning hollow eyes and one long pale bony hand? Really I could not decide which would be the more trying of the two.

By and by I began to recollect unwillingly all the frightful stories I had ever read; one in particular came back to me—the adventure of a foreign marshal who, after much industry, succeeded in invoking an evil spirit, which came bouncing into the room shaped like a gigantic ball, with, I *think,* a hideous face in the middle of it, and would not be got rid of until the horrified marshal had spent hours in hard praying and persistent exorcism!

What should I do if the Curse was a globular one and came rolling all round the room after me?

Then there was another appalling tale I had read in some magazine—a tale of a secret chamber, too, and in some respects a very similar case to my own, for there the heir of some great house had to go in and meet a mysterious aged person with strange eyes and an evil smile, who kept attempting to shake hands with him.

Nothing should induce me to shake hands with the Curse of the Catafalques, however apparently friendly I might find it.

But it was not very likely to be friendly, for it was one of those mystic powers of darkness which know nearly everything—it would detect me as an impostor directly, and what would become of me? I declare I almost resolved to confess all and sob out my deceit upon its bosom, and the only thing which made me pause was the reflection that probably the Curse did not possess a bosom.

By this time I had worked myself up to such a pitch of terror that I found it absolutely necessary to brace my nerves, and I did brace them. I emptied all the three decanters, but as Sir Paul's cellar was none of the best, the only result was that, while my courage and daring were not perceptibly heightened, I was conscious of feeling exceedingly unwell.

Tobacco, no doubt, would have calmed and soothed me, but I did not dare to smoke. For the Curse, being old-fashioned, might object to the smell of it, and I was anxious to avoid exciting its prejudices unnecessarily.

And so I simply sat in my chair and shook. Every now and then I heard steps on the frosty path outside: sometimes a rapid tread, as of some happy person bound to scenes of Christmas revelry, and little dreaming of the miserable wretch he was passing; sometimes the slow creaking tramp of the Fulham policeman on his beat.

What if I called him in and gave the Curse into custody—either for putting me in bodily fear (as it was undeniably doing), or for being found on the premises under suspicious circumstances?

There was a certain audacity about this means of cutting the knot that fascinated me at first, but still I did not venture to adopt it, thinking it most probable that the stolid constable would decline to interfere as soon as he knew the facts; and even if he did, it would certainly annoy Sir Paul extremely to hear of his Family Curse spending its Christmas in a police cell, and I felt instinctively that he would consider it a piece of unpardonable bad taste on my part.

So one hour passed. A few minutes after ten I heard more footsteps and voices in low consultation, as if a band of men had collected outside the railings. Could there be any indication without of the horrors these walls contained?

But no; the gaunt housefront kept its secret too well; they were merely the waits. They saluted me with the old carol, "God rest you, merry gentleman, let nothing you dismay!" which should have encouraged me, but it didn't and they followed that up by a wheezy but pathetic rendering of "The Mistletoe Bough."

For a time I did not object to them; while they were scraping and blowing outside I felt less abandoned and cut off from human help, and then they might arouse softer sentiments in the Curse upstairs by their seasonable strains: these things do happen at Christmas sometimes. But their performance was really so infernally bad that it was calculated rather to irritate than subdue any evil spirit, and very soon I rushed to the window and beckoned to them furiously to go away.

Unhappily, they thought I was inviting them indoors for refreshment, and came round to the gate, when they knocked and rang incessantly for a quarter of an hour.

This must have stirred the Curse up quite enough, but when they had gone, there came a man with a barrel organ, which was suffering from some complicated internal disorder, causing it to play its whole repertory at once, in maddening discords. Even the grinder himself seemed dimly aware that his instrument was not doing itself justice, for he would stop occasionally, as if to ponder or examine it. But he was evidently a sanguine person and had hopes of bringing it round by a little perseverance; so, as Parson's Green was well-suited by its quiet for this mode of treatment, he remained there till he must have reduced the Curse to a rampant and rabid condition.

He went at last, and then the silence that followed began to my excited fancy (for I certainly *saw* nothing) to be invaded by strange sounds that echoed about the old house. I heard sharp reports from the furniture, sighing moans in the draughty passages, doors opening and shutting, and—worse still—stealthy padding footsteps, both above and in the ghostly hall outside!

I sat there in an ice-cold perspiration, until my nerves required more bracing, to effect which I had recourse to the spirit-case.

And after a short time my fears began to melt away rapidly. What a ridiculous bugbear I was making of this thing after all! Was I not too hasty in setting it down as ugly and hostile before I had seen it . . . how did I know it was anything which deserved my horror?

Here a gush of sentiment came over me at the thought that it might be that for long centuries the poor Curse had been cruelly misunderstood—that it might be a *blessing* in disguise.

I was so affected by the thought that I resolved to go up at once and wish it a merry Christmas through the keyhole, just to show that I came in no unfriendly spirit.

But would not that seem as if I was afraid of it? I scorned the idea of being afraid. Why, for two straws, I would go straight in and pull its nose for it—if it *had* a nose!

I went out with this object, not very steadily, but before I had reached the top of the dim and misty staircase, I had given up all ideas of defiance, and merely intended to go as far as the corridor by way of a preliminary canter.

The coffin-lid door stood open, and I looked apprehensively down the corridor; the grim metal fittings on the massive door of the Gray Chamber were gleaming with a mysterious pale light, something between the phenomena obtained by electricity and the peculiar phosphorescence observable in a decayed shellfish; under the door I saw the reflection of a sullen red glow, and within I could hear sounds like the roar of a mighty wind, above which peals of fiendish mirth rang out at intervals, and were followed by a hideous dull clanking.

It seemed only too evident that the Curse was getting up the steam for our interview. I did not stay there long, because I was afraid that it might dart out suddenly and catch me eavesdropping, which would be a hopelessly bad beginning. I got back to the dining room, somehow; the fire had taken advantage of my short absence to go out, and I was surprised to find by the light of the fast-dimming lamp that it was a quarter to twelve already.

Only fifteen more fleeting minutes and then—unless I gave up Chlorine and her fortune forever—I must go up and knock at that awful door, and enter the presence of the frightful mystic Thing that was roaring and laughing and clanking on the other side!

Stupidly I sat and stared at the clock; in five minutes, now, I should be beginning my desperate duel with one of the powers of darkness—a thought which gave me sickening qualms.

I was clinging to the thought that I had still two precious minutes left—perhaps my last moments of safety and sanity—when the lamp expired with a gurgling sob, and left me in the dark.

I was afraid of sitting there all alone any longer, and besides, if I lingered, the Curse might come down and fetch me. The horror of this idea made me resolve to go up at once, especially as scrupulous punctuality might propitiate it.

Groping my way to the door, I reached the hall and stood there, swaying under the old stained-glass lantern. And then I made a terrible discovery. I was not in a condition to transact any business; I had disregarded Sir Paul's well-meant warning at dinner; I was not my own master. I was lost!

The clock in the adjoining room tolled twelve, and from without the distant steeples proclaimed in faint peals and chimes that it was Christmas morn. My hour had come!

Why did I not mount those stairs? I tried again and again, and fell down every time, and at each attempt I knew the Curse would be getting more and more impatient.

I was quite five minutes late, and yet, with all my eagerness to be punctual, I could *not* get up that staircase. It was a horrible situation, but it was not at its worst even then, for I heard a jarring sound above, as if heavy rusty bolts were being withdrawn.

The Curse was coming down to see what had become of me! I should have to confess my inability to go upstairs without assistance, and so place myself wholly at its mercy!

I made one more desperate effort, and then—and then, upon my word, I don't know how it was exactly—but, as I looked wildly about, I caught sight of my hat on the hat-rack below, and the thoughts it roused in me proved too strong for resistance. Perhaps it was weak of me, but I venture to think that very few men in my position would have behaved any better.

I renounced my ingenious and elaborate scheme forever, the door (fortunately for me) was neither locked nor bolted, and the next moment I was running for my life along the road to Chelsea, urged on by the fancy that the Curse itself was in hot pursuit.

For weeks after that I lay in hiding, starting at every sound, so fearful was I that the outraged Curse might track me down at last; all my worldly possessions were at Parson's Green, and I could not bring myself to write or call for them, nor indeed have I seen any of the Catafalques since that awful Christmas eve.

I wish to have nothing more to do with them, for I feel naturally that they took a cruel advantage of my youth and inexperience, and I shall always resent the deception and constraint to which I so nearly fell a victim.

But it occurs to me that those who may have followed my strange story with any curiosity and interest may be slightly disappointed at its conclusion, which I cannot deny is a lame and unsatisfactory one.

They expected, no doubt, to be told what the Curse's personal appearance is, and how it comports itself in that ghastly Gray Chamber, what it said to me, and what I said to it, and what happened after that.

This information, as will be easily understood, I cannot pretend to give, and, for myself, I have long ceased to feel the slightest curiosity on any of these points. But for the benefit of such as are less indifferent, I may suggest that almost any eligible bachelor would easily obtain the opportunities I failed to enjoy by simply calling at the old mansion at Parson's Green, and presenting himself to the baronet as a suitor for his daughter's hand.

I shall be most happy to allow my name to be used as a reference.

CHARLES DICKENS

THE STORY OF THE GOBLINS WHO STOLE A SEXTON

Charles Dickens's earliest Christmas story.

IN an old abbey town, down in this part of the country, a long, long while ago—so long, that the story must be a true one, because our great grandfathers implicitly believed it—there officiated as sexton and grave-digger in the churchyard, one Gabriel Grub. It by no means follows that because a man is a sexton, and constantly surrounded by emblems of mortality, therefore he should be a morose and melancholy man; your undertakers are the merriest fellows in the world; and I once had the honor of being on intimate terms with a mute, who in private life, and off duty, was as comical and jocose a little fellow as ever chirped out a devil-may-care song, without a hitch in his memory, or drained off the contents of a good stiff glass without stopping for breath. But, notwithstanding these precedents to the contrary, Gabriel Grub was an ill-conditioned, cross-grained, surly fellow—a morose and lonely man, who consorted with nobody but himself, and an old wicker bottle which fitted into his large deep waistcoat pocket—and who eyed each merry face, as it passed him by, with such a deep scowl of malice and ill-humor, as it was difficult to meet without feeling something the worse for.

A little before twilight, one Christmas eve, Gabriel shouldered his spade, lighted his lantern, and betook himself towards the old churchyard; for he had got a grave to finish by next morning, and feeling very low, he thought it might raise his spirits, perhaps, if he went on with his work at once. As he went his way, up the ancient street, he saw the cheerful light of the blazing fires gleam through the old casements, and heard the loud laugh and the cheerful shouts of those who were assembled around them; he marked the bustling preparations for next day's cheer, and smelt the numerous savory odors consequent thereupon, as they steamed up from the kitchen windows in clouds. All this was gall and wormwood to the heart of Gabriel Grub; and when groups of children bounded out of the houses, tripped across the road, and were met, before they could knock at the opposite door, by half a dozen curly-headed little rascals who crowded round them as they flocked upstairs to spend the evening in their Christmas games, Gabriel smiled grimly, and clutched the handle of his spade with a firmer grasp as he thought of measles, scarlet fever, thrush, hooping-cough, and a good many other sources of consolation besides.

In this happy frame of mind, Gabriel strode along: returning a short, sullen growl to the good-humored greetings of such of his neighbors as now and then passed him: until he turned into the dark lane which led to the churchyard. Now, Gabriel had been looking forward to reaching the dark lane, because it was, generally speaking, a nice, gloomy, mournful place, into which the townspeople did not much care to go, except in broad daylight, and when the sun was shining; consequently, he was not a little indignant to hear a young urchin roaring out some jolly song about a merry Christmas, in this very sanctuary, which had been called Coffin Lane ever since the days of the old abbey, and the time of the shaven-headed monks. As Gabriel walked on, and the voice drew nearer, he found it proceeded from a small boy, who was hurrying along, to join one of the little parties in the old street, and who, partly to keep himself company, and partly to prepare himself for the occasion, was shouting out the song at the highest pitch of his lungs. So Gabriel waited until the boy came up, and then dodged him into a corner, and rapped him over the head with his lantern, five or six times, to teach him to modulate his voice. And as the boy hurried away with his hand to his head, singing quite a different sort of tune, Gabriel Grub chuckled very heartily to himself, and entered the churchyard: locking the gate behind him.

He took off his coat, put down his lantern, and getting into the unfinished grave, worked at it for an hour or so with right good will. But the earth was hardened with the frost, and it was no very easy matter to break it up, and shovel it out; and although there was a moon, it was a very young one, and shed little light upon the grave, which was in the shadow of the church. At any other time, these obstacles would have made Gabriel Grub very moody and miserable, but he was so well pleased with having stopped the small boy's singing, that he took little heed of the scanty progress he had made, and looked down into the grave, when he had finished work for the night, with grim satisfaction: murmuring as he gathered up his things:

Brave lodgings for one, brave lodgings for one
A few feet of cold earth, when life is done;
A stone at the head, a stone at the feet,
A rich, juicy meal for the worms to eat;
Rank grass over head, and damp clay around,
Brave lodgings for one, these, in holy ground!

"Ho! ho!" laughed Gabriel Grub, as he sat himself down on a flat tombstone, which was a favorite resting-place of his; and drew forth his wicker bottle. "A coffin at Christmas! A Christmas-box. Ho! ho! ho!"

"Ho! ho! ho!" repeated a voice which sounded close behind him.

Gabriel paused in some alarm, in the act of raising the wicker bottle to his lips: and looked round. The bottom of the oldest grave about him was not more still and quiet than the churchyard in the pale moonlight. The cold hoarfrost glistened on the tombstones, and sparkled like rows of gems among the stone carvings of the old church. The snow lay hard and crisp upon the ground: and spread over the thickly strewn mounds of earth, so white and smooth a cover, that it seemed as if corpses lay there, hidden only by their winding sheets. Not the faintest rustle broke the profound tranquillity of the solemn scene. Sound itself appeared to be frozen up, all was so cold and still.

"It was the echoes," said Gabriel Grub, raising the bottle to his lips again.

"It was *not,*" said a deep voice.

Gabriel started up, and stood rooted to the spot with astonishment and terror; for his eyes rested on a form that made his blood run cold.

Seated on an upright tombstone, close to him, was a strange unearthly figure, whom Gabriel felt at once, was no being of this world. His long fantastic legs which might have reached the ground, were cocked up, and crossed after a quaint, fantastic fashion; his sinewy arms were bare; and his hands rested on his knees. On his short, round body, he wore a close covering, ornamented with small slashes; a short cloak dangled at his back; the collar was cut into curious peaks which served the goblin in lieu of ruff or neckerchief; and his shoes curled up at the toes into long points. On his head he wore a broad-brimmed sugar-loaf hat, garnished with a single feather. The hat was covered with the white frost; and the goblin looked as if he had sat on the same tombstone very comfortably, for two or three hundred years. He was sitting perfectly still; his tongue was put out, as if in derision; and he was grinning at Gabriel Grub with such a grin as only a goblin could call up.

"It was *not* the echoes," said the goblin.

Gabriel Grub was paralyzed, and could make no reply.

"What do you do here on Christmas eve?" said the goblin, sternly.

"I came to dig a grave, sir," stammered Gabriel Grub.

"What man wanders among graves and churchyards on such a night as this?" cried the goblin.

"Gabriel Grub! Gabriel Grub!" screamed a wild chorus of voices that seemed to fill the churchyard. Gabriel looked fearfully round—nothing was to be seen.

"What have you got in that bottle?" said the goblin.

"Hollands, sir," replied the sexton, trembling more than ever: for he had bought it of the smugglers, and he thought that perhaps his questioner might be in the excise department of the goblins.

"Who drinks Hollands alone, and in a churchyard, on such a night as this?" said the goblin.

"Gabriel Grub! Gabriel Grub!" exclaimed the wild voices again.

The goblin leered maliciously at the terrified sexton, and then raising his voice, exclaimed:

"And who, then, is our fair and lawful prize?"

To this inquiry the invisible chorus replied, in a strain that sounded like the voices of many choristers singing to the mighty swell of the old church organ—a strain that seemed borne to the sexton's ears upon a wild wind, and to die away as it passed onward—but the burden of the reply was still the same, "Gabriel Grub! Gabriel Grub!"

The goblin grinned a broader grin than before, as he said, "Well, Gabriel, what do you say to this?"

The sexton gasped for breath.

"What do you think of this, Gabriel?" said the goblin, kicking up his feet in the air on either side of the tombstone, and looking at the turned-up points with as much complacency as if he had been contemplating the most fashionable pair of Wellingtons in all Bond Street.

"It's—it's—very curious, sir," replied the sexton, half dead with fright; "very curious, and very pretty, but I think I'll go back and finish my work, sir, if you please."

"Work!" said the goblin, "what work?"

"The grave, sir; making the grave," stammered the sexton.

"Oh, the grave, eh?" said the goblin; "who makes graves at a time when all other men are merry, and takes a pleasure in it?"

Again the mysterious voices replied, "Gabriel Grub; Gabriel Grub!"

"I'm afraid my friends want you, Gabriel," said the goblin, thrusting his tongue farther into his cheek than ever—and a most astonishing tongue it was—"I'm afraid my friends want you, Gabriel," said the goblin.

"Under favor, sir," replied the horror-stricken sexton, "I don't think they can, sir; they don't know me, sir; I don't think the gentlemen have ever seen me, sir."

"Oh yes they have," replied the goblin; "we know the man with the sulky face and the grim scowl, that came down the street tonight, throwing his evil looks at the children, and grasping his burying spade the tighter. We know the man who struck the boy in the envious malice of his heart, because the boy could be merry, and he could not. We know him, we know him."

Here, the goblin gave a loud shrill laugh, which the echoes returned twentyfold: and throwing his legs up in the air, stood upon his head, or rather upon the very point of his sugar-loaf hat, on the narrow edge of the tombstone: whence he threw a summerset with extraordinary agility, right to the sexton's feet, at which he planted himself in the attitude in which tailors generally sit upon the shop-board.

"I—I—am afraid I must leave you, sir," said the sexton, making an effort to move.

"Leave us!" said the goblin, "Gabriel Grub going to leave us. Ho! ho! ho!"

As the goblin laughed, the sexton observed, for one instant, a brilliant illumination within the windows of the church, as if the whole building were lighted up; it disappeared, the organ pealed forth a lively air, and whole troops of goblins, the very counterpart of the first one, poured into the churchyard, and began playing at leap-frog with the tombstones: never stopping for an instant to take breath, but "overing" the highest among them, one after the other, with the most marvelous dexterity. The first goblin was a most astonishing leaper, and none of the others could come near him; even in the extremity of his terror the sexton could not help observing, that while his friends were content to leap over the common-sized gravestones, the first one took the family vaults, iron railings and all, with as much ease as if they had been so many street posts.

At last the game reached to a most exciting pitch; the organ played quicker and quicker; and the goblins leaped faster and faster: coiling themselves up, rolling head over heels upon the ground, and bounding over the tombstones like footballs. The sexton's brain whirled round with the rapidity of the motion he beheld, and his legs reeled beneath him, as the spirits flew before his eyes: when the goblin king, suddenly darting towards him, laid his hand upon his collar, and sunk with him through the earth.

When Gabriel Grub had had time to fetch his breath, which the rapidity of his descent had for the moment taken away, he found himself in what appeared to be a large cavern, surrounded on all sides by crowds of goblins, ugly and grim; in the center of the room, on an elevated seat, was stationed his friend of the churchyard; and close beside him stood Gabriel Grub himself, without the power of motion.

"Cold tonight," said the king of the goblins, "very cold. A glass of something warm, here!"

At this command, half a dozen officious goblins, with a perpetual smile upon their faces, whom Gabriel Grub imagined to be courtiers, on that account, hastily disappeared, and presently returned with a goblet of liquid fire, which they presented to the king.

"Ah!" cried the goblin, whose cheeks and throat were transparent, as he tossed down the flame, "This warms one, indeed! Bring a bumper of the same, for Mr. Grub."

It was in vain for the unfortunate sexton to protest that he was not in the habit of taking anything warm at night; one of the goblins held him while another poured the blazing liquid down his throat; the whole assembly screeched with laughter as he coughed and choked, and wiped away the tears which gushed plentifully from his eyes, after swallowing the burning draught.

"And now" said the king, fantastically poking the taper corner of his sugar-loaf hat into the sexton's eye, and thereby occasioning him the most exquisite pain: "And now show the man of misery and gloom, a few of the pictures from our great storehouse!"

As the goblin said this, a thick cloud which obscured the remoter end of the cavern, rolled gradually away, and disclosed, apparently at a great distance, a small and scantily furnished, but neat and clean apartment. A crowd of little children were gathered round a bright fire, clinging to their mother's gown, and gambolling around her chair. The mother occasionally rose, and drew aside the window-curtain, as if to look for some expected object; a frugal meal was ready spread upon the table; and an elbow-chair was placed near the fire. A knock was heard at the door: the mother opened it, and the children crowded round her, and clapped their hands for joy, as their father entered. He was wet and weary, and shook the snow from his garments, as the children crowded round him, and seizing his cloak, hat, stick, and gloves, with busy zeal, ran with them from the room. Then, as he sat down to his meal before the fire, the children climbed about his knee, and the mother sat by his side, and all seemed happiness and comfort.

But a change came upon the view, almost imperceptibly. The scene was altered to a small bedroom, where the fairest and youngest child lay dying; the roses had fled from his cheek, and the light from his eye; and even as the sexton looked upon him with an interest he had never felt or known before, he died. His young brothers and sisters crowded round his little bed, and seized his tiny hand, so cold and heavy; but they shrunk back from its touch, and looked with awe on his infant face; for calm and tranquil, as it was, and sleeping in rest and peace as the beautiful child seemed to be, they saw that he was dead, and they knew that he was an Angel looking down upon, and blessing them, from a bright and happy heaven.

Again the light cloud passed across the picture, and again the subject changed. The father and mother were old and helpless now, and the number of those about them was diminished more than half; but content and cheerfulness sat on every face, and beamed in every eye, as they crowded round the fireside, and told and listened to old stories of earlier and bygone days. Slowly and peacefully, the father sunk into the grave, and, soon after, the sharer of all his cares and troubles followed him to a place of rest. The few, who yet survived them, knelt by their tomb, and watered the green turf which covered it with their tears; then rose, and turned away: sadly and mournfully, but not with bitter cries, or despairing lamentations, for they knew that they should one day meet again; and once more they mixed with the busy world, and their content and cheerfulness were restored. The cloud settled upon the picture, and concealed it from the sexton's view.

"What do you think of *that?*" said the goblin, turning his large face towards Gabriel Grub.

Gabriel murmured out something about its being very pretty, and looked somewhat ashamed, as the goblin bent his fiery eyes upon him.

"*You* a miserable man!" said the goblin, in a tone of excessive contempt. "You!" He appeared disposed to add more, but indignation choked his utterance, so he lifted up one of his very pliable legs, and flourishing it above his head a little, to insure his aim, administered a good sound kick to Gabriel Grub; immediately after which, all the goblins in waiting, crowded round the wretched sexton, and kicked him without mercy: according to the established and invariable custom of courtiers upon earth, who kick whom royalty kicks, and hug whom royalty hugs.

"Show him some more!" said the king of the goblins.

At these words, the cloud was again dispelled, and a rich and beautiful landscape was disclosed to view—there is just such another, to this day, within half a mile of the old abbey town. The sun shone from out the clear blue sky, the water sparkled beneath his rays, and the trees looked greener, and the flowers more gay, beneath his cheering influence. The water rippled on, with a pleasant sound; the trees rustled in the light wind that murmured among their leaves; the birds sung upon the boughs; and the lark carolled on high, her welcome to the morning. Yes, it was morning: the bright, balmy morning of summer; the minutest leaf, the smallest blade of grass, was instinct with life. The ant crept forth to her daily toil, the butterfly fluttered and basked in the warm rays of the sun; myriads of insects spread their transparent wings, and reveled in their brief but happy existence. Man walked forth, elated with the scene; and all was brightness and splendor.

"*You* a miserable man!" said the king of the goblins, in a more contemptuous tone than before. And again the king of the goblins gave his leg a flourish; again it descended on the shoulders of the sexton; and again the attendant goblins imitated the example of their chief.

Many a time the cloud went and came, and many a lesson it taught to Gabriel Grub, who, although his shoulders smarted with pain from the frequent applications of the goblin's feet, looked on with an interest that nothing could diminish. He saw that men who worked hard, and earned their scanty bread with lives of labor, were cheerful and happy; and that to the most ignorant, the sweet face of nature was a never-failing source of cheerfulness and joy. He saw those who had been delicately nurtured, and tenderly brought up, cheerful under privations, and superior to suffering, that would have crushed many of a rougher grain, because they bore within their own bosoms the materials of happiness, contentment, and peace. He saw that women, the tenderest and most fragile of all God's creatures, were the oftenest superior to sorrow, adversity, and distress; and he saw that it was because they bore, in their own hearts, an inexhaustible well-spring of affection and devotion. Above all, he saw that men like himself, who snarled at the mirth and cheerfulness of others, were the foulest weeds on the fair surface of the earth; and setting all the good of the world against the evil, he came to the conclusion that it was a very decent and respectable sort of world after all. No sooner had he formed it, than the cloud which had closed over the last picture, seemed to settle on his senses, and lull him to repose. One by one, the goblins faded from his sight; and as the last one disappeared, he sunk to sleep.

The day had broken when Gabriel Grub awoke, and found himself lying, at full length on the flat gravestone in the churchyard, with the wicker bottle lying empty by his side, and his coat, spade, and lantern, all well whitened by the last night's frost, scattered on the ground. The stone on which he had first seen the goblin seated, stood bolt upright before him, and the grave at which he had worked, the night before, was not far off. At first, he began to doubt the reality of his adventures, but the acute pain in his shoulders when he attempted to rise, assured him that the kicking of the goblins was certainly not ideal. He was staggered again, by observing no traces of footsteps in the snow on which the goblins had played at leap-frog with the gravestones, but he speedily accounted for this circumstance when he remembered that, being spirits, they would leave no visible impression behind them. So, Gabriel Grub got on his feet as well as he could, for the pain in his back; and brushing the frost off his coat, put it on, and turned his face towards the town.

But he was an altered man, and he could not bear the thought of returning to a place where his repentance would be scoffed at, and his reformation disbelieved. He hesitated for a few moments; and then turned away to wander where he might, and seek his bread elsewhere.

The lantern, the spade, and the wicker bottle were found, that day, in the churchyard. There were a great many speculations about the sexton's fate, at first, but it was speedily determined that he had been carried away by the goblins; and there were not wanting some very credible witnesses who had distinctly seen him whisked through the air on the back of a chestnut horse blind of one eye, with the hindquarters of a lion, and the tail of a bear. At length all this was devoutly believed; and the new sexton used to exhibit to the curious, for a trifling emolument, a good-sized piece of the church weathercock which had been accidentally kicked off by the aforesaid horse in his aerial flight, and picked up by himself in the churchyard, a year or two afterwards.

Unfortunately, these stories were somewhat disturbed by the unlooked-for reappearance of Gabriel Grub himself, some ten years afterwards, a ragged, contented, rheumatic old man. He told his story to the clergyman, and also to the mayor; and in course of time it began to be received, as a matter of history, in which form it has continued down to this very day. The believers in the weathercock tale, having misplaced their confidence once, were not easily prevailed upon to part with it again, so they looked as wise as they could, shrugged their shoulders, touched their foreheads, and murmured something about Gabriel Grub having drank all the Hollands, and then fallen asleep on the flat tombstone; and they affected to explain what he supposed he had witnessed in the goblin's cavern, by saying that he had seen the world, and grown wiser. But this opinion, which was by no means a popular one at any time, gradually died off; and be the matter how it may, as Gabriel Grub was afflicted with rheumatism to the end of his days, this story has at least one moral, if it teach no better one—and that is, that if a man turn sulky and drink by himself at Christmas time, he may make up his mind to be not a bit the better for it; let the spirits be never so good, or let them be even as many degrees beyond proof, as those which Gabriel Grub saw in the goblin's cavern.

ELIZABETH WALTER

CHRISTMAS NIGHT

A young couple faces murderous terror on Christmas night.

"ON Christmas night all Christians sing." I don't know about that, but we were certainly singing, Mairi and I, as we came over the top of the Callow and saw the lights of Caringford five miles away in the valley below us. Clear roads, clear skies, and a hundred and forty miles still to London. The beauty of the night almost made up for having to leave Mairi's family in South Wales and drive back so that I could open in a new play on Boxing Night.

"We haven't seen another car since we left St. Devereux," Mairi said.

"That's because only rogues, vagabonds and actors are about."

"And only actors drive cars."

"I don't know. Some of the biggest rogues I know drive Rolls-Royces."

"We've still a way to go before we're in that class," Mairi said, and I could feel her dimpling in the darkness, "but at least we'll be seeing your name up in lights in the West End tomorrow night."

And at that moment the car gave a sudden lurch and began to bump rhythmically, and I said, "That's our offside rear tire gone," and got out to look at it. And of course it was.

Now I know every car carries a spare wheel and is required to do so by law and all the rest of it, but the fact is I didn't have one. I know I ought to have had and I'm not making excuses, but I'd left it to have a new tire fitted and in the rush of rehearsals and last-minute hitches, I hadn't had time to pick it up.

So there we were on top of the Callow, with no lights nearer than those of Carringford and a car we couldn't drive.

Mairi got out and stood beside me.

"What now, John?"

"We'll have to hire a car in Carringford."

"But everything closes at half past five even on weekdays."

"Not, presumably, the hotels. I'm not having you hanging about on a Welsh hillside. You'll get pneumonia again."

She'd had it two years ago and nearly died of it, and I wasn't taking any chances.

"We'll lock the car and start walking," I said, trying to sound masterful.

She looked down at her feet. "In these shoes?"

I'm familiar with the usual gripes about women's footwear, but I happen to like to see a girl in high heels and Mairi knows it. She hadn't packed anything beyond the delicate sandals she was wearing and a pair of fluffy bedroom mules. After all, for a thirty-six-hour trip home why bother, when we had all the family Christmas presents to take? Nevertheless, I must have sounded a bit ruffled as I suggested she should stay in the car.

"I'll get a taxi or hire a car—there must be something, even at Christmas—and come back and pick you up."

"No, John, I don't want to stay here." Her voice had a hysterical note.

"The only alternative is to walk."

"No, it isn't. There's an inn, I think. I'm almost certain."

"An inn in this benighted spot? Where?"

"Down there." She pointed to what appeared to be a cart track.

"There'll be nothing down there but a gate into a field."

"There's an inn," she said with an odd certainty. "I don't know how I know it, but I do."

I reflected that it must be a childhood memory. For much of her life Mairi had traveled between South Wales and London, first in her father's car, then in her own, now in mine. She knew the route backwards and I relied on her for navigation. If she said there was an inn, there probably was.

"Come on," I said, taking her arm and reaching for the powerful torch we always carry. "What are we waiting for?"

We didn't need the torch. I have never seen moonlight like it, and all from one small, high, brilliant globe. The furrows in the field, the twigs in the hedges, everything was rimed with frost. What was not black was silver. The stiff grass crunched under our feet. And we had not gone a hundred yards before the track curved and on our left was a two-storied, slate-roofed building.

"There," Mairi said a little breathlessly. "I told you there was an inn."

As we drew nearer we could see a sign swinging gently, but the place appeared to be closed.

"You forgot about Welsh licensing hours," I told her.

"We've been in England for the last fifteen miles."

I bowed to her superior knowledge. It was not yet ten o'-clock. But when I tried the inn door, it was unyielding. I lifted my hand to knock.

"John—don't!"

"What's the matter?" Mairi was clutching my arm.

"I don't like this place. Let's go away from here—quickly."

"I must say I've seen more prepossessing inns. But it's Hobson's choice, I'm afraid, love. We'll only stay long enough to use their phone."

"I don't think there's anyone at home."

"There's a light in that window." I pointed to one of the downstairs rooms which appeared to be shuttered on the inside. "It beats me how they make the place pay."

"Perhaps they don't."

"Then how do they keep going?"

"They may have other ways . . ."

My knocking drowned the rest of her sentence. It seemed to reverberate through the house. Then, somewhere within, a door opened and footsteps shuffled down the hall.

"Someone's coming," I said, but Mairi was looking at the sign, not listening.

"John, d'you see what this inn is called?"

I glanced up, but the inn sign was in shadow.

"It's called the Hanged Man," Mairi went on. "Isn't it horrible? It must be the most off-putting inn sign anywhere."

At that moment there was a dull creaking and moonlight fell upon the sign as it swung. There was indeed a crude representation of a gibbet from which a body hung. As the sign moved it was as though it was the gibbet creaking, swaying out of darkness into light. It was eerily lifelike, except that that is not the word for a dead body. I too was suddenly afraid of what might lie behind the inn's inhospitable door.

The landlord, when he appeared, did nothing to reassure me. He was squat and scowling and none too clean. I apologized for disturbing him if he was not open, and asked if I might use the phone.

"There's no phone here."

The absence of telephone wires endorsed his statement. I felt he thought I was a fool.

"Perhaps we could at least come in and have a drink if you're open."

He grudgingly held the door.

Inside it was all wainscot and low ceilings. The room on the right was the bar, stone-flagged, with a sullen fire smouldering in the open hearth and a couple of oak settles drawn up at right angles. It was unwelcoming to say the least. We were the only customers. The shuttered window was bare. Above the bar a paraffin lamp cast the only illumination and fought an unequal fight against the shadows.

I ordered a beer and Mairi a gin and tonic, though what she got was a gin and ginger ale. The landlord claimed he was out of tonic.

"Ah," I said, "you've had a busy night."

He missed the irony, and once again I felt myself a fool in his eyes. To recover, I said: "You're very much off the beaten track. Do you get many customers?"

"There's always them as remembers the way," he answered. His eyes were on Mairi as he spoke.

I didn't altogether care for the way he looked at her, but I had to keep in with him.

"Since you've no phone," I said, "and our car's broken down and we've no means of getting in to Carringford, do you think you could put us up for the night?"

"Ah," he said noncommittally.

"Unless you know of anywhere else?"

"Nothing nearer than the Tram Inn at Garton."

I turned to Mairi. "Where's that?"

"At the end of the old tramway that used to run over the hills from South Wales. They used it for hauling slate at one time. Garton's a good three miles."

"We might as well stay here, then."

"If mine host will give us a bed."

"Landlord, can you put us up?" I asked again with some asperity.

He did not answer directly. "Long time since anyone stayed here."

"That means it's damp and there are bedbugs," Mairi said under her breath.

"But you can stay if you want," the landlord continued. "I'd best go and see about a bed."

We heard the stairs creak as he ascended, and then a floorboard groaned overhead. Evidently, he was single-handed. I wondered he wasn't melancholy mad. When I said so, Mairi gave a hysterical giggle. "Perhaps he is. Oh John, I hate this place. It's so primitive. Do you suppose there's a bathroom? I thought licensed premises had to conform to a certain standard, but I've never seen anything like this."

"It's probably so out of the way the inspectors missed it. You'd never expect to find an inn here. Except of course that you did."

She shivered. "I just knew it was here. I don't understand it. I must have come some time with Dad."

"The place mightn't look so bad in daylight."

"No, but it would feel as bad. Don't you notice it, John—how cold it is, and evil?"

"You're being fanciful," I said.

I never knew an actor who wasn't superstitious, but Mairi had us all beat. No doubt it was her Celtic blood, but her extraordinary sensitivity amounted at times to ESP. At other times it amounted to nothing and I called her fanciful. I hoped this was one of those times as I poked the smoky fire, which merely became smokier, and teased her about her premonitions and dreams.

No circumstances would cause me to describe the return of our landlord as welcome, though this time he was trying to smile. I couldn't honestly say it improved his appearance, but at least it showed goodwill.

"Well, sir and madam, we're all ready for you," he said, rubbing his hands as though he had a treat in store. "And how about a glass of mulled wine as a nightcap? It would warm the cockles of your heart."

I looked enquiringly at Mairi. It seemed to me the landlord did the same, but his eyes rested on the diamond pendant she was wearing, which caught the light as she moved. It had cost a lot and some people said I was crazy, but a combination of a big West End part, our fifth wedding anniversary and Christmas had caused me to give my natural extravagance free rein. If a man can't buy his wife jewelry occasionally, what's the good of having a wife, and money and prospects and one foot on the ladder, and all the rest of it? I counted the money well spent, but I didn't care for the way mine host was eyeing the pendant. I was about to refuse his offer of mulled wine when he said ingratiatingly: "On the house."

Perhaps a refusal would seem churlish. It would certainly help Mairi to get warm. I thanked him and he produced it at once. It must have been mulling in the kitchen and for the moment was too hot to touch. Mine host also produced a large candle in an old-fashioned candlestick and prepared to light the way upstairs. Clasping our mugs, we followed him like children up to the room above the bar.

There was a washstand in the corner and nothing else except a high old-fashioned double bed covered with a white honeycomb quilt which looked spotless, with one corner invitingly turned down. There was a bolster and a positive mountain of pillows and three steps to help you climb into bed. As we watched, our host set the candle down upon a small night table we had not noticed and withdrew two flannel-wrapped hot bricks from the bed. He stood there holding them like weights and bowed slightly.

"I hope you sleep well, sir and madam, and I wish you a very good night."

The door latched behind him. Mairi, who had been examining the bed, exclaimed, "John, feathers! It's a real old-fashioned feather bed."

"They don't exactly go in for all mod. cons. at the Hanged Man," I observed ruefully, surveying the washstand and wondering if the morning would produce hot water for a shave.

Mairi was already nestling among the feathers and sipping her mulled wine. Without more ado I joined her, after flinging back the shutters so that the moonlight flooded in. The room was as bright as day, and with this mock daylight the inn seemed to have become alive. Not only could I hear the groaning sigh as the sign of the Hanged Man moved uneasily below our window, but there were all sorts of creaks and cracks from boards inside the house. When an owl hooted, seemingly in the chimney, I jumped almost out of my skin. I drank a little of the wine but it had grown tepid and I did not care for the taste. Mairi was asleep already, snuggled deep in the feather bed. Gradually I let its warmth suffuse me and felt myself relax. I was drowning in feathers, sinking deeper, ever deeper. The last thing I remembered was the scent of lavender from the sheets.

I don't know what wakened me, but my eyes went at once to the door latch. It was still in exactly the same place. Reassured, I let my gaze rove round the room and to the window. The moon had gone but the stars were large and clear. And then, as my eyes went back to the door, I felt my scalp prickle. The latch had risen an inch silently, and as I watched it moved again.

I looked at Mairi sleeping peacefully and slid my hand under the pillow at her head. The pendant was there, where I had told her to put it. I had no doubt he had come for that. For who else could the visitor be but our ungenial landlord who thought he saw an easy way of compensating for lost trade? While I was wondering whether to shout for nonexistent help or walk boldly forward and face him, the door itself began to move.

I glanced at my watch. It was two o'clock in the morning, the time when all the vital forces run low. No less a general than Napoleon had praised the possessors of two o'clock courage, but I was not numbered in their ranks. The panic that gripped me was far worse than first-night nerves, and it came to me uncomfortably that last-night nerves might be a better term. Did the landlord intend violence in any case, or would he resort to it only if challenged? Was I actor enough to call his bluff?

The door had now opened about a foot. At any moment I expected to see the landlord's head peer round. And then, faint but drawing steadily nearer, came one of the commonest of twentieth-century sounds. Someone in the early hours of Boxing Day morning was driving a car down the track that led to the Hanged Man.

I don't know whether I or our sinister landlord was the more startled, but on our respective sides of the door, we froze. Then, as the car drew up outside the inn, our latch fell gently into place, and an instant later there was a thunderous knocking downstairs as the car-driver demanded admittance. Very quietly I slipped out of bed.

The car was a yellow Austin, and the registration number began KCJ. The rest was in shadow and I couldn't see it, and all I could see of the driver was the balding top of his head. As I watched, the inn door evidently opened and a shaft of light streamed forth. I had time enough to glimpse our landlord and to note that he was still fully dressed. I could not catch a word of the conversation, but the balding man came inside and I heard him with the landlord in the bar-room just below us as I crept back to bed and dozed the rest of the night.

When next I woke it was seven-thirty, though not a soul was astir. In little more than twelve hours I was due to open in the West End of London. I could not linger here.

I shook Mairi gently by the shoulder. "Wake up, we've got to go."

She looked at me blankly. "There are no horses . . ."

Obviously she was still in the land of dreams.

"Quite right, sweetheart. We're going to walk," I said lightly. "And since the landlord isn't up, I'm not waiting for him. Get your clothes on and let's go."

To be honest, I was only too anxious to avoid the landlord. I did not know what I might say. Of course I could prove nothing and he would say I had imagined the door opening, yet if that car had not come I was convinced we should have been robbed, perhaps murdered. I led the way downstairs.

The stairs creaked and groaned and we made no attempt to be quiet. Despite this, no one came. I left the landlord what I hoped was fair recompense on the bar counter, and we stepped out into the frosty air. The yellow Austin was still parked underneath the inn sign, only now it glistened with frost.

"So we weren't the only visitors," Mairi said, surprise showing.

"You were asleep when he came."

Briefly I described the nocturnal arrival, though without mentioning the incident of the door.

"I suppose the poor fellow was lost," Mairi said as we stumbled along the cart track. "Otherwise he'd never have left the road."

"Either that or he remembered the place, as you did."

"I didn't remember it."

"But you were positive it was there."

"That's different."

I did not bother to ask why because at that moment a car came along the road. I hailed it and explained our plight. In no time we had a lift into Carringford and I was rousing a grumpy garage proprietor and telling him the tale of our flat tire. Even so, it was ten before we were on the road to London and I drove fast all the way. Thereafter I was caught up in the excitement of an opening, and knew nothing about the murder till next day.

Mairi brought me breakfast in bed next morning, and the papers. I knew from her eyes that the notices were good. We turned to them eagerly, strewing papers all over the bedroom. Several singled me out by name. We hugged ourselves and each other in the small, safe, egotistical world of success. The usual gloomy headlines meant nothing. It was some time before we turned to the front page.

Even then, it was while I was on the telephone, accepting congratulations with a falsely practiced air, that a small item datelined Carringford caught my attention and then held me riveted.

It described how the body of the seasonably-named Mr. Noel

Hutchins, aged 42, had been discovered savagely battered in a field five miles from Carringford. Near him his car had been found abandoned. It was in perfect working order and there was no indication why it had been left. Mr. Hutchins, a bachelor, had been driving home alone from a late-night party, but there was no excess alcohol in his blood. Why had he stopped and where had he been murdered? Who had driven his car off the road? One theory was that he had given a lift to his killer, but as he was known to have had little money with him, it was impossible to say if he had been robbed. Police were anxious to contact anyone who might have seen his yellow Austin, registration number KCJ 7333, on the 26th between the hours of 1 A.M. and 11 A.M., at which time the body had been found.

I pushed the paper across to Mairi, mouthed "He was at the Hanged Man," and strove to terminate my telephone conversation which had reached its end some time ago.

As I put the receiver down, Mairi looked up at me. "His car was certainly there at seven-thirty when we left."

"Yes, but where was he? What happened to him after his two o'clock arrival?"

"Oh John, you don't think . . ."

"I don't know what to think, but I don't trust that landlord. He was trying to get into our room. I'll swear he was after your pendant, only the arrival of Mr. Hutchins disturbed him. We owe the poor fellow a lot."

"I don't know what you're talking about."

"No, sweetheart, you were asleep."

Briefly I told her what had happened.

"Yes," she said thoughtfully, "it fits. That wine was drugged. I suspected it. I don't usually sleep heavily like that."

"And I hardly touched mine," I said, remembering, "which is why I was instantly awake. There may be some innocent explanation, but mine host had better give it to the police."

The inspector who came in answer to my telephone call to the local police station was accompanied by a sergeant who took down everything I said. He made no comment and indeed seemed to know no more about the case than he could have read in the papers, but he promised to be in touch. The upshot was that the next day, after the matinee, I was told an Inspector Reece would like to see me and was waiting in my dressing-room. I was tired and resentful of this intrusion. In the worst of moods I went along.

Inspector Reece was a small man with an accent like Mairi's father's. It is one I find difficult not to catch. Before long it sounded as if I were rehearsing Fluellen, and I was mortally afraid Inspector Reece would take offense. But he didn't; he merely took me through my statement at a brisk pace, asking an occasional question, and then tapping his pencil and looking thoughtful.

"What did you say the inn was called, sir?" he said at last, after a pause.

"The Hanged Man."

"Funny name, isn't it? You would not expect many customers with a name like that."

"There weren't many. My wife and I saw no one but the landlord."

"Ah yes. The landlord. Could you describe him, sir?"

"Squat, thickset, unprepossessing."

"Too vague, sir, I'm afraid. His name now, did you hear it mentioned?"

"No."

"You're very sure of that."

"He didn't tell us his name and there was no one else to do so. We never saw another soul."

"Except Mr. Hutchins," the inspector reminded me. "You say he arrived very late."

"Around two o'clock in the morning. I know because I looked at my watch."

"You were awake, then?"

"Yes. You know how it is—strange beds."

"But your wife—she was not awake?"

"No, she'd had a nightcap. Some mulled wine that sent her off."

"Mulled wine, now. There can't be many inns where that is offered."

"I told you, we think it was drugged."

"Yes, well, it might be an effective vehicle, but strangely old-fashioned."

"The Hanged Man *was* old-fashioned. I'd call it primitive."

"So you did. The very word." The inspector glanced at my statement. "Now, sir, where was the Hanged Man?" He leaned forward with peculiar intensity as he asked me, as though my answer mattered a lot.

"Well, we'd come over the Callow—"

"How far over?" he interrupted.

"I don't think I could say. Over the brow, to a point where we could see Carringford. But we hadn't come very far down."

The inspector repeated my shaky location. I said sharply: "I expect my wife would know. She's been traveling that road since she was a schoolgirl. It was she who found the Hanged Man."

"We shall certainly ask her," Inspector Reece said drily. "Your own directions are a little imprecise. And the truth is, there's no inn at the spot you mention, neither the Hanged Man nor anything else."

I looked at him in astonishment. "But we spent the night there."

"Yes, sir. So you say."

"Well, there's no other inn we could have mistaken it for, is there? Not with a name like that."

"The nearest inn is the Tram Inn at Garton."

"It certainly wasn't the Tram. The landlord mentioned it and my wife knew it. She said it was three miles away."

"Yes, it's about that from the spot you're describing."

"And we didn't spend the night at the Tram."

"No, sir. We've already checked."

Suddenly I was angry. "You think we're not telling the truth."

"It's true enough that your car developed a flat tire on the Carringford side of the Callow. The garage proprietor confirms that."

"You *have* been doing your homework."

"It's our duty to find out facts," he said stiffly, slightly emphasizing the last word. "And you and your wife are the only people to have admitted seeing Mr. Hutchins and his car between the early hours of Boxing Day morning when he left his friends' party and eleven o'clock when his body was found. Now, sir, why exactly did you come forward?"

I said equally stiffly, "It is every citizen's duty to help the police."

"True enough, but some people place a pretty liberal interpretation upon it. Enjoy the notoriety, you might say."

"I assure you I've no need to seek more limelight."

"No, sir, they tell me you've made a hit. Nevertheless, I shall have to ask you and your wife as good citizens to tear yourself away from the capital and come back to Carringford. On the spot and by daylight you will perhaps be better able to identify the place where you spent Christmas night."

"But the play—"

"I'm aware of your commitments," he said smoothly, "but you don't work a seven-day week. I'll be on my way now to see your wife and leave you to rest before your next performance."

He stood up and I deliberately hesitated before doing likewise.

"About Carringford," he said, "would Sunday suit?"

Everything was different. Gray, low skies, air dank and moisture-laden, Carringford invisible in a miasma of river mist. When we got out of the car at the point the inspector indicated, I accepted his word that this was where we had parked on the Callow, but I might have been a thousand miles away.

The inspector was accompanied by a sergeant and a constable. The constable never said a word the whole time. The sergeant was a local man, and as he led the way confidently towards the cart track I had the feeling that he knew the terrain better than his superior. He gave me a sympathetic look.

The inspector paused at the beginning of the cart track. "Now, sir," he said, "where's your inn?"

"Down here," Mairi said with sudden confidence. "I remember."

It was she who led the way.

After about a quarter of a mile the track curved gently. Just beyond the bend a small piece of ground had been fenced off and covered with a tarpaulin.

"Where we found Hutchins's car," the inspector said.

"It was parked outside the inn when we saw it."

"Then someone drove it here."

"They didn't," Mairi said softly, in a little-girl-lost sort of voice. "This is where the Hanged Man was."

On either side of the track ploughed fields stretched emptily.

"You're being fanciful," I said gently.

"I am not. The inn was here."

"Then they did a quick job of demolition," the inspector said.

I had been accused once of seeking the publicity which association with a murder case can give. I did not care for the thought that we should soon be accused of frivolous time-wasting, or even of obstructing the police.

"I was surprised myself that there should be an inn down a cart track," I told the inspector, "but my wife was positive. And there certainly was an inn. A two-storied, slate-roofed building like dozens I've seen round here. It was primitive; no phone or electricity, and lit by candles and lamps, but it existed as true as I stand here. They even put hot bricks in our bed."

"There *was* an inn round about here once, sir," the sergeant said hesitantly. "I've heard my grandfather speak of it, but it was pulled down a hundred years ago."

"What was it called?"

"I don't know, sir, but it wasn't the Hanged Man, that's for sure."

"But why have an inn on a cart track in open country?" I asked him.

He smiled. "It must seem funny now, but you see this wasn't always a cart track. It's all that's left of the old tramway to South Wales."

"With the Tram Inn at the bottom," Mairi said, understanding dawning.

"That's right, ma'm, but this was a convenient stopping place. The beginning of the downhill run or the end of the first climb, depending on which way you were going. It must have done good business once. But of course, after they closed the tramway the inn was stuck in the midst of nowhere and there wasn't the trade any more. They hung on for a time because there was talk of using the old tramway as the route for a new road over the Callow, but in the end—" he gestured—"the new road went elsewhere."

I looked at the muddy, rutted track and thought how once its rails had gleamed darkly on drizzle-dull days like this, or shone silver in the Christmas moonlight, or glinted in the mid-day sun. And now—this. The earth reclaimed her own with a vengeance, nature triumphing over man's short primacy just as she was asserting herself over what had been railway lines in my boyhood and were now fast becoming sunken lanes.

Inspector Reece brought us back to the present. "I fail to see," he said, "how a building pulled down a hundred years ago can have been mysteriously resurrected to enable a murder to take place."

"I don't either, sir," the sergeant said, "but there was an inn here once, so the lady's not being entirely—" he glanced at me—"fanciful."

A sudden chill breeze started blowing.

Mairi had gone very white.

"I told you there was an atmosphere of evil about the place, John."

"Yes, love, I know you did. My wife," I explained to the inspector, "is exceedingly sensitive to atmosphere. If a murder was being committed in the vicinity—and we must suppose that it was—it is not surprising that she picked up some reverberations."

"Indeed?" the inspector said. "The jury may be interested to hear it, but they won't be convinced, I'm afraid."

Any more than I am, we could hear him adding.

He said abruptly, "We'd better go back. But I'd be obliged if you could stay on until tomorrow, in case something else comes up."

Or in case you decide to tell the truth and stop fooling, his unspoken thought said loudly.

We drove thoughtfully and rather slowly back into Carringford.

That night neither Mairi nor I slept well, despite the fact that the Red Lion at Carringford is a first-class hotel. It was a wild night, for the breeze we had noticed that morning had become a high wind by sunset, hunting down clouds against a livid sky. All night it blew gustily through the streets, setting doors banging and dustbin lids clattering, and rising sometimes to a long, mournful howl that sounded strangely like a wolf. It dashed scuds of raindrops against the window, and then, when we looked out, parted the racing clouds to show us a high and pallid moon.

Yet the tumult was within me rather than without. What had become of the Hanged Man? How could an inn whose every physical impression was remarkably vivid, vanish so utterly? I had that indeterminate aggressive feeling of one who has been in some way tricked. And as a result the police suspected me of being a vulgar seeker after notoriety—and perhaps of something worse. Did they think Mairi and I were in some way concerned in Noel Hutchins's murder? True, we had no motive, but neither had anyone else. It seemed a completely purposeless crime. He must have given a lift to a madman. God alone knew what went wandering about the roads of the Welsh Border after dark.

We were finishing a late breakfast when we were told that Sergeant Price was waiting to see us. I asked them to bring him in. He sat down shyly and accepted coffee. We waited for him to begin.

He looked from one to the other of us, and a smile spread over his face. "The inspector asked me to tell you, sir, that for the moment he doesn't need to see either of you again."

"You mean we can start back to London after breakfast instead of waiting till after lunch?"

"If you so wish, sir, though there's one or two things in Carringford worth seeing."

"I dare say, but we've had enough of the place." I remembered too late that he was a local. "In other circumstances, perhaps."

"Are you any nearer to catching the murderer?" Mairi asked to distract attention.

"Not really." He smiled a slow, secretive smile. "Perhaps we're never going to catch him."

"What makes you say that?" I asked.

"Hunch. Oh, I know policemen aren't supposed to have hunches." He mimicked the inspector. " 'The jury might be interested, but they won't believe you, I'm afraid.' But I've found out a bit more about the Hanged Man, if you'd care to hear it."

I spoke for both of us. "Of course we would."

"The inn was pulled down, like I told you, about a hundred years ago. It was already derelict and local folk said it was haunted."

"I'm not surprised," Mairi said, "with a name like the Hanged Man."

"Oh, that wasn't its name when it was an inn. The inn was called the Peacock. It acquired the other name afterwards, first as a nickname and then some joker hung up a sign. Not surprising, perhaps, since the last landlord was hanged for murder."

"How do you know all this?" I asked.

"Local history's always been an interest of mine. Industrial archaeology, really—like the route of the old tramway or of the canal that used to link us with Gloucester, but the local history bit comes in. I'd heard of the inn in connection with the tramway, and also some things my grandfather knew, so I looked in the library first thing as soon as it opened. They've an interesting local collection in there."

"And what about this landlord?"

"Well, it seems that his name was Prosser—Prosser of the Peacock—and so long as the tramway was open he did quite a bit of trade, with the men coming over with full trucks but returning with empties, but when the tramway closed he fell on hard times. It wasn't the same for the Tram Inn down at the bottom, because that's in Garton and on the road, but the Peacock was high and dry on the hillside and no one any longer went by. Prosser hung on for a year or two in hopes that the new road over the Callow would bring him business, but when they drove it through it was half a mile to the west. Soon after that, in desperation, Prosser committed his first murder."

Mairi and I spoke in unison. "His first!"

"Oh yes, sir, he did several. Anyone staying overnight at the inn who looked to have a bit of money about him was likely to end his journey there. The place was so isolated that no one ever heard anything, and Prosser used to turn the horses loose so his victims couldn't get away."

I looked at Mairi oddly. "You said something about there being no horses when first I woke you up."

"Did I? I don't remember."

"I thought you were dreaming, of course."

"So I was. I had nightmares all night. I told you the place was evil. What happened to Prosser in the end?"

The sergeant cleared his throat. "He committed one murder too many. A young lady, the last of 'em was. But she was rich and had influential connections who raised a hue and cry."

"And she was found?"

"Her and the others. But it was for her murder Prosser was hanged."

I thought of the drugged wine, the lifting latch, and the way the landlord had eyed Mairi's pendant, and a shiver went down my spine.

"I don't know what it has to do with the murder of Hutchins," I said to the sergeant, "but I think there's something you should know."

And I filled in some details I had omitted in my statement to the inspector.

"What d'you make of it?" I asked at the end.

He met my gaze squarely. "I reckon Hutchins did you a good turn by coming, but it's not a matter for the police."

"But why did he come there?"

"Why did you, sir?"

"You know that. Our car broke down. And my wife must have had a faint recollection of some story about the inn."

"Perhaps the same went for Mr. Hutchins."

I heard the landlord's voice: "There's always them as remembers the way."

"You don't think his murder will be solved, do you?" I challenged the sergeant.

He shrugged. "That's for the inspector to say. But I know what I think, and I'll warrant you do too, sir. I'd best be getting on my way."

As we escorted him to the door, Mairi said, "It's dreadful to think of that horrible inn resurrecting at Christmas."

"That's when they say round here the graves do gape."

"Oh no," I said, dredging up lines from *Hamlet,* "at that season 'no spirit dare walk abroad.' "

"Very comforting," the sergeant observed drily, "but we say the twelve nights of Christmas are the most haunted of the year. That's when the Wild Hunt rides—Cwn Annwn, the Welsh call it. It was out last night by the sound of it. Don't tell me you didn't hear."

I thought of the wind with its mournful, lupine howling, and the torn clouds racing like wolves across the moon. I had heard of the ghostly huntsman and his pack, but I had not thought of them in this connection.

I looked significantly from Mairi to the sergeant. "We'll be glad to be getting back to London. Soon."

So far as I know, the killer of poor Noel Hutchins is still unapprehended. A verdict of willful murder was returned against a person or persons unknown. But the story had one curious and unexpected addendum, which came about in this way.

I sent Sergeant Price and his wife two front stall tickets and invited them backstage after the show. They were as excited as children when they joined Mairi and me and one or two other members of the cast for drinks in my dressing room, and made no secret of the fact.

At one point in the socializing I became aware that Sergeant Price was trying to draw me aside. "Got something here you might like to see," he said portentously, producing a wallet as thick as a small book.

From it he extracted a photograph of a drawing. "The original's in the library," he said. "It's Prosser's last victim. I came across it when I was delving into him a bit more deeply and had this taken special. I thought you'd be interested."

It was a drawing of a girl in the costume of the eighteen-forties or 'fifties: poke bonnet, and sloping shoulders beneath a shawl; the kind of thing you see in Christmas cards and Dickens illustrations and say, "How pretty." But in this case that wasn't all.

The room swam and I sat down weakly. Beneath the bonnet's brim frilled with lace, dark eyes looked out at me, a soft round chin and a dimple. I was looking at Mairi's face.

Arthur Machen

A NEW CHRISTMAS CAROL

Nothing is certain but death and taxes.

SCROOGE was undoubtedly getting on in life, to begin with. There is no doubt whatever about that. Ten years had gone by since the spirit of old Jacob Marley had visited him, and the Ghosts of Christmas Past, Christmas Present, and Christmas Yet to Come had shown him the error of his mean, niggardly, churlish ways, and had made him the merriest old boy that ever walked on 'Change with a chuckle, and was called "Old Medlar" by the young dogs who never reverenced anybody or anything.

And, not a doubt of it, the young dogs were in the right. Ebenezer Scrooge *was* a meddler. He was always ferreting about into other peoples' business; so that he might find out what good he could do them. Many a hard man of affairs softened as he thought of Scrooge and of the old man creeping round to the countinghouse where the hard man sat in despair, and thought of the certain ruin before him.

"My dear Mr. Hardman," old Scrooge had said, "not another word. Take this draft for thirty thousand pounds, and use it as none knows better. Why, you'll double it for me before six months are out."

He would go out chuckling on that, and Charles the waiter, at the old City tavern where Scrooge dined, always said that Scrooge was a fortune for him and to the house. To say nothing of what Charles got by him; everybody ordered a fresh supply of hot brandy and water when his cheery, rosy old face entered the room.

It was Christmastide. Scrooge was sitting before his roaring fire, sipping at something warm and comfortable, and plotting happiness for all sorts of people.

"I won't bear Bob's obstinacy," he was saying to himself—the firm was Scrooge and Cratchit now—"he does all the work, and it's not fair for a useless old fellow like me to take more than a quarter share of the profits."

A dreadful sound echoed through the grave old house. The air grew chill and sour. The something warm and comfortable grew cold and tasteless as Scrooge sipped it nervously. The door flew open, and a vague but fearful form stood in the doorway.

"Follow me," it said.

Scrooge is not at all sure what happened then. He was in the streets. He recollected that he wanted to buy some sweetmeats for his little nephews and nieces, and he went into a shop.

"Past eight o'clock, sir," said the civil man. "I can't serve you."

He wandered on through the streets that seemed strangely altered. He was going westward, and he began to feel faint. He thought he would be the better for a little brandy and water, and he was just turning into a tavern when all the people came out and the iron gates were shut with a clang in his face.

"What's the matter?" he asked feebly of the man who was closing the doors.

"Gone ten," the fellow said shortly, and turned out all the lights.

Scrooge felt sure that the second mince-pie had given him indigestion, and that he was in a dreadful dream. He seemed to fall into a deep gulf of darkness, in which all was blotted out. When he came to himself again it was Christmas Day, and the people were walking about the streets.

Scrooge, somehow or other, found himself among them. They smiled and greeted one another cheerfully, but it was evident that they were not happy. Marks of care were on their faces, marks that told of past troubles and future anxieties. Scrooge heard a man sigh heavily just after he had wished a neighbor a Merry Christmas. There were tears on a woman's face as she came down the church steps, all in black.

"Poor John!" she was murmuring. "I am sure it was the wearing cark of money troubles that killed him. Still, he is in heaven now. But the clergyman said in his sermon that heaven was only a pretty fairy tale." She wept anew.

All this disturbed Scrooge dreadfully. Something seemed to be pressing on his heart.

"But," said he, "I shall forget all this when I sit down to dinner with Nephew Fred and my niece and their young rascals."

It was late in the afternoon; four o'clock and dark, but in capital time for dinner. Scrooge found his nephew's house. It was as dark as the sky; not a window was lighted up. Scrooge's heart grew cold.

He knocked and knocked again, and rang a bell that sounded as faint and far as if it had rung in a grave.

At last a miserable old woman opened the door for a few inches and looked out suspiciously.

"Mr. Fred?" said she. "Why, he and his missus have gone off to the Hotel Splendid, as they call it, and they won't be home till midnight. They got their table six weeks ago! The children are away at Eastbourne."

"Dining in a tavern on Christmas day!" Scrooge murmured. "What terrible fate is this? Who is so miserable, so desolate, that he dines at a tavern on Christmas day? And the children at Eastbourne!"

The air grew misty about him. He seemed to hear as though from a great distance the voice of Tiny Tim, saying "God help us, every one!"

Again the Spirit stood before him. Scrooge fell upon his knees.

"Terrible Phantom!" he exclaimed. "Who and what are thou? Speak, I entreat thee."

"Ebenezer Scrooge," replied the Spirit in awful tones. "I am the Ghost of thc Christmas of 1920. With me I bring the demand note of the Commissioners of Income Tax!"

Scrooge's hair bristled as he saw the figures. But it fell out when he saw that the Apparition had feet like those of a gigantic cat.

"My name is Pussyfoot. I am also called Ruin and Despair," said the Phantom, and vanished.

With that Scrooge awoke and drew back the curtains of his bed.

"Thank God!" he uttered from his heart. "It was but a dream!"

A. N. L. Munby

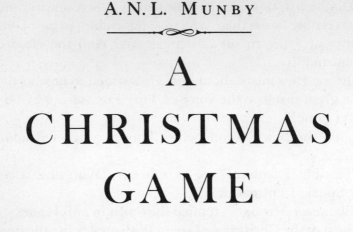

A CHRISTMAS GAME

A game in the dark has a grisly outcome.

THE old country doctor who told me these strange events has died during the late war at the age of about eighty-five. He was a medical student at the time of the incidents which he related, so they can be assigned to the late seventies of the last century. I made profuse notes of his narrative, and I give it, as far as possible, in his own words.

I was spending Christmas with my family in Dorset—my father was a solicitor in Dorchester, and we lived in a comfortable Victorian house about three miles south of the town. The party in the house was a large one. It included my mother and her two unmarried sisters—my Aunts Emily and Gertrude—my younger brother Edward, who was then a schoolboy at Blundell's, and my two small sisters, Bella and Felicity, aged sixteen and ten respectively. In addition, we had staying with us our young cousin Giles; and a number of young people in the neighborhood were constantly coming to see us, so everything indicated that we should have a festive Christmas holiday. I myself, the eldest son, was a medical student in London, and I arrived home on the afternoon of December the 22nd. Rather to my surprise my father was away when I got there, for he led a fairly leisurely existence, and normally took a clear week off for Christmas. I was told, however, that he had had to go to Exeter on business and would be returning that night.

It was about nine o'clock when I heard the wheels of our dogcart on the drive and I ran out to greet my father. I was astonished to see that he was not alone; for nothing had been said about his returning with a guest. However, a tall, elderly man dismounted with him, very much muffled up, who was introduced to me as Mr. Fenton. My father asked me to take the dogcart round to the yard and to see to the horse, and he passed into the house with the stranger. When I returned, I met my mother in the hall. She seemed to have lost some of her normal placidity.

"Really," she said, "your dear father is the most impulsive man. He met Mr. Fenton in Exeter, and apparently he knew him years and years ago. On hearing that he had nowhere to go for Christmas, he asked him to come and stay with us. He *is* so hospitable, and says that he couldn't bear the thought of anyone spending Christmas alone at an inn. I know that I ought to feel the same, but I *had* been looking forward so much to having just the family round me, and however nice Mr. Fenton may be, he will still be a stranger. However, we must just make the best of it. Giles will have to move into Edward's room. . . ." And she digressed into domestic affairs.

In the drawing room I was first able to get a proper view of our guest. He was old, I should think sixty-five, but he carried himself well. His face was bronzed and he had a high color; his nose was aquiline and he had a patrician air about him. His expression was not a kindly one—it was hard, even forbidding in repose, and I could picture him as being given to fits of imperious anger. Altogether I fully shared my mother's regrets that such a stranger should have been introduced into our family circle at the Christmas season. Nevertheless, he greeted me politely and expressed his gratitude that my father had taken pity on his solitary condition, and he said that he hoped his presence would not in any way interfere with our plans. As a matter of fact, he proved a singularly unobtrusive guest, and seemed quite content to withdraw to my father's study with his book and his cigar, or to take long, solitary walks. At meals he took his share in the family small talk and made himself quite a favorite with my aunts.

It was at a meal—dinner on Christmas eve—that I committed inadvertently what seemed to be a *faux pas*. Something in our guest's conversation had given me the idea that he had traveled extensively. In some way or other discussion at table had turned itself to the topic of New Zealand, and in order to bring Mr. Fenton into the conversation, I asked him if he had ever been there. He replied with the curt monosyllable "Yes" and at once changed the subject. I caught a warning glance from my father's eye at the top of the table, and he gave an almost imperceptible shake of the head. After dinner he drew me to one side.

"I shouldn't raise the topic of New Zealand with Mr. Fenton," he said. "I have done so myself on one occasion and he obviously found it distasteful. I know that he spent some years as a young man in the Colonial service, and I believe now that I remember hearing that some sort of scandal was circulating at the time of his retirement. I never knew the details—it was the merest rumor and nearly thirty years ago now."

"When did you know him before?" I asked.

"As a boy," he replied. "His father owned considerable property in these parts, but he made a number of unwise speculations in railway stocks and died a comparatively poor man. That was no doubt the reason why his son went into the Colonial service. He has really changed very little since I first knew him. I recognized him at once."

Christmas day passed pleasantly enough. No doubt modern children would have found it intolerably dull, but we were content with simpler pleasures. The whole household went to church in the morning, and after luncheon the young people went for a walk with the dogs. It was not until we'd had our tea that the serious business of the day began. We all went into the drawing room, where the Christmas tree had been set up; the servants filed in under the watchful eye of Watkins, our old butler, and we all received our presents. I was gratified to get a sovereign, neatly wrapped in tissue paper, from Mr. Fenton, and my younger brother and two sisters received half a sovereign apiece from the same source. He seemed to be entering into the spirit of the occasion, and was quite genial at dinner, which followed at six. After the meal my smallest sister, Felicity, was sent up to bed, which occasioned a few tears, and the rest of us proceeded to play various games, such as Dumb Crambo and Forfeits, and the evening passed merrily.

At half past eleven we started to play a game which had become almost a family institution. It was simple in the extreme. The lights were extinguished and a screen was drawn in front of the fire; then my father began to tell us a horrid tale, which gave rise to many delicious shudders. We children knew it almost by heart, but it never lost its appeal. It was my role to assist him in this, by passing round in the darkness certain objects which illustrated the story. I expect our modern psychoanalysts would say that it was harmful to the young, but in those days, thank God, we weren't burdened with that sort of moonshine. I still recall the plot of my father's tale. It described how a lonely traveler in North America had to pass through a dark, almost impenetrable forest. Night overtook him before he had reached his destination, and he became aware that stealthy footsteps were following him. Suddenly he heard the dreaded sound of the Indian's war whoop, and he was surrounded by a band of yelling savages who despatched him with their tomahawks. The abandoned wretches proceeded to dismember the corpse—first the scalp was removed. This was my cue to pass round the circle an old strip of a fur rug, which was greeted with much giggling and with exclamations of disgust from my aunts. Then my father described how the tongue of the victim was cut out, and I sent passing from hand to hand a small padded wash-leather bag, which I had carefully damped with glycerine. Finally the unfortunate man's eyes were gouged out, and this was the signal for my *pièce de résistance.* Two large muscatelle grapes had been peeled and I picked them up to hand them to my neighbor. This was Mr. Fenton. He seemed unwilling to receive them, but I found his left hand in the darkness and thrust into it the slimy horrors. To my astonishment he gave an inarticulate half-strangled cry of disgust, and rising from his seat he snatched aside the firescreen and hurled the grapes into the flames. Then he took a step back and slumped into his chair, breathing heavily. An embarrassed silence fell upon the room, broken by my father's anxious query of "Are you all right, Fenton?" There was no reply. In the flickering firelight I could see my father fumbling with a lamp. As the light came up we could see that our guest was lolling back in his chair with his head drooping at an unnatural angle. He was very pale and his eyes were closed. I expect you can imagine the confusion that broke out. My sister burst into tears, and one of my aunts started to scream hysterically, until my mother led her from the room. My father sent my cousin Giles posthaste for the doctor, and in the meantime he tried to revive Fenton with brandy. In the midst of all this, I was the only one present who looked into the fire. I suppose I wondered subconsciously why our guest had reacted so strangely to the grapes I had passed him. Anyhow I bent down to look into the grate for them. You won't believe me when I say what I saw. I swear that instead of grapes there was a pair of eyes, sizzling and sputtering in the flames. I know I wasn't mistaken, and I know they were human eyes. I'd seen enough in the dissecting room to make no error about that. I was dreadfully shocked, but in some curious way I didn't question the evidence of my senses. I realized that I had come face to face with something outside the scope of my comprehension—something in which all my scientific training would be of no avail. I resolved to keep my discovery to myself—for I could visualize the effect that any disclosure on my part would have upon that overwrought room. So I seized the poker and brought the flaming logs tumbling down, and those dreadful relics were buried from sight.

All this took only a few seconds, and I was quickly helping my father to revive the prostrate man. A cursory examination showed that he was the victim of some sort of stroke—a condition beyond the range of my elementary medical knowledge. I was therefore relieved when Giles returned in a few minutes with the doctor, who was a near neighbor. He seemed to take a grave view of our guest's appearance. Under his direction we carried the unconscious figure up to his bedroom and undressed him, leaving him alone in the doctor's care.

By this time it was very late. The other members of the household had gone quickly off to their beds, and I went to my room, where I sat down for a few minutes to try to collect my thoughts. The house was now almost silent, and I was oppressed by my extraordinary experience. I tried to persuade myself that I'd been the victim of some sort of optical illusion—that the eyes had existed only in my imagination; but I had seen them so distinctly—the pupil, the iris, every detail. They had been dark brown, almost black. The more I thought about it, the more I was appalled and dismayed. The transition from the cheerful atmosphere of the Christmas party had been terrifyingly abrupt. It was as though a curtain had been lifted for a moment, and beyond it I had glimpsed another world, exempted from the laws of Nature. I recalled an old piece of ecclesiastical dogma that I'd heard quoted, "God may work above Nature, but never contrary to Nature." If I had observed a miracle, it had certainly no Divine origin.

My meditations were interrupted by a noise from downstairs, the intermittent scratching and whining of a dog, and I recollected that in the excitement of the evening, no one had put our spaniel, Danny, outside before locking up. I went down and let him out through the door in the drawing room, which led on to the terrace. Then, as I had a few moments to wait I lit the lamp and seated myself on the sofa. The idea of waiting in that room without a light did not appeal to me. The fire had died to a few glowing embers, and whatever had been put there had been utterly consumed.

The minutes passed and I became impatient. I went to the door and whistled, but Danny did not come. He was normally a most obedient dog, and his behavior seemed quite unaccountable. Suddenly he began to howl, low at first but increasing in mournful intensity, making an eerie sound that sent shivers down my spine. I realized that he had gone down the drive into the shrubbery, and I called him again sharply, but again with no result. Seriously irritated, I went out to find him and after some difficulty I located him in the laurels. He was still whining and whimpering when I came upon him, and as he paid no attention to my command to follow me back to the house, I stooped and picked him up. I was surprised to find that he was trembling violently, and as soon as he was in my arms he pushed his head inside my jacket and kept it there, while his body twitched and quaked. I turned towards the house and took a few steps up the drive. Then I stopped as though transfixed.

I had left the garden door of the drawing room open, and through it the light was streaming out on to the terrace. Into this ray of light a figure was moving, approaching the open door with faltering steps. It became silhouetted in the doorway, and I was able to see its outlines clearly. It was a fantastic, incredible form to see in the familiar setting of my Dorset home. It was not a white man. I could see the gleam of a golden-brown body and a head covered with glossy black hair. One side of the face was visible and it was heavily tattooed. A short skirt of rush or flax was its sole covering, and its feet were bare. In one hand it held a stick, and I realized that it was blind, for it tapped gently upon the pavingstones and felt its way towards the door. In another moment it had passed into the room and was lost to my view.

I silently changed my position in order to see more, and in doing so I came nearer to the house. The figure came once more into my range of vision, and I saw that it was on its knees before the chair in which our guest had been sitting, and that it was searching feverishly upon the floor, groping blindly round the chairlegs with clawlike hands. I was near enough to hear it give a deep sigh of vexation as it found nothing. Then it turned to the remains of the fire and with fascinated horror I watched it plunge its hands into the still glowing embers and pull them out on to the hearth. It scrabbled in the red-hot ashes for a moment or two, then it gave a low cry, almost heart-rending in its bitterness and despair. No soul in limbo could have given vent to a sound more fraught with desolation. As I stood watching, it rose silently to its feet and moved across the room, out of my sight once more.

For some reason I was no longer afraid, just amazed and curious. I take no particular credit for this; I divined in some obscure way that the apparition, or whatever it may have been, was not malevolent to myself. So you need not think that I was exceptionally brave when I tell you that I strode quickly across the terrace and in through the door. The room was deserted; a second's glance told me this, and as I stood there the inner door of the room opened and my father came in. If the strange visitant had left, it could only have done so by thc door at which he entered, and he must surely have passed it in the passage.

"Did you see anyone as you came in here?" I asked.

My father frowned and replied sharply. "What are you talking about? Why on earth don't you go to bed? Shut the door and go upstairs at once. It's nearly two o'clock."

I glanced at the fireplace before replying. There were the embers, scattered about the hearth—unshatterable testimony that my eyes had not deceived me. But I didn't say anything to my father about it. I went somewhat in awe of him, as did many sons at that date, and there was no very complete and frank understanding between us. I feared his anger and I feared his ridicule: I knew that any revelation on my part must bring both upon my head. So I stammered out something about having let the dog out, holding out the now quiescent Danny as evidence for my words. Then I quickly locked up. My father waited until I'd finished.

"Fenton's pretty bad, I'm afraid," he said; "but the doctor says that there's a chance of recovery. I'm glad I asked him here. I wouldn't like to think of any friend of mine being taken ill staying alone at some inn. I'm sorry that it has spoilt our Christmas, though."

We went up the stairs together, and on the landing my father wished me good night. As he did so, we heard a confused noise from Fenton's room. The old man must have recovered consciousness, for we could perceive quite distinctly his rather high, querulous tones intermingled with the quieter phrases of the doctor. As we listened the patient's voice became louder and we caught his words.

"Keep him off—keep him away," he was shouting, "for God's sake, don't let him come near me."

Some reassuring remarks of the doctor's followed, but Fenton didn't seem to be pacified.

"Can't you see him?" he cried. "Over there by the window!" His voice became shriller and he lapsed into some foreign language that I did not understand. The doctor's tones became louder and more authoritative as he said:

"Lie down, sir, lie down. I tell you there's nothing there. I assure you that there's no one in the room but you and myself."

I looked questioningly at my father for direction, but he shook his head and said:

"I don't think we'd better go in. There's nothing we can do. Leave it to the doctor."

He was interrupted by another series of cries, culminating in the sound of a struggle, as though Fenton were being forcibly held down upon his bed. Then, quite suddenly, there was utter silence for a period of perhaps two minutes. We waited, straining our ears. Our vigil was broken by the door being opened; the doctor stood upon the threshold, looking pale and tired.

"I'm afraid he's gone," he said simply. Then, as my father stepped forward, he held up his hand and added:

"I should not go inside. The poor devil was in the grip of some terrifying hallucination at the end, and he didn't have a very peaceful passage. His appearance would only upset you. You go off to bed. I'll make all the necessary arrangements."

We obeyed and tiptoed quietly away. When I got to my room I found that I still had Danny in my arms, and very glad I was of his company for the remainder of that night.

It must have been quite ten years later, when I was qualified and in practice at Cheltenham, that I met a man who knew Fenton's name. He was a retired sheep farmer who had spent twenty-five years in New Zealand, and though he was too young to have known Fenton personally, he knew him by repute. It was from him that I learned some details of the scandal that surrounded Fenton's retirement from the Colonial service. Dark stories of his ruthlessness and brutality as an administrator had for a time been circulating, but finally there had been an incident which the authorities could not ignore. Under Fenton's direction an alleged malefactor had been subjected to torture, in order to wring a confession from him. When other methods had failed, he had been threatened with blinding, and upon his still remaining obdurate, this dire threat had been carried out. A subsequent enquiry had established the native's innocence, but for the sake of British prestige there had been no public denunciation of the public servant, who had so grossly exceeded his powers. Fenton's only punishment was to be sent home. But though his retribution was light at the hands of men, it would seem that finally he was called to account before a different and a higher court.

FRANK R. STOCKTON

THE GREAT STAIRCASE AT LANDOVER HALL

A young man falls in love on Christmas eve.

I WAS spending a few days in the little village of Landover, simply for the purpose of enjoying the beautiful scenery of the neighborhood. I had come up from Mexico because the weather was growing too warm in that region, and I was glad of the chance to vary my interesting and sometimes exciting travels with a little rest in the midst of this rural quiet.

It was early summer, and I had started out for an afternoon walk, when, just upon the outskirts of the village, my attention was attracted by a little group at a gateway which opened upon the road. There were two women and an elderly man. The women appeared to be taking leave of the man, and one of them frequently put her handkerchief to her eyes. I walked slowly, because I did not wish to intrude upon what seemed to be an affecting leave-taking; so when I reached the gate the women had gone, but the man was still standing there, looking after them.

Glancing over the low fence, I saw a very pretty grove, apparently not well kept, and some distance back, among the trees, a large, old house. The man was looking at me with a curiosity which country people naturally betray when they see a stranger, and, as I was glad to have someone to talk to, I stopped.

"Is this one of the old family mansions of Landover?" I asked. He was a good-looking man, with the air of a head gardener.

"It is not *one* of them, sir," he answered; "it is the only one in the village. It is called Landover Hall, and the other houses growed up around it."

"Who owns it?" I asked.

"That is hard to say, sir," he said, with a grim smile; "though perhaps I could tell you in the course of a couple of weeks. The family who lived there is dead and gone, and everything in it is to be sold at auction."

I became interested, and asked some questions, which the man was very willing to answer. It was an old couple who had owned it, he said. The husband had died the previous year, and the wife about ten days ago. The heirs were a brother and sister living out in Colorado, and, as they had never seen the house, and cared nothing about it, or about anything that was in it, they had written that they wished everything to be sold, and the money sent to them as soon as possible.

"And that is the way it stands," said the old man. "Next week there is to be a sale of the personal property—a 'vandoo' we call it out here—and every movable thing in the house and grounds is to be sold to the highest bidder; and mighty little the things will bring, it's my opinion. Then the house will be sold, as soon as anybody can be found who wants it."

"Then there is no one living in the house at present?" said I.

"Nobody but me," he answered. "That was the cook and her

daughter, the chambermaid, who just left here. There is a black man who attends to the horses and cows, but he will go when they are sold; and very soon I will go too, I suppose."

"Have you lived here long?" I asked.

"Pretty near all my life," said he.

I was greatly interested in old houses, and I asked the man if I might look at the place.

"I have not had any orders to show it," he said; "but, as everything is for sale, I suppose the sooner people see the household goods the better; there's many a bit of old furniture, candlesticks, and all that sort of thing, which strangers might like to buy. Oh, yes; you can come in if you like."

I shall not attempt to describe the delightful hour I spent in that old house and in the surrounding grounds. There was a great piazza in front; a wide hall stretched into the interior of the mansion, with a large fireplace on one side and a noble staircase at the further end, a single flight of stairs running up to a platform, and then branching off on each side to the second floor. On the landing stood one of the tallest clocks I have ever seen. There were portraits on the walls, and here and there a sporting picture, interspersed with antlers and foxes' heads mounted on panels, with the date of the hunt inscribed beneath. There was an air of largeness and gravity about the furniture in the hall, which was very pleasing to me, and when I entered the long drawing room I found it so filled with books and bric-à-brac of the olden days, with many quaint furnishings, that, had I been left to myself, even the long summer afternoon would not have sufficed for their examination. Upstairs was the same air of old-fashioned comfort. The grounds—the grass rather long, and the bushes untrimmed—were shaded by some grand old trees, and beyond there were gardens and some green pasture-fields.

I did not take the walk that I had proposed to myself. When I left the old house I inquired the name of the agent who had charge of the estate, and then I went back to the village inn, where I sat communing with myself for the rest of the afternoon and all the evening.

I was not yet thirty, I had a good fortune, and I had travelled until I was tired of moving about the world. Often I had had visions of a home, but they had been very vague and fanciful ones. Now, for the first time in my life, I had seen a home for which I really might care; a house to which I might bring only my wearing apparel, and then sit down surrounded by everything I needed, not even excepting books.

Immediately after breakfast I repaired to the office of Mr. Marchmay, the lawyer who had charge of the property. I stayed there a long time. Mr. Marchmay took dinner with me at the inn, and in the evening we sent a telegram to Colorado. I made a proposition to buy everything for cash, and the price agreed upon between Mr. Marchmay and myself was considerably higher than could have been expected had the property been sold at auction. It is needless to say that my offer was quickly accepted, and in less than a week from the day I had first seen the old house I became its owner. The cook and the housemaid, who had retired in tears from its gateway, were sent for, and reinstalled in their offices; the black man who had charge of the horses and cows continued to take care of them, and old Robert Flake was retained in the position of head gardener and general caretaker, which he had held for so many years.

That summer was a season of delight to me, and even when autumn arrived, and there was a fire in the great hall, I could not say that I had fully explored and examined my home and its contents. I had had a few bachelor friends to visit me, but for the greater part of the time I had lived alone. I liked company, and expected to have people about me, but so long as the novelty of my new possessions and my new position continued I was company enough for myself.

At last the holiday season came around, and I was still alone. I had invited a family of old friends to come and make the house lively and joyous, but they had been prevented from doing so. I afterward thought of asking some of my neighbors to eat their Christmas dinner in the old house, but I found that they all had ties and obligations of their own with which I should not seek to interfere. And thus it happened that late on Christmas eve I sat by myself before a blazing fire in the hall, quietly smoking my pipe. The servants were all in bed, and the house was as quiet as if it contained no living being.

For the first time since I lived in that house I began to feel lonely, and I could not help smiling when I thought that there was no need of my feeling lonely if I wished it otherwise. For several years I had known that there were mothers in this country, and even in other countries, who had the welfare of their daughters at heart, and who had not failed to let me know the fact; I had also known that there were young women, without mothers, who had their own welfare at heart, and to whom a young man of fortune was an object of interest; but there was nothing in these recollections which interested me in these lonely moments.

The great clock on the landing-place began to strike, and I counted stroke after stroke; when there were twelve I turned to see whether I had made a mistake, and if it were now really Christmas day. But before my eyes had reached the face of the clock I saw that I was mistaken in supposing myself alone. At the top of the broad flight of stairs there stood a lady.

I pushed back my chair and started to my feet. I know my mouth was open and my eyes staring. I could not speak; I doubt if I breathed.

Slowly the lady descended the stairs. There were two tall lamps on the newel-posts, so that I could see her distinctly. She was young, and she moved with the grace of perfect health. Her gown was of an olden fashion, and her hair was dressed in the style of our ancestors. Her attire was simple and elegant, but it was evident that she was dressed for a festive occasion.

Down she came, step by step, and I stood gazing, not only with my eyes, but, I may say, with my whole heart. I had never seen such grace; I had never seen such beauty.

She reached the floor, and advanced a few steps toward me; then she stopped. She fixed her large eyes upon me for a moment, and then turned them away. She gazed at the fire, the walls, the ceiling, and the floor. There came upon her lovely features an almost imperceptible smile, as though it gave her pleasure thus to stand and look about her.

As for me, I was simply entranced. Vision or no vision, spirit from another world or simply a mist of fancy, it mattered not.

She approached a few steps nearer, and fixed her eyes upon mine. I trembled as I stood. Involuntarily the wish of my heart came to my lips. "If—" I exclaimed.

"If what?" she asked, quickly.

I was startled by the voice. It was rich, it was sweet, but there was something in its intonation which suggested the olden time. I cannot explain it. It was like the perfume from an ancient wardrobe opened a hundred years after a great-grandmother had closed and locked it, when even the scent of rose and lavender was only the spirit of something gone.

"Oh, if you were but real!" I said.

She smiled, but made no reply. Slowly she passed around the great hall, coming so near me at one time that I could almost have touched her. She looked up at the portraits, stopping before some old candlesticks upon a bracket, apparently examining everything with as much pleasure as I had looked upon them when first they became mine.

When she had made the circuit of the hall, she stood as if reflecting. Fearful that she might disappear, and knowing that a spirit must be addressed if one would hear it speak, I stepped toward her. I had intended to ask her if she were, or rather ever had been, the lady of this house, why she came, and if she bore a message, but in my excitement and infatuation I forgot my purpose; I simply repeated my former words—"Oh, if you were but real!"

"Why do you say that?" she asked, with a little gentle petulance. "I am not real, as you must know. Shall I tell you who I was, and why I am here?"

I implored her to do so. She drew a little nearer the fire. "It is so bright and cheerful," she said. "It is many, many years since I have seen a fire in this hall. The old people who lived in this house so long never built a fire here—at least on Christmas eve."

I felt inclined to draw up a chair and ask her to sit down, but why need a ghost sit? I was afraid of making some mistake. I stood as near her as I dared, eagerly ready to listen.

"I was mistress of this house," she said. "That was a long, long time ago. You can see my portrait hanging there."

I bowed. I could not say that it was her portrait. An hour before, I had looked upon it as a fine picture; now it seemed to be the travesty of a woman beyond the reach of pigments and canvas.

"I died," she continued, "when I was but twenty-five, and but four years married. I had a little girl three years old, and the very day before I left this world I led her around this hall and tried to make her understand the pictures. That is her portrait on this other wall."

I turned, and following the direction of her graceful hand my eyes fell upon the picture of an elderly lady with silvered hair and benignant countenance.

"Your daughter?" I gasped.

"Yes," she answered; "she lived many years after my death. Over there, nearer the door, you may see the picture of her daughter—the plump young girl with the plumed hat."

Now, to my great surprise, she asked me to take a seat. "It seems ungracious," she remarked, "that in my own house I should be so inhospitable as to keep you standing. And yet it is not my house; it is yours."

Obedient to her command, for such I felt it to be, I resumed my seat, and to my delight she took a chair not far from me. Seated, she seemed more graceful and lovely than when she stood. Her shapely hands lay in her lap; soft lace fell over them, like tender mist upon a cloud. As she looked at me her eyes were raised.

"Does it distress you that this house should now be mine?" I asked.

"Oh, no, no," she answered, with animation; "I am very glad

of it. The elderly couple who lived here before you were not to my liking. Once a year, on Christmas eve, I am privileged to spend one hour in this house, and, although I have never failed to be here at the appointed time, it has been years, as I told you, since I saw a fire on that hearth and a living being in this hall. I knew you were here, and I am very glad of it. It pleases me greatly that one is living here who prizes this old place as I once prized it. This mansion was built for me by my husband, upon the site of a smaller house, which he removed. The grounds about it, which I thought so lovely, are far more lovely now. For four years I lived here in perfect happiness, and now one hour each year something of that happiness is renewed."

Ordinarily I have good control of my actions and of my emotions, but at this moment I seemed to have lost all power over myself; my thoughts ran wild. To my amazement, I became conscious that I was falling in love—in love with something which did not exist; in love with a woman who once had been. It was absurd; it was ridiculous; but there was no power within me which could prevent it.

After all, this rapidly growing passion was not altogether absurd. She was an ideal which far surpassed any ideal I had ever formed for the mistress of my home. More than that, she had really been the mistress of this house, which was now my home. Here was a vision of the past, fully revealed to my eyes. As the sweet voice fell upon my ears, how could I help looking upon it as something real, listening to it as something real, and loving it as something real.

I think she perceived my agitation; she looked upon me wonderingly.

"I hoped very much," she said, "that you would be in this hall when I should come down tonight, but I feared that I should disturb you, that perhaps I might startle or—"

I could not restrain myself. I rose and interrupted her with passionate earnestness.

"Startle or trouble me!" I exclaimed. "Oh, gracious lady, you have done but one thing to me tonight—you have made me love you! Pardon me; I cannot help it. Do not speak of impossibilities, of passionate ravings, of unmeaning words. Lady, I love you; I may not love you as you are, but I love you as you were. No happiness on earth could equal that of seeing you real—the mistress of this house, and myself the master."

She rose, drew back a little, and stood looking at me. If she had been true flesh and blood she could not have acted more naturally.

For some moments there was silence, and then a terrible thought came into my head. Had I a right to speak to her thus, even if she were but the vision of something that had been? She had told me of her husband; she had spoken of her daughter; but she had said no word which would give me reason to believe that little girl was fatherless when her mother led her around the hall and explained to her the family portraits. Had I been addressing my wild words of passion to one whose beauty and grace, when they were real and true, belonged to another? Had I spoken as I should not have spoken, even to the vision of a well-loved wife? I trembled with apprehension.

"Pardon me," I said, "if I have been imprudent. Remember that I know so little about you, even as you were."

When she answered there was nothing of anger in her tone, but she spoke softly, and with, I thought, a shade of pity.

"You have said nothing to offend me, but every word you have spoken has been so wild and so far removed from sense and reason that I am unable to comprehend your feelings."

"They are easy to understand!" I exclaimed. "I have seen my ideal of the woman I could love. I love you; that is all! Again I say it, and I say it with all my heart: Would you were real! Would you were real!"

She smiled. I am sure *now* she understood my passion. I am sure she expected it. I am sure that she pitied me.

Suddenly a change of expression came over her face; a beaming interest shone from her eyes; she took some steps toward me.

"I told you," said she, speaking quickly, "that what you have said seems to be without sense or reason, and yet it may mean something. I assure you that your words have been appreciated. I know that each one of them is true and comes from your heart. And now listen to me while I tell you—" At that moment the infernal clock upon the landing-place struck one. It was like the crash of doom. I stood alone in the great hall.

The domestics in that old house supposed that I spent Christmas day alone; but they were mistaken, for wherever I went my fancy pictured near me the beautiful vision of the night before. She walked with me in the crisp morning air; I led her through the quiet old rooms, and together we went up the great staircase and stood before the clock—the clock that I had blessed for striking twelve and cursed for striking one. At dinner she sat opposite me in a great chair which I had had placed there—"for the sake of symmetry," as I told my servants. After what had happened, it was impossible for me to be alone.

The day after Christmas old Mr. Marchmay came to call upon me. He was so sorry that I had been obliged to spend Christmas day all by myself. I fairly laughed as I listened to him.

There were things I wanted him to tell me if he could, and I plied him with questions. I pointed to the portrait of the lady near the chimney-piece, and asked him who she was.

"That is Mrs. Evelyn Heatherton, first mistress of this house; I have heard a good deal about her. She was very unfortunate. She lost her life here in this hall on Christmas eve. She was young and beautiful, and must have looked a good deal like that picture."

I forgot myself. "I don't believe it," I said. "It does not seem to me that that portrait could have been a good likeness of the real woman."

"You may know more about art than I do, sir," said he. "It has always been considered a fine picture; but of course she lived before my time. As I was saying, she died here in this hall. She was coming downstairs on Christmas eve; there were a lot of people here in the hall waiting to meet her. She stepped on something on one of the top steps—a child's toy, perhaps—and lost her footing. She fell to the bottom and was instantly killed—killed in the midst of youth, health, and beauty."

"And her husband," I remarked, "was he—"

"Oh, he was dead!" interrupted Mr. Marchmay. "He died when his daughter was but a mere baby. By the way," said the old gentleman, "it seems rather funny that the painting over there—that old lady with the gray hair—is the portrait of that child. It is the only one there is, I suppose."

I did not attend to these last words. My face must have glowed with delight as I thought that I had not spoken to her as I should not. If I had known her to be real, I might have said everything which I had said to the vision of what she had been.

The old man went on talking about the family. That sort of thing interested him very much, and he said that, as I owned the house, I ought to know everything about the people who formerly lived there. The Heathertons had not been fortunate. They had lost a great deal of money, and, some thirty years before, the estate had passed out of their hands and had been bought by a Mr. Kennard, a distant connection of the family, who, with his wife, had lived there until very recently. It was to a nephew and niece of old Mr. Kennard that the property had descended. The Heathertons had nothing more to do with it.

"Are there any members of the family left?" I asked.

"Oh yes!" said Mr. Marchmay. "Do you see that portrait of a girl with a feather in her hat? She is a granddaughter of that Evelyn Heatherton up there. She is an old woman now and a widow, and she it was who sold the place to the Kennards. When the mortgages were paid she did not have much left, but she manages to live on it. But I tell you what you ought to do, sir: you ought to go to see her. She can tell you lots of stories of this place, for she knows more about the Heathertons than anyone living. She married a distant cousin, who had the family name; but he was a poor sort of a fellow, and he died some fifteen years ago. She has talked to me about your having the old house, and she said that she hoped you would not make changes and tear down things. But of course she would not say anything like that to you; she is a lady who attends to her own business."

"Where does she live?" I asked. "I should like, above all things, to go and talk to her."

"It is the third house beyond the church," said Mr. Marchmay. "I am sure she will be glad to see you. If you can make up your mind to listen to long stories about the Heathertons you will give her pleasure."

The next day I made the call. The house was neat, but small and unpretentious—a great drop from the fine hall I now possessed.

The servant informed me that Mrs. Heatherton was at home, and I was shown into the little parlor—light, warm, and pleasantly furnished. In a few minutes the door opened, and I rose, but no old lady entered.

Struck dumb by breathless amazement, I beheld Evelyn Heatherton coming into the room!

I could not understand; my thoughts ran wild. Had someone been masquerading? Had I dreamed on Christmas eve, or was I dreaming now? Had my passionate desire been granted? Had that vision become real? I was instantly convinced that what I saw before me was true and real, for the lady advanced toward me and held out her hand. I took it, and it was the hand of an actual woman.

Her mother, she said, begged that I would excuse her; she was not well and was lying down. Mr. Marchmay had told them that I was coming, and that I wanted to know something about the old house; perhaps she might be able to give me a little information.

Almost speechless, I sat down, and she took a chair not far from me. Her position was exactly that which had been taken by the vision of her great-grandmother on Christmas eve. Her hands were crossed in her lap, and her large blue eyes were slightly upraised to mine. She was not dressed in a robe of olden days, nor was her hair piled up high on her head in bygone fashion, but she was Evelyn Heatherton, in form and feature and in quiet grace. She was some years younger, and she lacked the dignity of a woman who had been married, but she was no stranger to me; I had seen her before.

Encouraged by my rapt attention, she told me stories of the old house where her mother had been born, and all that she knew of her great-grandmother she related with an interest that was almost akin to mine. "People tell me," she said, "that I am growing to look like her, and I am glad of it, for my mother gave me her name."

I sat and listened to the voice of this beautiful girl, as I had listened to the words which had been spoken to me by the vision of her ancestress. If I had not known that she was real, and that there was no reason why she should vanish when the clock should strike, I might have spoken as I spoke to her great-grandmother. I remained entranced, enraptured, and it was only when the room began to grow dark that I was reminded that it was incumbent upon me to go.

But I went again, again, and again, and after a time it so happened that I was in that cottage at least once every day. The old lady was very gracious; it was plain enough that her soul was greatly gratified to know that the present owner of her old home—the house in which she had been born—was one who delighted to hear the family stories, and who respected all their traditions.

I need not tell the story of Evelyn and myself. My heart had been filled with a vision of her personality before I had seen her. At the first moment of our meeting my love for her sprung into existence as the flame bursts from a match. And she could not help but love me. Few women, certainly not Evelyn Heatherton, could resist the passionate affection I offered her. She did not tell me this in words, but it was not long before I came to believe it.

It was one afternoon in spring that old Mrs. Heatherton and her daughter came to visit me in my house—the home of their ancestors. As I walked with them through the halls and rooms

I felt as if they were the ladies of the manor, and that I was the recipient of their kind hospitality.

Mrs. Heatherton was in the dining room, earnestly examining some of the ancestral china and glass, and Evelyn and I stood together in the hall, almost under the portrait which hung near the chimney-piece. She had been talking of the love and reverence she felt for this old house. "Evelyn," said I, "if you love this house and all that is in it, will you not take it, and have it for your own? And will you not take me and love me, and have me for your own?"

I had my answer before the old lady came out of the dining-room. She was reading the inscription on an old silver loving-cup when we went in to her and told her that again Evelyn Heatherton was to be the mistress of the old mansion.

We were married in the early winter, and after a journey in the South we came back to the old house, for I had a great desire that we should spend the holidays under its roof.

It was Christmas eve, and we stood together in the great hall, with a fire burning upon the hearth as it had glowed and crackled a year before. It was some minutes before twelve, and, purposely, I threw my arms around my dear wife and turned her so that she stood with her back to the great staircase. I had never told her of the vision I had seen; I feared to do so; I did not know what effect it might have upon her. I cared for her so earnestly and tenderly that I would risk nothing, but I felt that I must stand with her in that hall on that Christmas eve, and I believed that I could do so without fear or self-reproach.

The clock struck twelve. "Look up at your great-grandmother, Evelyn," I said; "it is fit that you should do so at this time." In obedience to my wishes her eyes were fixed upon the old portrait, and, at the same time, looking over her shoulder, my eyes fell upon the vision of the first Evelyn Heatherton descending the stairs. Upon her features was a gentle smile of welcome and of pleasure. So she must have looked when she went out of this world in health and strength and womanly bloom.

The vision reached the bottom of the stairs and came toward us. I stood expectant, my eyes fixed upon her noble countenance.

"It seems to me," said my Evelyn, "as if my great-grandmother really looked down upon us; as if it made her happy to think that—"

"Is this what you meant?" said I, speaking to the lovely vision, now so near us.

"Yes," was the answer; "it is what I meant, and I am rejoiced. I bless you and I love you both," and as she spoke two fair and shadowy hands vere extended over our heads. No one can hear the voice of a spirit except those to whom it speaks, and my wife thought that my words had been addressed to her.

"Yes," said my Evelyn; "I mean that we should be standing here in her old home, and that your arm should be around me."

I looked again. There was no one in the hall, except my Evelyn and myself.

JOHN KENDRICK BANGS

THE WATER GHOST OF HARROWBY HALL

A family's Christmas is dampened each year by a ghost.

THE trouble with Harrowby Hall was that it was haunted, and, what was worse, the ghost did not content itself with merely appearing at the bedside of the afflicted person who saw it, but persisted in remaining there for one mortal hour before it would disappear.

It never appeared except on Christmas eve, and then as the clock was striking twelve, in which respect alone was it lacking in that originality which in these days is a *sine qua non* of success in spectral life. The owners of Harrowby Hall had done their utmost to rid themselves of the damp and dewy lady who rose up out of the best bedroom floor at midnight, but without avail. They had tried stopping the clock, so that the ghost would not know when it was midnight; but she made her appearance just the same, with that fearful miasmatic personality of hers, and there she would stand until everything about her was thoroughly saturated.

Then the owners of Harrowby Hall calked up every crack in the floor with the very best quality of hemp, and over this were placed layers of tar and canvas; the walls were made waterproof, and the doors and windows likewise, the proprietors having conceived the notion that the unexorcised lady would find it difficult to leak into the room after these precautions had been taken; but even this did not suffice. The following Christmas eve she appeared as promptly as before, and frightened the occupant of the room quite out of his senses by sitting down alongside of him and gazing with her cavernous blue eyes into his; and he noticed, too, that in her long, aqueously bony fingers bits of dripping seaweed were entwined, the ends hanging down, and these ends she drew across his forehead until he became like one insane. And then he swooned away, and was found unconscious in his bed the next morning by his host, simply saturated with seawater and fright, from the combined effects of which he never recovered, dying four years later of pneumonia and nervous prostration at the age of seventy-eight.

The next year the master of Harrowby Hall decided not to have the best spare bedroom opened at all, thinking that perhaps the ghost's thirst for making herself disagreeable would be satisfied by haunting the furniture, but the plan was as unavailing as the many that had preceded it.

The ghost appeared as usual in the room—that is, it was supposed she did, for the hangings were dripping wet the next morning, and in the parlor below the haunted room a great damp spot appeared on the ceiling. Finding no one there, she immediately set out to learn the reason why, and she chose none other to haunt than the owner of the Harrowby himself. She found him in his own cozy room drinking whiskey—whiskey undiluted—and felicitating himself upon having foiled her ghostship, when all of a sudden the curl went out of his hair, his whiskey bottle filled and overflowed, and he was himself in a condition similar to that of a man who has fallen into a water-butt. When he recovered from the shock, which was a painful one, he saw before him the lady of the cavernous eyes and seaweed fingers. The sight was so unexpected and so terrifying that he fainted, but immediately came to, because of the vast amount of water in his hair, which, trickling down over his face, restored his consciousness.

Now it so happened that the master of Harrowby was a brave man, and while he was not particularly fond of interviewing ghosts, especially such quenching ghosts as the one before him, he was not to be daunted by an apparition. He had paid the lady the compliment of fainting from the effects of his first surprise, and now that he had come to he intended to find out a few things he felt he had a right to know. He would have liked to put on a dry suit of clothes first, but the apparition declined to leave him for an instant until her hour was up, and he was forced to deny himself that pleasure. Every time he would move she would follow him, with the result that everything she came in contact with got a ducking. In an effort to warm himself up he approached the fire, an unfortunate move as it turned out, because it brought the ghost directly over the fire, which immediately was extinguished. The whiskey became utterly valueless as a comforter to his chilled system, because it was by this time diluted to a proportion of ninety percent of water. The only thing he could do to ward off the evil effects of his encounter he did, and that was to swallow ten two-grain quinine pills, which he managed to put into his mouth before the ghost had time to interfere. Having done this, he turned with some asperity to the ghost, and said:

"Far be it from me to be impolite to a woman, madam, but I'm hanged if it wouldn't please me better if you'd stop these infernal visits of yours to this house. Go sit out on the lake, if you like that sort of thing; soak the water-butt, if you wish; but do not, I implore you, come into a gentleman's house and saturate him and his possessions in this way. It is damned disagreeable."

"Henry Hartwick Oglethorpe," said the ghost, in a gurgling voice, "you don't know what you are talking about."

"Madam," returned the unhappy householder, "I wish that remark were strictly truthful. I was talking about you. It would be shillings and pence—nay, pounds, in my pocket, madam, if I did not know you."

"That is a bit of specious nonsense," returned the ghost, throwing a quart of indignation into the face of the master of Harrowby. "It may rank high as repartee, but as a comment upon my statement that you do not know what you are talking about, it savors of irrelevant impertinence. You do not know that I am compelled to haunt this place year after year by inexorable fate. It is no pleasure to me to enter this house, and ruin and mildew everything I touch. I never aspired to be a shower-bath, but it is my doom. Do you know who I am?"

"No, I don't," returned the master of Harrowby. "I should say you were the Lady of the Lake, or Little Sallie Waters."

"You are a witty man for your years," said the ghost.

"Well, my humor is drier than yours ever will be," returned the master.

"No doubt. I'm never dry. I am the Water Ghost of Harrowby Hall, and dryness is a quality entirely beyond my wildest hope. I have been the incumbent of this highly unpleasant office for two hundred years tonight."

"How the deuce did you ever come to get elected?" asked the master.

"Through a suicide," replied the specter. "I am the ghost of that fair maiden whose picture hangs over the mantelpiece in the drawing room. I should have been your great-great-great-great-great-aunt if I had lived, Henry Hartwick Oglethorpe, for I was the own sister of your great-great-great-great-grandfather."

"But what induced you to get this house into such a predicament?"

"I was not to blame, sir," returned the lady. "It was my father's fault. He it was who built Harrowby Hall, and the haunted chamber was to have been mine. My father had it furnished in pink and yellow, knowing well that blue and gray formed the only combination of color I could tolerate. He did it merely to spite me, and, with what I deem a proper spirit, I declined to live in the room; whereupon my father said I could live there or on the lawn, he didn't care which. That night I ran from the house and jumped over the cliff into the sea."

"That was rash," said the master of Harrowby.

"So I've heard," returned the ghost. "If I had known what the consequences were to be I should not have jumped; but I really never realized what I was doing until after I was drowned. I had been drowned a week when a sea nymph came to me and informed me that I was to be one of her followers forever afterwards, adding that it should be my doom to haunt Harrowby Hall for one hour every Christmas eve throughout the rest of eternity. I was to haunt that room on such Christmas eves as I found it inhabited; and if it should turn out not to be inhabited, I was and am to spend the allotted hour with the head of the house."

"I'll sell the place."

"That you cannot do, for it is also required of me that I shall appear as the deeds are to be delivered to any purchaser, and divulge to him the awful secret of the house."

"Do you mean to tell me that on every Christmas eve that I don't happen to have somebody in that guest chamber, you are going to haunt me wherever I may be, ruining my whiskey, taking all the curl out of my hair, extinguishing my fire, and soaking me through to the skin?" demanded the master.

"You have steated the case, Oglethorpe. And what is more," said the water ghost, "it doesn't make the slightest difference where you are, if I find that room empty, wherever you may be I shall douse you with my spectral pres—"

Here the clock struck one, and immediately the apparition faded away. It was perhaps more of a trickle than a fade, but as a disappearance it was complete.

"By St. George and his Dragon!" ejaculated the master of Harrowby, wringing his hands. "It is guineas to hot-cross buns that next Christmas there's an occupant of the spare room, or I spend the night in a bathtub."

But the master of Harrowby would have lost his wager had there been any one there to take him up, for when Christmas eve came again he was in his grave, never having recovered from the cold contracted that awful night. Harrowby Hall was closed, and the heir to the estate was in London, where to him in his chambers came the same experience that his father had gone through, saving only that, being younger and stronger, he survived the shock. Everything in his rooms was ruined—his clocks were rusted in the works; a fine collection of watercolor drawings was entirely obliterated by the onslaught of the water ghost; and what was worse, the apartments below his were drenched with the water soaking through the floors, a damage for which he was compelled to pay, and which resulted in his being requested by his landlady to vacate the premises immediately.

The story of the visitation inflicted upon his family had gone abroad, and no one could be got to invite him out to any function save afternoon teas and receptions. Fathers of daughters declined to permit him to remain in their houses later than eight o'clock at night, not knowing but that some emergency might arise in the supernatural world which would require the unexpected appearance of the water ghost in this on nights other than Christmas eve, and before the mystic hour when weary churchyards, ignoring the rules which are supposed to govern polite society, begin to yawn. Nor would the maids themselves have aught to do with him, fearing the destruction by the sudden incursion of aqueous femininity of the costumes which they held most dear.

So the heir of Harrowby Hall resolved, as his ancestors for several generations before him had resolved, that something must be done. His first thought was to make one of his servants occupy the haunted room at the crucial moment; but in this he failed, because the servants themselves knew the history of that room and rebelled. None of his friends would consent to sacrifice their personal comfort to his, nor was there to be found in all England a man so poor as to be willing to occupy the doomed chamber on Christmas eve for pay.

Then the thought came to the heir to have the fireplace in the room enlarged, so that he might evaporate the ghost at its first appearance, and he was felicitating himself upon the ingenuity of his plan, when he remembered what his father had told him—how that no fire could withstand the lady's extremely contagious dampness. And then he bethought him of steam-pipes. These, he remembered, could lie hundreds of feet deep in water, and still retain sufficient heat to drive the water away in vapor; and as a result of this thought the haunted room was heated by steam to a withering degree, and the heir for six months attended daily the Turkish baths, so that when Christmas eve came he could himself withstand the awful temperature of the room.

The scheme was only partially successful. The water ghost appeared at the specified time, and found the heir of Harrowby prepared; but hot as the room was, it shortened her visit by no more than five minutes in the hour, during which time the nervous system of the young master was wellnigh shattered, and the room itself was cracked and warped to an extent which required the outlay of a large sum of money to remedy. And worse than this, as the last drop of the water ghost was slowly sizzling itself out on the floor, she whispered to her would-be conqueror that his scheme would avail him nothing, because there was still water in great plenty where she came from, and that next year would find her rehabilitated and as exasperatingly saturating as ever.

It was then that the natural action of the mind, in going from one extreme to the other, suggested to the ingenious heir of Harrowby the means by which the water ghost was ultimately conquered, and happiness once more came within the grasp of the house of Oglethorpe.

The heir provided himself with a warm suit of fur underclothing. Donning this with the furry side in, he placed over it a rubber garment, tightfitting, which he wore just as a woman wears a jersey. On top of this he placed another set of underclothing, this suit made of wool, and over this was a second rubber garment like the first. Upon his head he placed a light and comfortable diving helmet, and so clad, on the following Christmas eve he awaited the coming of his tormentor.

It was a bitterly cold night that brought to a close this twenty-fourth day of December. The air outside was still, but the temperature was below zero. Within all was quiet, the servants of Harrowby Hall awaiting with beating hearts the outcome of their master's campaign against his supernatural visitor.

The master himself was lying on the bed in the haunted room, clad as has already been indicated, and then—

The clock clanged out the hour of twelve.

There was a sudden banging of doors, a blast of cold air swept through the halls, the door leading into the haunted chamber flew open, a splash was heard, and the water ghost was seen standing at the side of the heir of Harrowby, from whose outer dress there streamed rivulets of water, but whose own person deep down under the various garments he wore was as dry and as warm as he could have wished.

"Ha!" said the young master of Harrowby. "I'm glad to see you."

"You are the most original man I've met, if that is true," returned the ghost. "May I ask where did you get that hat?"

"Certainly, madam," returned the master, courteously. "It is a little portable observatory I had made for just such emergencies as this. But, tell me, is it true that you are doomed to follow me about for one mortal hour—to stand where I stand, to sit where I sit?"

"That is my delectable fate," returned the lady.

"We'll go out on the lake," said the master, starting up.

"You can't get rid of me that way," returned the ghost. "The water won't swallow me up; in fact, it will just add to my present bulk."

"Nevertheless," said the master, firmly, "we will go out on the lake."

"But, my dear sir," returned the ghost, with a pale reluctance, "it is fearfully cold out there. You will be frozen hard before you've been out ten minutes."

"Oh no, I'll not," replied the master. "I am very warmly dressed. Come!" This last in a tone of command that made the ghost ripple.

And they started.

They had not gone far before the water ghost showed signs of distress.

"You walk too slowly," she said. "I am nearly frozen. My knees are so stiff now I can hardly move. I beseech you to accelerate your step."

"I should like to oblige a lady," returned the master, courteously, "but my clothes are rather heavy, and a hundred yards an hour is about my speed. Indeed, I think we would better sit down here on this snowdrift and talk matters over."

"Do not! Do not do so, I beg!" cried the ghost. "Let me move on. I feel myself growing rigid as it is. If we stop here, I shall be frozen stiff."

"That madam," said the master slowly, and seating himself on an ice-cake—"that is why I have brought you here. We have been on this spot just ten minutes; we have fifty more. Take your time about it, madam, but freeze, that is all I ask of you."

"I cannot move my right leg now," cried the ghost, in despair, "and my overskirt is a solid sheet of ice. Oh, good, kind Mr. Oglethorpe, light a fire, and let me go free from these icy fetters."

"Never, madam. It cannot be. I have you at last."

"Alas!" cried the ghost, a tear trickling down her frozen cheek. "Help me, I beg. I congeal!"

"Congeal, madam, congeal!" returned Oglethorpe, coldly. "You have drenched me and mine for two hundred and three years, madam. Tonight you have had your last drench."

"Ah, but I shall thaw out again, and then you'll see. Instead of the comfortably tepid, genial ghost I have been in my past, sir, I shall be iced water," cried the lady, threateningly.

"No, you won't, either," returned Oglethorpe; "for when you are frozen quite stiff, I shall send you to a cold-storage warehouse, and there shall you remain an icy work of art forever more."

"But warehouses burn."

"So they do, but this warehouse cannot burn. It is made of asbestos and surrounding it are fireproof walls, and within those walls the temperature is now and shall forever be 416 degrees below the zero point; low enough to make an icicle of any flame in this world—or the next," the master added, with an ill-suppressed chuckle.

"For the last time let me beseech you. I would go on my knees to you, Oglethorpe, were they not already frozen. I beg of you do not doo—"

Here even the words froze on the water ghost's lips and the clock struck one. There was a momentary tremor throughout the ice-bound form, and the moon, coming out from behind a cloud, shone down on the rigid figure of a beautiful woman sculptured in clear, transparent ice. There stood the ghost of Harrowby Hall, conquered by the cold, a prisoner for all time.

The heir of Harrowby had won at last, and today in a large storage house in London stands the frigid form of one who will never again flood the house of Oglethorpe with woe and seawater.

As for the heir of Harrowby, his success in coping with a ghost has made him famous, a fame that still lingers about him, although his victory took place some twenty years ago; and so far from being unpopular with the fair sex, as he was when we first knew him, he has not only been married twice, but is to lead a third bride to the altar before the year is out.

ROSEMARY TIMPERLEY

CHRISTMAS MEETING

A ghost from the past? . . . or the future?

I HAVE never spent Christmas alone before.

It gives me an uncanny feeling, sitting alone in my "furnished room," with my head full of ghosts, and the room full of voices of the past. It's a drowning feeling—all the Christmases of the past coming back in a mad jumble: the childish Christmas, with a house full of relations, a tree in the window, sixpences in the pudding, and the delicious, crinkly stocking in the dark morning; the adolescent Christmas, with mother and father, the War and the bitter cold, and the letters from abroad; the first really grown-up Christmas, with a lover—the snow and the enchantment, red wine and kisses, and the walk in the dark before midnight, with the grounds so white, and the stars diamond bright in a black sky—so many Christmases through the years.

And, now, the first Christmas alone.

But not quite loneliness. A feeling of companionship with all the other people who are spending Christmas alone—millions of them—past and present. A feeling that, if I close my eyes, there will be no past or future, only an endless present which *is* time, because it is all we ever have.

Yes, however cynical you are, however irreligious, it makes you feel queer to be alone at Christmas time.

So I'm absurdly relieved when the young man walks in. There's nothing romantic about it—I'm a woman of nearly fifty, a spinster schoolma'am with grim, dark hair, and myopic eyes that once were beautiful, and he's a kid of twenty, rather unconventionally dressed with a flowing, wine-colored tie and black velvet jacket, and brown curls which could do with a taste of the barber's scissors. The effeminacy of his dress is belied by his features—narrow, piercing, blue eyes, and arrogant, jutting nose and chin. Not that he looks strong. The skin is fine-drawn over the prominent features, and he is very white.

He bursts in without knocking, then pauses, says: "I'm so sorry. I thought this was my room." He begins to go out, then hesitates and says: "Are you alone?"

"Yes."

"It's—queer, being alone at Christmas, isn't it? May I stay and talk?"

"I'd be glad if you would."

He comes right in, and sits down by the fire.

"I hope you don't think I came in here on purpose. I really did think it was my room," he explains.

"I'm glad you made the mistake. But you're a very young person to be alone at Christmas time."

"I wouldn't go back to the country to my family. It would hold up my work. I'm a writer."

"I see." I can't help smiling a little. That explains his rather unusual dress. And he takes himself so seriously, this young man! "Of course, you mustn't waste a precious moment of writing," I say with a twinkle.

"No, not a moment! That's what my family won't see. They don't appreciate urgency."

"Families are never appreciative of the artistic nature."

"No, they aren't," he agrees seriously.

"What are you writing?"

"Poetry and a diary combined. It's called *My Poems and I,* by Francis Randel. That's my name. My family says there's no point in my writing, that I'm too young. But I don't feel young. Sometimes I feel like an old man, with too much to do before he dies."

"Revolving faster and faster on the wheel of creativeness."

"Yes! Yes, exactly! You understand! You must read my work some time. Please read my work! Read my work!" A note of desperation in his voice, a look of fear in his eyes, makes me say:

"We're both getting much too solemn for Christmas day. I'm going to make you some coffee. And I have a plum cake."

I move about, clattering cups, spooning coffee into my percolator. But I must have offended him, for, when I look round, I find he has left me. I am absurdly disappointed.

I finish making coffee, however, then turn to the bookshelf in the room. It is piled high with volumes, for which the landlady has apologized profusely: "Hope you don't mind the books, Miss, but my husband won't part with them, and there's nowhere else to put them. We charge a bit less for the room for that reason."

"I don't mind," I said. "Books are good friends."

But these aren't very friendly-looking books. I take one at random. Or does some strange fate guide my hand?

Sipping my coffee, inhaling my cigarette smoke, I begin to read the battered little book, published, I see, in Spring, 1852. It's mainly poetry—immature stuff, but vivid. Then there's a kind of diary. More realistic, less affected. Out of curiosity, to see if there are any amusing comparisons, I turn to the entry for Christmas day, 1851. I read:

"My first Christmas day alone. I had rather an odd experience. When I went back to my lodgings after a walk, there was a middle-aged woman in my room. I thought, at first, I'd walked into the wrong room, but this was not so, and later, after a pleasant talk, she—disappeared. I suppose she was a ghost. But I wasn't frightened. I liked her. But I do not feel well tonight. Not at all well. I have never felt ill at Christmas before."

A publisher's note followed the last entry:

FRANCIS RANDEL DIED FROM A SUDDEN HEART ATTACK ON THE NIGHT OF CHRISTMAS DAY, 1851. THE WOMAN MENTIONED IN THIS FINAL ENTRY IN HIS DIARY WAS THE LAST PERSON TO SEE HIM ALIVE. IN SPITE OF REQUESTS FOR HER TO COME FORWARD, SHE NEVER DID SO. HER IDENTITY REMAINS A MYSTERY.

WILLIAM D. O' CONNOR

THE GHOST

A Boston doctor regains the Christmas spirit.

AT the West End of Boston is a quarter of some fifty streets, more or less, commonly known as Beacon Hill.

It is a rich and respectable quarter, sacred to the abodes of Our First Citizens. The very houses have become sentient of its prevailing character of riches and respectability; and, when the twilight deepens on the place, or at high noon, if your vision is gifted, you may see them as long rows of Our First Giants, with very corpulent or very broad fronts, with solid-set feet of sidewalk ending in square-toed curbstone, with an air about them as if they had thrust their hard hands into their wealthy pockets forever, with a character of arctic reserve, and portly dignity, and a well-dressed, full-fed, self-satisifed, opulent, stony, repellant aspect to each, which says plainly: "I belong to a rich family, of the very highest respectability."

History, having much to say of Beacon Hill generally, has, on the present occasion, something to say particularly of a certain street which bends over the eminence, sloping steeply down to its base. It is an old street—quaint, quiet, and somewhat picturesque. It was young once, though—having been born before the Revolution, and was then given to the city by its father, Mr. Middlecott, who died without heirs, and did this much for posterity. Posterity has not been grateful to Mr. Middlecott. The street bore his name till he was dust, and then got the more aristocratic epithet of Bowdoin. Posterity has paid him by effacing what would have been his noblest epitaph. We may expect, after this, to see Faneuil Hall robbed of its name, and called Smith Hall! Republics are proverbially ungrateful. What safer claim to public remembrance has the old Huguenot, Peter Faneuil, than the old Englishman, Mr. Middlecott? Ghosts, it is said, have risen from the grave to reveal wrongs done them by the living; but it needs no ghost from the grave to prove the proverb about republics.

Bowdoin street only differs from its kindred, in a certain shady, grave, old-fogy, fossil aspect, just touched with a pensive solemnity, as if it thought to itself, "I'm getting old but I'm highly respectable; that's a comfort." It has, moreover, a dejected, injured air, as if it brooded solemnly on the wrong done to it by taking away its original name, and calling it Bowdoin; but, as if, being a very conservative street, it was resolved to keep a cautious silence on the subject, lest the Union should go to pieces. Sometimes it wears a profound and mysterious look, as if it could tell something if it had a mind to, but thought it best not. Something of the ghost of its father—it was the only child he ever had!—walking there all the night, pausing at the corners to look up at the signs, which bear a strange name, and wringing his ghostly hands in lamentation at the wrong done his memory! Rumor told it in a whisper, many years ago. Perhaps it was believed by a few of the oldest inhabitants of the city; but the highly respectable quarter never heard of it; and, if it had, would not have been bribed to believe it, by any sum. Some one had said that some very old person had seen a phantom there. Nobody knew who some one was. Nobody knew who the very old person was. Nobody knew who had seen it; nor when; nor how. The very rumor was spectral.

All this was many years ago. Since then it has been reported that a ghost was seen there one bitter Christmas eve, two or three years back. The twilight was already in the street; but the evening lamps were not yet lighted in the windows, and the roofs and chimney-tops were still distinct in the last clear light of the dropping day. It was light enough, however, for one to read, easily, from the opposite sidewalk, "Dr. C. Renton," in black letters, on the silver plate of a door, not far from the gothic portal of the Swedenborgian church. Near this door stood a misty figure, whose sad, spectral eyes floated on vacancy, and whose long, shadowy white hair, lifted like an airy weft in the streaming wind. That was the ghost! It stood near the door a long time, without any other than a shuddering motion, as though it felt the searching blast, which swept furiously from the north up the declivity of the street, rattling the shutters in its headlong passage. Once or twice, when a passer-by, muffled warmly from the bitter air, hurried past, the phantom shrank closer to the wall, till he was gone. Its vague, mournful face seemed to watch for someone. The twilight darkened, gradually; but it did not flit away. Patiently it kept its piteous look fixed in one direction—watching—watching; and, while the howling wind swept frantically through the chill air, it still seemed to shudder in the piercing cold.

A light suddenly kindled in an opposite window. As if touched by a gleam from the lamp, or as if by some subtle interior illumination, the specter became faintly luminous, and a thin smile seemed to quiver over its features. At the same moment, a strong, energetic figure—Dr. Renton, himself—came in sight, striding down the slope of the pavement to his own door, his overcoat thrown back, as if the icy air were a tropical warmth to him, his hat set on the back of his head, and the loose ends of a 'kerchief about his throat, streaming in the nor'wester. The wind set up a howl the moment he came in sight, and swept upon him; and a curious agitation began on the part of the phantom. It glided rapidly to and fro, and moved in circles, and then, with the same swift, silent motion, sailed toward him, as if blown thither by the gale. Its long, thin arms, with something like a pale flame spiring from the tips of the slender fingers, were stretched out, as in greeting, while the wan smile played over its face; and when he rushed by, unheedingly, it made a futile effort to grasp the swinging arms with which he appeared to buffet back the buffeting gale. Then it glided on by his side, looking earnestly into his countenance, and moving its pallid lips with agonized rapidity, as if it said: "Look at me—speak to me—speak to me—see me!" But he kept his course with unconscious eyes, and a vexed frown on his bold, white forehead, betokening an irritated mind. The light that had shone in the figure of the phantom, darkened slowly, till the form was only a pale shadow. The wind had suddenly lulled, and no longer lifted its white hair. It still glided on with him, its head drooping on its breast, and its long arms hanging by its side; but when he reached the door, it suddenly sprang before him, gazing fixedly into his eyes, while a convulsive motion flashed over its grief-worn features, as if it had shrieked out a word. He had his foot on the step at the moment. With a start, he put his gloved hand to his forehead, while the vexed look went out quickly on his face. The ghost watched him breathlessly. But the irritated expression came back to his countenance more resolutely than before, and he began to fumble in his pocket for a latchkey, muttering petulantly, "What the devil is the matter with me now!" It seemed to him that a voice had cried, clearly, yet as from afar, "Charles Renton!"—his own name. He had heard it in his startled mind; but, then, he knew he was in a highly wrought state of nervous excitement, and his medical science, with that knowledge for a basis, could have reared a formidable fortress of explanation against any phenomenon, were it even more wonderful than this.

He entered the house; kicked the door to; pulled off his overcoat; wrenched off his outer 'kerchief; slammed them on a branch of the clothes tree; banged his hat on top of them; wheeled about; pushed in the door of his library; strode in, and, leaving the door ajar, threw himself into an easy chair, and sat there in the fire-reddened dusk, with his white brows knit, and his arms tightly locked on his breast. The ghost had followed him, sadly, and now stood motionless in a corner of the room, its spectral hands crossed on its bosom, and its white locks drooping down.

It was evident Dr. Renton was in a bad humor. The very library caught contagion from him, and became grouty and somber. The furniture was grim, and sullen, and sulky; it made ugly shadows on the carpet and on the wall, in allopathic quantity; it took the red gleams from the fire on its polished surfaces, in homeopathic globules, and got no good from them. The fire itself peered out sulkily from the black bars of the grate, and seemed resolved not to burn the fresh deposit of black coals at the top, but to take this as a good time to remember that those coals had been bought in the summer at five dollars a ton—under price, mind you—when poor people, who cannot buy at advantage, but must get their firing in the winter, would then have given nine or ten dollars for them. And so (glowered the fire), I am determined to think of that outrage, and not to light them, but to go out myself directly! And the fire got into such a spasm of glowing indignation over the injury that it lit a whole tier of black coals with a series of little explosions, before it could cool down, and sent a crimson gleam over the moody figure of its owner in the easy chair, and over the solemn furniture, and into the shadowy corner filled by the ghost.

The specter did not move when Dr. Renton arose and lit the chandelier. It stood there, still and gray, in the flood of mellow light. The curtains were drawn, and the twilight without had deepened into darkness. The fire was now burning in despite of itself, fanned by the wintry gusts, which found their way down the chimney. Dr. Renton stood with his back to it, his hands behind him, his bold white forehead shaded by a careless lock of black hair, and knit sternly; and the same frown in his handsome, open, searching dark eyes. Tall and strong, with an erect port, and broad, firm shoulders, high, resolute features, a commanding figure garbed in aristocratic black, and not yet verging into the proportions of obesity—take him for all in all, a very fine and favorable specimen of the solid men of Boston. And seen in contrast (oh! could he but have known it!) with the attenuated figure of the poor, dim ghost!

Hark! a very light foot on the stairs—a rich rustle of silks. Everything still again—Dr. Renton looking fixedly, with great sternness, at the half-open door, from whence a faint, delicious perfume floats into the library. Somebody there, for certain. Somebody peeping in with very bright, arch eyes. Dr. Renton knew it, and prepared to maintain his ill humor against the invader. His face became triply armed with severity for the encounter. That's Netty, I know, he thought. His daughter. So it was. In she bounded. Bright little Netty! Gay little Netty! A dear and sweet little creature, to be sure, with a delicate and pleasant beauty of face and figure, it needed no costly silks to grace or heighten. There she stood. Not a word from her merry lips, but a smile which stole over all the solitary grimness of the library, and made everything better, and brighter, and fairer, in a minute. It floated down into the cavernous humor of Dr. Renton, and the gloom began to lighten directly—though he would not own it, nor relax a single feature. But the wan ghost in the corner lifted its head to look at her, and slowly brightened as to something worthy a spirit's love, and a dim phantom's smiles. Now then, Dr. Renton! the lines are drawn, and the time is coming. Be martial, sir, as when you stand in the ranks of the cadets on training days! Steady, and stand the charge! So he did. He kept an inflexible frown as she glided toward him, softly, slowly, with her bright eyes smiling into his, and doing dreadful execution.

Then she put her white arms around his neck, laid her dear, fair head on his breast, and peered up archly into his stern visage. Spite of himself, he could not keep the fixed lines on his face from breaking confusedly into a faint smile. Somehow or other, his hands came from behind him, and rested on her head. There! That's all. Dr. Renton surrendered at discretion! One of the solid men of Boston was taken after a desperate struggle—internal, of course—for he kissed her, and said, "Dear little Netty!" And so she was.

The phantom watched her with a smile, and wavered and brightened as if about to glide to her; but it grew still, and remained.

"Pa in the sulks tonight?" she asked, in the most winning, playful, silvery voice.

"Pa's a fool," he answered in his deep chest-tones, with a vexed good humor; "and you know it."

"What's the matter with pa? What makes him be a great bear? Papa'sy, dear," she continued, stroking his face with her little hands, and patting him, very much as Beauty might have patted the Beast after she fell in love with him—or, as if he were a great baby. In fact, he began to look then as if he were.

"Matter? Oh! everything's the matter, little Netty. The world goes round too fast. My boots pinch. Somebody stole my umbrella last year. And I've got a headache." He concluded this fanciful abstract of his grievances by putting his arms around her, and kissing her again. Then he sat down in the easy-chair, and took her fondly on his knee.

"Pa's got a headache! It is t-o-o bad, so it is," she continued in the same soothing, winning way, caressing his bold, white brow with her tiny hands. "It's a horrid shame, so it is! P-o-o-r pa. Where does it ache, papa-sy, dear? In the forehead? Cerebrum or cerebellum, papa-sy? Occiput or sineiput, deary?"

"Bah! you little quiz," he replied, laughing and pinching her cheek, "none of your nonsense! And what are you dressed up in this way for, tonight? Silks, and laces, and essences, and what not! Where are you going, fairy?"

"Going out with mother for the evening, Dr. Renton," she replied briskly; "Mrs. Larrabee's party, papa-sy. Christmas eve, you know. And what are you going to give me for a present, tomorrow, pa-sy?"

"Tomorrow will tell, little Netty."

"Good! And what are you going to give me, so that I can make *my* presents, Beary?"

"Ugh!" but he growled it in fun, and had a pocketbook out from his breast pocket directly after. Fives—tens—twenties—fifties—all crisp, and nice, and new bank notes.

"Will that be enough, Netty?" He held up a twenty. The smiling face nodded assent, and the bright eyes twinkled.

"No, it won't. But *that* will," he continued, giving her a fifty.

"Fifty dollars, Globe Bank, Boston!" exclaimed Netty, making great eyes at him. "But we must take all we can get, pa-sy; mustn't we? It's too much, though. Thank you all the same, pa-sy, nevertheless." And she kissed him, and put the bill in a little bit of a portemonnaie with a gay laugh.

"Well done, I declare!" he said, smilingly. "But you're going to the party?"

"Pretty soon, pa."

He made no answer; but sat smiling at her. The phantom watched them, silently.

"What made pa so cross and grim, tonight? Tell Netty—do," she pleaded.

"Oh! because;—everything went wrong with me, today. There." And he looked as sulky, at that moment, as he ever did in his life.

"No, no, pa-sy; that won't do. I want the particulars," continued Netty, shaking her head, smilingly.

"Particulars! Well, then, Miss Nathalie Renton," he began, with mock gravity, "your professional father is losing some of his oldest patients. Everybody is in ruinous good health; and the grass is growing in the graveyards."

"In the wintertime, papa?—smart grass!"

"Not that I want practice," he went on, getting into soliloquy; "or patients, either. A rich man who took to the profession simply for the love of it, can't complain on that score. But to have an interloping she-doctor take a family I've attended ten years, out of my hands, and to hear the hodge-podge gabble about physiological laws, and woman's rights, and no taxation without representation, they learn from her—well, it's too bad!"

"Is that all, pa-sy? Seems to me, *I'd* like to vote, too," was Netty's piquant rejoinder.

"Hoh! I'll warrant," growled her father. "Hope you'll vote the Whig ticket, Netty, when you get your rights."

"Will the Union be dissolved, then, pa-sy—when the Whigs are beaten?"

"Bah! you little plague," he growled, with a laugh. "But, then, you women don't know anything about politics. So, there. As I was saying, everything went wrong with me today. I've been speculating in railroad stock, and singed my fingers. Then, old Tom Hollis outbid me, today, at Leonard's on a rare medical work I had set my eyes upon having. Confound him! Then, again, two of my houses are tenantless, and there are folks in two others that won't pay their rent, and I can't get them out. Out they'll go, though, or I'll know why. And, to crown all—um-m. And I wish the devil had him! as he will."

"Had who, Beary-papa?"

"Him. I'll tell you. The street floor of one of my houses in Hanover street lets for an oyster-room. They keep a bar there, and sell liquor. Last night they had a grand row—a drunken fight, and one man was stabbed, it's thought fatally."

"O, father!" Netty's bright eyes dilated with horror.

"Yes. I hope he won't die. At any rate, there's likely to be a stir about the matter, and my name will be called into question, then, as I'm the landlord. And folks will make a handle of it, and there'll be the deuce to pay, generally."

He got back the stern, vexed frown, to his face, with the anticipation, and beat the carpet with his foot. The ghost still watched from the angle of the room, and seemed to darken, while its features looked troubled.

"But, father," said Netty, a little tremulously, "I wouldn't let my houses to such people. It's not right; is it? Why, it's horrid to think of men getting drunk, and killing each other!"

Dr. Renton rubbed his hair into disorder, with vexation, and then subsided into solemnity.

"I know it's not exactly right, Netty; but I can't help it. As I said before, I wish the devil had that barkeeper. I ought to have ordered him out long ago, and then this wouldn't have happened. I've increased his rent twice, hoping to get rid of him so; but he pays without a murmur; and what am I to do? You see, he was an occupant when the building came into my hands, and I let him stay. He pays me a good, round rent; and, apart from his cursed traffic, he's a good tenant. What can I do? It's a good thing for him, and it's a good thing for me, pecuniarily. Confound him. Here's a nice rumpus brewing!"

"Dear pa, I'm afraid it's not a good thing for you," said Netty, caressing him, and smoothing his tumbled hair. "Nor for him either. I wouldn't mind the rent he pays you. I'd order him out. It's bad money. There's blood on it."

She had grown pale, and her voice quivered. The phantom glided over to them, and laid its spectral hand upon her forehead. The shadowy eyes looked from under the misty hair into the doctor's face, and the pale lips moved as if speaking the words heard only in the silence of his heart—"hear her, hear her!"

"I must think of it," resumed Dr. Renton, coldly. "I'm resolved, at all events, to warn him that if anything of this kind occurs again, he must quit at once. I dislike to lose a profitable tenant; for no other business would bring me the sum his does. Hang it, everybody does the best he can with his property—why shouldn't I?"

The ghost, standing near them, drooped its head again on its breast, and crossed its arms. Netty was silent. Dr. Renton continued, petulantly:

"A precious set of people I manage to get into my premises. There's a woman hires a couple of rooms for a dwelling, overhead, in that same building, and for three months I haven't got a cent from her. I know these people's tricks. Her month's notice expires tomorrow, and out she goes."

"Poor creature!" sighed Netty.

He knit his brow, and beat the carpet with his foot, in vexation.

"Perhaps she can't pay you, pa," trembled the sweet, silvery voice. "You wouldn't turn her out in this cold winter, when she can't pay you—would you, pa?"

"Why don't she get another house, and swindle someone else?" he replied, testily; "there's plenty of rooms to let."

"Perhaps she can't find one, pa," answered Netty.

"Humbug!" retorted her father; "I know better."

"Pa, dear, if I were you, I'd turn out that rumseller, and let the poor woman stay a little longer; just a little, pa."

"Shan't do it. Hah! that would be scattering money out of both pockets. Shan't do it. Out she shall go; and as for him—well, he'd better turn over a new leaf. There, let us leave the subject, darling. It vexes me. How did we contrive to get into this train. Bah!"

He drew her closer to him, and kissed her forehead. She sat quietly, with her head on his shoulder, thinking very gravely.

"I feel queerly today, little Netty," he began, after a short pause. "My nerves are all high-strung with the turn matters have taken."

"How is it, papa? The headache?" she answered.

"Y-e-s—n-o—not exactly; I don't know," he said dubiously; then, in an absent way, "it was that letter set me to think of him all day, I suppose."

"Why, pa, I declare," cried Netty, starting up, "if I didn't forget all about it, and I came down expressly to give it to you! Where is it? Oh! here it is."

She drew from her pocket an old letter, faded to a pale yellow, and gave it to him. The ghost started suddenly.

"Why, bless my soul! it's the very letter! Where did you get that, Nathalie?" asked Dr. Renton.

"I found it on the stairs after dinner, pa."

"Yes, I do remember taking it up with me; I must have dropped it," he answered, musingly, gazing at the superscription. The ghost was gazing at it, too, with startled interest.

"What beautiful writing it is, pa," murmured the young girl. "Who wrote it to you? It looks yellow enough to have been written a long time since."

"Fifteen years ago, Netty. When you were a baby. And the hand that wrote it has been cold for all that time."

He spoke with a solemn sadness, as if memory lingered with the heart of fifteen years ago, on an old grave. The dim figure by his side had bowed its head, and all was still.

"It is strange," he resumed, speaking vacantly and slowly, "I have not thought of him for so long a time, and today—especially this evening—I have felt as if he were constantly near me. It is a singular feeling."

He put his left hand to his forehead, and mused—his right clasped his daughter's shoulder. The phantom slowly raised its head, and gazed at him with a look of unutterable tenderness.

"Who was he, father?" she asked with a hushed voice.

"A young man—an author—a poet. He had been my dearest friend, when we were boys; and, though I lost sight of him for years—he led an erratic life—we were friends when he died. Poor, poor fellow! Well, he is at peace."

The stern voice had saddened, and was almost tremulous. The spectral form was still.

"How did he die, father?"

"A long story, darling," he replied gravely, "and a sad one. He was very poor and proud. He was a genius—that is, a person without an atom of practical talent. His parents died, the last, his mother, when he was near manhood. I was in college then. Thrown upon the world, he picked up a scanty subsistence with his pen, for a time. I could have got him a place in the counting-house, but he would not take it; in fact, he wasn't fit for it. You can't harness Pegasus to the cart, you know. Besides, he despised mercantile life—without reason, of course; but he was always notional. His love of literature was one of the rocks he foundered on. He wasn't successful; his best compositions were too delicate—fanciful—to please the popular taste; and then he was full of the radical and fanatical notions which infected so many people at that time in New England, and infect them now, for that matter; and his sublimated, impracticable ideas and principles, which he kept till his dying day, and which, I confess, alienated me from him, always staved off his chances of success. Consequently, he never rose above the drudgery of some employment on newspapers. Then he was terribly passionate, not without cause, I allow; but it wasn't wise. What I mean is this: if he saw, or if he fancied he saw, any wrong or injury done to anyone, it was enough to throw him into a frenzy; he would get black in the face and absolutely shriek out his denunciations of the wrongdoer. I do believe he would have visited his own brother with the most unsparing invective, if that brother had laid a harming finger on a street-beggar, or a colored man, or a poor person of any kind. I don't blame the feeling; though with a man like him, it was very apt to be a false or mistaken one; but, at any rate, its exhibition wasn't sensible. Well, as I was saying, he buffeted about in this world a long time, poorly paid, fed, and clad; taking more care of other people than he did of himself. Then mental suffering, physical exposure, and want killed him."

The stern voice had grown softer than a child's. The same look of unutterable tenderness brooded on the mournful face of the phantom by his side; but its thin, shining hand was laid upon his head, and its countenance had undergone a change. The form was still undefined; but the features had become distinct. They were those of a young man, beautiful and wan, and marked with great suffering.

A pause had fallen on the conversation, in which the father and daughter heard the solemn sighing of the wintry wind around the dwelling. The silence seemed scarcely broken by the voice of the young girl.

"Dear father, this was very sad. Did you say he died of want?"

"Of want, my child. Of hunger and cold. I don't doubt it. He had wandered about, as I gather, houseless for a couple of days and nights. It was in December, too. Someone found him, on a rainy night, lying in the street, drenched and burning with fever, and had him taken to the hospital. It appears that he had always cherished a strange affection for me, though I had grown away from him; and in his wild ravings he constantly mentioned my name, and they sent for me. That was our first meeting after two years. I found him in the hospital—dying. Heaven can witness that I felt all my old love for him return then, but he was delirious, and never recognized me. And, Nathalie, his hair—it had been coal-black, and he wore it very long, he wouldn't let them cut it either; and as they knew no skill could save him, they let him have his way—his hair was then as white as snow! God alone knows what that brain must have suffered to blanch hair which had been as black as the wing of a raven!"

He covered his eyes with his hand, and sat silently. The fingers of the phantom still shone dimly on his head, and its white locks drooped above him, like a weft of light.

"What was his name, father?" asked the pitying girl.

"George Feval. The very name sounds like fever. He died on Christmas eve, fifteen years ago this night. It was on his deathbed, while his mind was tossing on a sea of delirious fancies, that he wrote me this long letter—for to the last, I was uppermost in his thoughts. It is a wild, incoherent thing, of course—a strange mixture of sense and madness. But I have kept it as a memorial of him. I have not looked at it for years; but this morning I found it among my papers, and somehow it has been in my mind all day."

He slowly unfolded the faded sheets, and sadly gazed at the writing. His daughter had risen from her half-recumbent posture, and now bent her graceful head over the leaves. The phantom covered its face with its hands.

"What a beautiful manuscript it is, father!" she exclaimed. "The writing is faultless."

"It is, indeed," he replied. "Would he had written his life a fairly!"

"Read it, father," said Nathalie.

"No—but I'll read you a detached passage here and there,' he answered, after a pause. "The rest you may read yoursel some time, if you wish. It is painful to me. Here's the beginning

"My Dear Charles Renton:—Adieu, and adieu. It is Christmas eve, and I an going home. I am soon to exhale from my flesh, like the spirit of a broken flower Exultemus forever!

"It is very wild. His mind was in a fever-craze. Here is a passage that seems to refer to his own experience of life:

"Your friendship was dear to me. I give you true love. Stocks and returns. You are rich, but I did not wish to be your bounty's pauper. Could I beg? I had my work to do for the world, but oh! the world has no place for souls that can only love and suffer. How many miles to Babylon? Threescore and ten. Not so far—not near so far! Ask starvelings—they know.

. . .

I wanted to do the world good and the world has killed me, Charles."

"It frightens me," said Nathalie, as he paused.

"We will read no more," he replied somberly. "It belongs to the psychology of madness. To me, who knew him, there are gleams of sense in it, and passages where the delirium of the language is only a transparent veil on the meaning. All the remainder is devoted to what he thought important advice to me. But it's all wild and vague. Poor—poor George!"

The phantom still hid its face in its hands, as the doctor slowly turned over the pages of the letter. Nathalie, bending over the leaves, laid her finger on the last, and asked—"What are those closing sentences, father? Read them."

"Oh! that is what he called his 'last counsel' to me. It's as wild as the rest—tinctured with the prevailing ideas of his career. First he says, 'Farewell—farewell;' then he bids me take his 'counsel into memory on Christmas day;' then, after enumerating all the wretched classes he can think of in the country, he says. 'These are your sisters and your brothers—love them all.' Here he says, 'O friend, strong in wealth for so much good, take my last counsel. In the name of the Savior, I charge you be true and tender to mankind.' He goes on to bid me 'live and labor for the fallen, the neglected, the suffering, and the poor'; and finally ends by advising me to help upset any, or all, institutions, laws, and so forth, that bear hardly on the fag-ends of society; and tells me that what he calls 'a service to humanity' is worth more to the doer than a service to anything else, or than anything we can gain from the world. Ah, well! poor George."

"But isn't all that true, father?" said Netty; "it seems so."

"H'm," he murmured through his closed lips. Then, with a vague smile, folding up the letter, meanwhile, he said, "Wild words, Netty, wild words. I've no objection to charity, judiciously given; but poor George's notions are not mine. Every man for himself, is a good general rule. Every man for humanity, as George has it, and in his acceptation of the principle, would send us all to the almshouse pretty soon. The greatest good of the greatest number—that's my rule of action. There are plenty of good institutions for the distressed, and I'm willing to help support 'em, and do. But as for making a martyr of one's self, or tilting against the necessary evils of society, or turning philanthropist at large, or any quixotism of that sort, I don't believe in it. We didn't make the world, and we can't mend it. Poor George. Well—he's at rest. The world wasn't the place for him."

They grew silent. The specter glided slowly to the wall, and stood as if it were thinking what, with Dr. Renton's rule of action, was to become of the greatest good of the smallest number. Nathalie sat on her father's knee, thinking only of George Feval, and of his having been starved and grieved to death.

"Father," said Nathalie, softly, "I felt, while you were reading the letter, as if he were near us. Didn't you? The room was so light and still, and the wind sighed so."

"Netty, dear, I've felt that all day, I believe," he replied. "Hark! there is the doorbell. Off goes the spirit-world, and here comes the actual. Confound it! Someone to see me, I'll warrant, and I'm not in the mood."

He got into a fret at once. Netty was not the Netty of an hour ago, or she would have coaxed him out of it. But she did not notice it now in her abstraction. She had risen at the tinkle of the bell, and seated herself in a chair. Presently a nose, with a great pimple on the end of it, appeared at the edge of the door, and a weak, piping voice said, reckless of the proper tense, "there was a woman wanted to see you, sir."

"Who is it, James?—no matter, show her in."

He got up with the vexed scowl on his face, and walked the room. In a minute the library door opened again, and a pale, thin, rigid, frozen-looking little woman, scantily clad, the weather being considered, entered, and dropped a curt, awkward bow to Dr. Renton.

"Oh! Mrs. Miller. Good evening, ma'am. Sit down," he said, with a cold, constrained civility.

The little woman faintly said, "Good evening, Dr. Renton," and sat down stiffly, with her hands crossed before her, in the chair nearest the wall. This was the obdurate tenant, who had paid no rent for three months, and had a notice to quit, expiring tomorrow.

"Cold evening, ma'am," remarked Dr. Renton, in his hard way.

"Yes, sir, it is," was the cowed, awkward answer.

"Won't you sit near the fire, ma'am," said Netty, gently; "you look cold."

"No, miss, thank you. I'm not cold," was the faint reply. She was cold, though, as well she might be with her poor, thin shawl, and open bonnet, in such a bitter night as it was outside. And there was a rigid, sharp, suffering look in her pinched features that betokened she might have been hungry, too.

"Poor people don't mind the cold weather, miss," she said,

with a weak smile, her voice getting a little stronger. "They have to bear it, and they get used to it."

She had not evidently borne it long enough to effect the point of indifference. Netty looked at her with a tender pity. Dr. Renton thought to himself—Hoh!—blazoning her poverty—manufacturing sympathy already—the old trick—and steeled himself against any attacks of that kind, looking jealously, meanwhile, at Netty.

"Well, Mrs. Miller," he said, "what is it this evening? I suppose you've brought me my rent."

The little woman grew paler, and her voice seemed to fail on her quivering lips. Netty cast a quick, beseeching look at her father.

"Nathalie, please to leave the room." We'll have no nonsense carried on here, he thought, triumphantly, as Netty rose, and obeyed the stern, decisive order, leaving the door ajar behind her.

He seated himself in his chair, and resolutely put his right leg up to rest on his left knee. He did not look at his tenant's face, determined that her piteous expressions (got up for the occasion, of course) should be wasted on him.

"Well, Mrs. Miller," he said again.

"Dr. Renton," she began, faintly gathering her voice as she proceeded, "I have come to see you about the rent. I am very sorry, sir, to have made you wait, but we have been unfortunate."

"Sorry, ma'am," he replied, knowing what was coming; "but your misfortunes are not my affair. We all have misfortunes, ma'am. But we must pay our debts, you know."

"I expected to have got money from my husband before this, sir," she resumed, "and I wrote to him. I got a letter from him today, sir, and it said that he sent me fifty dollars a month ago, in a letter; and it appears that the post-office is to blame, or somebody, for I never got it. It was nearly three months' wages, sir, and it is very hard to lose it. If it hadn't been for that, your rent would have been paid long ago, sir."

"Don't believe a word of *that* story," thought Dr. Renton, sententiously.

"I thought, sir," she continued, emboldened by his silence, "that if you would be willing to wait a little longer, we would manage to pay you soon, and not let it occur again. It has been a hard winter with us, sir; firing is high, and provisions, and everything; and we're only poor people, you know, and it's difficult to get along."

The doctor made no reply.

"My husband was unfortunate, sir, in not being able to get employment here," she resumed; "his being out of work, in the autumn, threw us all back, and we've got nothing to depend on but his earnings. The family that he's in now, sir, don't give him very good pay—only twenty dollars a month, and his board—but it was the best chance he could get, and it was either go to Baltimore with them, or stay at home and starve, and so he went, sir. It's been a hard time with us, and one of the children is sick, now, with a fever, and we don't hardly know how to make out a living. And so, sir, I have come here this evening, leaving the children alone, to ask you if you wouldn't be kind enough to wait a little longer, and we'll hope to make it right with you in the end."

"Mrs. Miller," said Dr. Renton, with stern composure, "I have no wish to question the truth of any statement you may make; but I must tell you plainly, that I can't afford to let my houses for nothing. I told you a month ago, that if you couldn't pay me my rent, you must vacate the premises. You know very well that there are plenty of tenants who are able and willing to pay when the money comes due. You *know* that."

He paused as he said this, and, glancing at her, saw her pale lips falter. It shook the cruelty of his purpose a little, and he had a vague feeling that he was doing wrong. Not without a proud struggle, during which no word was spoken, could he beat it down. Meanwhile, the phantom had advanced a pace toward the center of the room.

"That is the state of the matter, ma'am," he resumed, coldly.

"People who will not pay me my rent must not live in my tenements. You must move out. I have no more to say."

"Dr. Renton," she said faintly, "I have a sick child—how can I move now? Oh! sir, it's Christmas eve—don't be hard with us!"

Instead of touching him, this speech irritated him beyond measure. Passing all considerations of her difficult position involved in her piteous statement, his anger flashed at once on her implication that he was unjust and unkind. So violent was his excitement that it whirled away the words that rushed to his lips, and only fanned the fury that sparkled from the whiteness of his face in his eyes.

"Be patient with us, sir," she continued; "we are poor, but we mean to pay you; and we can't move now in this cold weather; please, don't be hard with us, sir."

The fury now burst out on his face in a red and angry glow, and the words came.

"Now, attend to me!" He rose to his feet. "I will not hear any more from you. I know nothing of your poverty, nor of the condition of your family. All I know is that you owe me three months' rent, and that you can't or won't pay me. I say, therefore, leave the premises to people who can and will. You have had your legal notice; quit my house tomorrow; if you don't, your furniture shall be put in the street. Mark me—tomorrow!"

The phantom had rushed into the center of the room. Standing, face to face with him—dilating—blackening—its whole form shuddering with a fury to which his own was tame—the semblance of a shriek upon its flashing lips, and on its writhing features, and an unearthly anger streaming from its bright and terrible eyes—it seemed to throw down, with its tossing arms, mountains of hate and malediction on the head of him whose words had smitten poverty and suffering, and whose heavy hand was breaking up the barriers of a home.

Dr. Renton sank again into his chair. His tenant—not a woman!—not a sister in humanity!—but only his tenant; she sat crushed and frightened by the wall. He knew it vaguely. Conscience was battling in his heart with the stubborn devils that had entered there. The phantom stood before him, like a dark cloud in the image of a man. But its darkness was lightening slowly, and its ghostly anger had passed away.

The poor woman, paler than before, had sat mute and trembling, with all her hopes ruined. Yet her desperation forbade her to abandon the chances of his mercy, and she now said:

"Dr. Renton, you surely don't mean what you have told me. Won't you bear with me a little longer, and we will yet make it all right with you?"

"I have given you my answer," he returned, coldly; "I have no more to add. I never take back anything I say—never!"

It was true. He never did—never! She half rose from her seat as if to go; but weak and sickened with the bitter result of her visit, she sunk down again with her head bowed. There was a pause. Then, solemnly gliding across the lighted room, the phantom stole to her side with a glory of compassion on its wasted features. Tenderly, as a son to a mother, it bent over her; its spectral hands of light rested upon her in caressing and benediction; its shadowy fall of hair, once blanched by the anguish of living and loving, floated on her throbbing brow; and resignation and comfort not of this world, sank upon her spirit, and consciousness grew dim within her, and care and sorrow seemed to die.

He who had been so cruel and so hard, sat silent in black gloom. The stern and sullen mood from which had dropped but one fierce flash of anger, still hung above the heat of his mind, like a dark rack of thundercloud. It would have burst anew into a fury of rebuke, had he but known his daughter was listening at the door, while the colloquy went on. It might have flamed violently, had his tenant made any further attempt to change his purpose. She had not. She had left the room meekly, with the same curt, awkward bow that marked her entrance. He recalled her manner very indistinctly; for a feeling, like a mist, began to gather in his mind, and make the occurrences of moments before uncertain.

Alone, now, he was yet oppressed with a sensation that

something was near him. Was it a spiritual instinct? for the phantom stood by his side. It stood silently, with one hand raised above his head, from which a pale flame seemed to flow downward to his brain; its other hand pointed movelessly to the open letter on the table beside him.

He took the sheets from the table, thinking, at the moment, only of George Feval; but the first line on which his eye rested was, "In the name of the Savior, I charge you, be true and tender to mankind!" and the words touched him like a low voice from the grave. Their penetrant reproach pierced the hardness of his heart. He tossed the letter back on the table. The very manner of the act accused him of an insult to the dead. In a moment he took up the faded sheets more reverently, but only to lay them down again.

He had not been well that day, and he now felt worse than before. The pain in his head had given place to a strange sense of dilation, and there was a silent, confused riot in his fevered brain, which seemed to him like the incipience of insanity. Striving to divert his mind from what had passed, by reflection on other themes, he could not hold his thoughts; they came teeming but dim, and slipped and fell away; and only the one circumstance of his recent cruelty, mixed with remembrance of George Feval, recurred and clung with vivid persistence. This tortured him. Sitting there, with arms tightly interlocked, he resolved to wrench his mind down by sheer will upon other things; and a savage pleasure at what at once seemed success, took possession of him. In this mood, he heard soft footsteps and the rustle of festal garments on the stairs, and had a fierce complacency in being able to clearly apprehend that it was his wife and daughter going out to the party. In a moment, he heard the controlled and even voice of Mrs. Renton—a serene and polished lady with whom he had lived for years in cold and civil alienation, both seeing as little of each other as possible. With a scowl of will upon his brow, he received her image distinctly into his mind, even to the minutia of the dress and ornaments he knew she wore, and felt an absolutely savage exultation in his ability to retain it. Then came the sound of the closing of the hall door and the rattle of receding wheels, and somehow it was Nathalie and not his wife that he was holding so grimly in his thought, and with her, salient and vivid as before, the tormenting remembrance of his tenant, connected with the memory of George Feval. Springing to his feet, he walked the room.

He had thrown himself on a sofa, still striving to be rid of his remorseful visitations, when the library door opened, and the inside man appeared, with his hand held bashfully over his nose. It flashed on him at once, that his tenant's husband was the servant of a family like this fellow; and, irritated that the whole matter should be thus broadly forced upon him in another way, he harshly asked him what he wanted. The man only came in to say that Mrs. Renton and the young lady had gone out for the evening, but that tea was laid for him in the dining room. He did not want any tea, and if anybody called, he was not at home. With this charge, the man left the room, closing the door behind him.

If he could but sleep a little! Rising from the sofa, he turned the lights of the chandelier low, and screened the fire. The room was still. The ghost stood, faintly radiant, in a remote corner. Dr. Renton lay down again, but not to repose. Things he had forgotten of his dead friend, now started up again in remembrance, fresh from the grave of many years; and not one of them but linked itself by some mysterious bond to something connected with his tenant, and became an accusation.

He had lain thus for more than an hour, feeling more and more unmanned by illness, and his mental excitement fast becoming intolerable, when he heard a low strain of music, from the Swedenborgian chapel, hard by. Its first impression was one of solemnity and rest, and its first sense, in his mind, was of relief. Perhaps it was the music of an evening meeting; or it might be that the organist and choir had met for practice. Whatever its purpose, it breathed through his heated fancy like a cool and fragrant wind. It was vague and sweet and wandering at first, straying on into a strain more mysterious and melancholy, but very shadowy and subdued, and evoking the innocent and tender moods of early youth before worldliness had hardened around his heart. Gradually, as he listened to it, the fires in his brain were allayed, and all yielded to a sense of coolness and repose. He seemed to sink from trance to trance of utter rest, and yet was dimly aware that either something in his own condition, or some supernatural accession of tone, was changing the music from its proper quality to a harmony more infinite and awful. It was still low and indeterminate and sweet, but had unaccountably and strangely swelled into a gentle and somber dirge, incommunicably mournful, and filled with a dark significance that touched him in his depth of rest with a secret tremor and awe. As he listened, rapt and vaguely wondering, the sense of his tranced sinking seemed to come to an end, and with the feeling of one who had been descending for many hours, and at length lay motionless at the bottom of a deep, dark chasm; he heard the music fail and cease.

A pause, and then it rose again, blended with the solemn voices of the choir, sublimed and dilated now, reaching him as though from weird night gulfs of the upper air, and charged with an overmastering pathos as of the lamentations of angels. In the dimness and silence, in the aroused and exalted condition of his being, the strains seemed unearthly in their immense and desolate grandeur of sorrow, and their mournful and dark significance was now for him. Working within him the impression of vast, innumerable, fleeing shadows, thick-crowding memories of all the ways and deeds of an existence fallen from its early dreams and aims, poured across the midnight of his soul, and under the streaming melancholy of the dirge, his life showed like some monstrous treason. It did not terrify or madden him; he listened to it rapt utterly as in some deadening ether of dream; yet feeling to his inmost core all its powerful grief and accusation, and quietly aghast at the sinister consciousness it gave him. Still it swelled, gathering and sounding on into yet mightier pathos, till all at once it darkened and spread wide in wild despair, and aspiring again into a pealing agony of supplication, quivered and died away in a low and funereal sigh.

The tears streamed suddenly upon his face; his soul lightened and turned dark within him; and as one faints away, so consciousness swooned, and he fell suddenly down a precipice of sleep. The music rose again, a pensive and holy chant, and sounded on to its close, unaffected by the action of his brain, for he slept and heard it no more. He lay tranquilly, hardly seeming to breathe, in motionless repose. The room was dim and silent, and the furniture took uncouth shapes around him. The red glow upon the ceiling, from the screened fire, showed the misty figure of the phantom kneeling by his side. All light had gone from the spectral form. It knelt beside him, mutely, as in prayer. Once it gazed at his quiet face with a mournful tenderness, and its shadowy hands caressed his forehead. Then it resumed its former attitude, and the slow hours crept by.

At last it rose and glided to the table, on which lay the open letter. It seemed to try to lift the sheets with its misty hands—but vainly. Next it essayed the lifting of a pen which lay there—but failed. It was a piteous sight, to see its idle efforts on these shapes of grosser matter, which appeared now to have to it but the existence of illusions. Wandering about the shadowy room, it wrung its phantom hands as in despair.

Presently it grew still. Then it passed quickly to his side, and stood before him. He slept calmly. It placed one ghostly hand above his forehead, and, with the other pointed to the open letter. In this attitude its shape grew momentarily more distinct. It began to kindle into brightness. The pale flame again flowed from its hand, streaming downward to his brain. A look of trouble darkened the sleeping face. Stronger—stronger; brighter—brighter; until, at last, it stood before him, a glorious shape of light, with an awful look of commanding love in its shining features—and the sleeper sprang to his feet with a cry!

The phantom had vanished. He saw nothing. His first impression was, not that he had dreamed, but that, awaking in the familiar room, he had seen the spirit of his dead friend, bright and awful by his side, and that it had gone! In the flash of that quick change, from sleeping to waking, he had detected, he thought, the unearthly being that, he now felt, watched him from behind the air, and it had vanished! The library was the same as in the moment of that supernatural revealing; the open letter lay upon the table still; only *that* was gone which had made these common aspects terrible. Then, all the hard, strong skepticism of his nature, which had been driven backward by the shock of his first conviction, recoiled, and rushed within him, violently struggling for its former vantage ground; till, at length, it achieved the foothold for a doubt. Could he have dreamed? The ghost, invisible, still watched him. Yes—a dream—only a dream; but, how vivid—how strange! With a slow thrill creeping through his veins—the blood curdling at his heart—a cold sweat starting on his forehead, he stared through the dimness of the room. All was vacancy.

With a strong shudder, he strode forward, and turned up the flames of the chandelier. A flood of garish light filled the apartment. In a moment, remembering the letter to which the phantom of his dream had pointed, he turned and took it from the table. The last page lay upward, and every word of the solemn counsel at the end seemed to dilate on the paper, and all its mighty meaning rushed upon his soul. Trembling in his own despite, he laid it down and moved away. A physician, he remembered that he was in a state of violent nervous excitement, and thought that when he grew calmer its effects would pass from him. But the hand that had touched him had gone down deeper than the physician, and reached what God had made.

He strove in vain. The very room, in its light and silence, and the lurking sentiment of something watching him, became terrible. He could not endure it. The devils in his heart, grown pusillanimous, cowered beneath the flashing strokes of his aroused and terrible conscience. He could not endure it. He must go out. He will walk the streets. It is not late—it is but ten o'clock. He will go.

The air of his dream still hung heavily about him. He was in the street—he hardly remembered how he had got there, or when; but there he was, wrapped up from the searching cold, thinking, with a quiet horror in his mind, of the darkened room he had left behind, and haunted by the sense that something was groping about there in the darkness, searching for him. The night was still and cold. The full moon was in the zenith. Its icy splendor lay on the bare streets, and on the walls of the dwellings. The lighted oblong squares of curtained windows, here and there, seemed dim and waxen in the frigid glory. The familiar aspect of the quarter had passed away, leaving behind only a corpselike neighborhood, whose huge, dead features, staring rigidly through the thin, white shroud of moonlight that covered all, left no breath upon the stainless skies. Through the vast silence of the night he passed along; the very sound of his footfalls was remote to his muffled sense.

Gradually, as he reached the first corner, he had an uneasy feeling that a thing—a formless, unimaginable thing—was dogging him. He had thought of going down to his club room; but he now shrank from entering, with this thing near him, the lighted rooms where his set were busy with cards and billiards, over their liquors and cigars, and where the heated air was full of their idle faces and careless chatter, lest someone should bawl out that he was pale, and ask him what was the matter, and he should answer, tremblingly, that something was following him, and was near him then! He must get rid of it first; he must walk quickly, and baffle its pursuit by turning sharp corners, and plunging into devious streets and crooked lanes, and so lose it!

It was difficult to reach through memory to the crazy chaos of his mind on that night, and recall the route he took while haunted by this feeling; but he afterward remembered that, without any other purpose than to baffle his imaginary pursuer, he traversed at a rapid pace a large portion of the moonlit city;

always (he knew not why) avoiding the more populous thoroughfares, and choosing unfrequented and tortuous byways, but never ridding himself of that horrible confusion of mind in which the faces of his dead friend and the pale woman were strangely blended, nor of the fancy that he was followed. Once, as he passed the hospital where Feval died, a faint hint seemed to flash and vanish from the clouds of his lunacy, and almost identify the dogging goblin with the figure of his dream; but the conception instantly mixed with a disconnected remembrance that this was Christmas eve, and then slipped from him, and was lost. He did not pause there, but strode on. But just there, what had been frightful became hideous. For at once he was possessed with the conviction that the thing that lurked at a distance behind him, was quickening its movement, and coming up to seize him. The dreadful fancy stung him like a goad, and, with a start, he accelerated his flight, horribly conscious that what he feared was slinking along in the shadow, close to the dark bulks of the houses, resolutely pursuing, and bent on overtaking him. Faster! His footfalls rang hollowly and loud on the moonlit pavement, and in contrast with their rapid thuds he felt it as something peculiarly terrible that the furtive thing behind, slunk after him with soundless feet. Faster, faster! Traversing only the most unfrequented streets, and at that late hour of a cold winter night, he met no one, and with a terrifying consciousness that his pursuer was gaining on him, he desperately strode on. He did not dare to look behind, dreading less what he might see, than the momentary loss of speed the action might occasion. Faster, faster, faster! And all at once he knew that the dogging thing had dropped its stealthy pace and was racing up to him. With a bound he broke into a run, seeing, hearing, heeding nothing, aware only that the other was silently louping on his track two steps to his one; and with that frantic apprehension upon him, he gained the next street, flung himself around the corner with his back to the wall, and his arms convulsively drawn up for a grapple; and felt something rush whirring past his flank, striking him on the shoulder as it went by, with a buffet that made a shock break through his frame. That shock restored him to his senses. His delusion was suddenly shattered. The goblin was gone. He was free.

He stood panting, like one just roused from some terrible dream, wiping the reeking perspiration from his forehead and thinking confusedly and wearily what a fool he had been. He felt he had wandered a long distance from his house, but had no distinct perception of his whereabouts. He only knew he was in some thinly-peopled street, whose familiar aspect seemed lost to him in the magical disguise the superb moonlight had thrown over all. Suddenly a film seemed to drop from his eyes, as they became riveted on a lighted window, on the opposite side of the way. He started, and a secret terror crept over him, vaguely mixed with the memory of the shock he had felt as he turned the last corner, and his distinct, awful feeling that something invisible had passed him. At the same instant he felt, and thrilled to feel, a touch, as of a light finger, on his cheek. He was in Hanover street. Before him was the house—the oyster room staring at him through the lighted transparencies of its two windows, like two square eyes, below; and his tenant's light in a chamber above! The added shock which this discovery gave to the heaving of his heart, made him gasp for breath. Could it be? Did he still dream? While he stood panting and staring at the building, the city clocks began to strike. Eleven o'clock; it was ten when he came away; how he must have driven! His thoughts caught up the word. Driven—by what? Driven from his house in horror, through street and lane, over half the city—driven—hunted in terror, and smitten by a shock here! Driven—driven! He could not rid his mind of the word, nor of the meaning it suggested. The pavements about him began to ring and echo with the tramp of many feet, and the cold, brittle air was shivered with the noisy voices that had roared and bawled applause and laughter at the National Theatre all the evening, and were now singing and howling homeward. Groups of rude men, and ruder boys, their breaths steaming in the icy air, began to tramp by, jostling him as they passed, till he was forced to draw back to the wall, and give them the sidewalk. Dazed and giddy, in cold fear, and with the returning sense of something near him, he stood and watched the groups that pushed and tumbled in through the entrance of the oyster room, whistling and chattering as they went, and banging the door behind them. He noticed that some came out presently, banging the door harder, and went, smoking and shouting, down the street. Still they poured in and out, while the street was startled with their stimulated riot, and the barroom within echoed their trampling feet and hoarse voices. Then, as his glance wandered upward to his tenant's window, he thought of the sick child, mixing this hideous discord in the dreams of fever. The word brought up the name and the thought of his dead friend. "In the name of the Savior, I charge you be true and tender to mankind!" The memory of these words seemed to ring clearly, as if a voice had spoken them, above the roar that suddenly rose in his mind. In that moment he felt himself a wretched and most guilty man. He felt that his cruel words had entered that humble home, to make desperate poverty more desperate, to sicken sickness, and to sadden sorrow. Before him was the dram-shop, let and licensed to nourish the worst and most brutal appetites and instincts of human natures, at the sacrifice of all their highest and holiest tendencies. The throng of tipplers and drunkards was swarming through its hopeless door, to gulp the fiery liquor whose fumes give all shames, vices, miseries, and crimes, a lawless strength and life, and change the man into the pig or tiger. Murder was done, or nearly done, within those walls last night. Within those walls no good was ever done; but, daily, unmitigated evil, whose results were reaching on to torture unborn generations. He had consented to it all! He could not falter, or equivocate, or evade, or excuse. His dead friend's words rang in his conscience like the trump of the judgment angel. He was conquered.

Slowly, the resolve to instantly go in uprose within him, and with it a change came upon his spirit, and the natural world, sadder than before, but sweeter, seemed to come back to him. A great feeling of relief flowed upon his mind. Pale and trembling still, he crossed the street with a quick, unsteady step, entered a yard at the side of the house, and, brushing by a host of white, rattling specters of frozen clothes, which dangled from lines in the enclosure, mounted some wooden steps, and rang the bell. In a minute he heard footsteps within, and saw the gleam of a lamp. His heart palpitated violently as he heard the lock turning, lest the answerer of his summons might be his tenant. The door opened, and, to his relief, he stood before a rather decent-looking Irishman, bending forward in his stocking feet, with one boot and a lamp in his hand. The man stared at him from a wild head of tumbled red hair, with a half smile round his loose open mouth, and said, "Begorra!" This was a second floor tenant.

Dr. Renton was relieved at the sight of him; but he rather failed in an attempt at his rent-day suavity of manner, when he said:

"Good evening, Mr. Flanagan. Do you think I can see Mrs. Miller tonight?"

"She's up *there,* docther, anyway." Mr. Flanagan made a sudden start for the stairs, with the boot and lamp at arm's length before him, and stopped as suddenly. "Yull go up?—or wud she come down to ye?" There was as much anxious indecision in Mr. Flanagan's general aspect, pending the reply, as if he had to answer the question himself.

"I'll go up, Mr. Flanagan," returned Dr. Renton, stepping in, after a pause, and shutting the door. "But I'm afraid she's in bed."

"Naw—she's not, sur." Mr. Flanagan made another feint with the boot and lamp at the stairs, but stopped again in curious bewilderment, and rubbed his head. Then, with another inspiration, and speaking with such velocity that his words ran into each other, pell-mell, he continued: "Th' small girl's sick, sur. Begorra, I wer just pullin' on th' boots tuh gaw for the docther, in th' nixt streth, an' summons him to her relehf, fur it's bad she is. A'id better be goan." Another start, and a movement to put on the boot instantly, baffled by his getting the lamp into the leg of it, and involving himself in difficulties in trying to get it out again without dropping either, and stopped finally by Dr. Renton.

"You needn't go, Mr. Flanagan. I'll see to the child. Don't go."

He stepped slowly up the stairs, followed by the bewildered Flanagan. All this time Dr. Renton was listening to the racket from the barroom. Clinking of glasses, rattling of dishes, trampling of feet, oaths and laughter, and a confused din of coarse voices, mingling with boisterous calls for oysters and drink, came, hardly deadened by the partition walls, from the haunt below, and echoed through the corridors. Loud enough within—louder in the street without, where the oysters and drink were reeling and roaring off to brutal dreams. People trying to sleep here; a sick child upstairs. Listen! "*Two* stew! *One* roast! *Four* ale! Hurry 'em up! *Three* stew! *In* number six! *One* fancy—*two* roast! *One* sling! *Three* brandy—*hot! Two* stew! *One* whisk' *skin!* Hurry 'em up! *What* yeh *'bout! Three* brand' punch—*hot! Four* stew! *What-*ye-e-h 'bout! *Two* gin-cock-t'il! *One* stew! Hu-r-r-y 'em up!" Clashing, rattling, cursing, swearing, laughing, shouting, trampling, stumbling, driving, slamming, of doors. "Hu-r-r-y 'em up."

"Flanagan," said Dr. Renton, stopping at the first landing, "do you have this noise every night?"

"Naise? Hoo! Divil a night, docther, but I'm wehked out ov me bed wid 'em, Sundays an' all. Sure didn't they murdher wan of 'em, out an' out, last night!"

"Is the man dead?"

"Dead? Troth he is. An' cowld."

"H'm"—through his compressed lips. "Flanagan, you needn't come up. I know the door. Just hold the light for me here. There, that'll do. Thank you." He whispered the last words from the top of the second flight.

"Are ye there, docther?" Flanagan anxious to the last, and trying to peer up at him with the lamplight in his eyes.

"Yes. That'll do. Thank you!" in the same whisper. Before

he could tap at the door, then darkening in the receding light, it opened suddenly, and a big Irish woman bounced out, and then whisked in again, calling to someone in an inner room: "Here he is, Mrs. Mill'r," and then bounced out again, with a "Walk royt in, if *you* plaze; here's the choild"—and whisked in again, with a "Sure an' Jehms was quick;" never once looking at him, and utterly unconscious of the presence of her landlord. He had hardly stepped into the room and taken off his hat, when Mrs. Miller came from the inner chamber with a lamp in her hand. How she started! With her pale face grown suddenly paler, and her hand on her bosom, she could only exclaim: "Why, it's Dr. Renton!" and stand, still and dumb, gazing with a frightened look at his face, whiter than her own. Whereupon Mrs. Flanagan came bolting out again, with wild eyes and a sort of stupefied horror in her good, coarse, Irish features; and then, with some uncouth ejaculation, ran back, and was heard to tumble over something within, and tumble something else over in her fall, and gather herself up with a subdued howl, and subside.

"Mrs. Miller," began Dr. Renton, in a low, husky voice, glancing at her frightened face, "I hope you'll be composed. I spoke to you very harshly and rudely tonight; but I really was not myself—I was in anger—and I ask your pardon. Please to overlook it all, and—but I will speak of this presently; now—I am a physician; will you let me look now at your sick child?"

He spoke hurriedly, but with evident sincerity. For a moment her lips faltered; then a slow flush came up, with a quick change of expression on her thin, worn face, and, reddening to painful scarlet, died away in a deeper pallor.

"Dr. Renton," she said, hastily, "I have no ill-feeling for you, sir, and I know you were hurt and vexed—and I know you have tried to make it up to me again, sir—secretly. I know who it was, now; but I can't take it, sir. You must take it back. You know it was you sent it, sir?"

"Mrs. Miller," he replied, puzzled beyond measure, "I don't understand you. What do you mean?"

"Don't deny it, sir. Please not to," she said imploringly, the tears starting to her eyes. "I am very grateful—indeed I am. But I can't accept it. Do take it again."

"Mrs. Miller," he replied, in a hasty voice, "what do you mean? I have sent you nothing—nothing at all. I have, therefore, nothing to receive again."

She looked at him fixedly, evidently impressed by the fervor of his denial.

"You sent me nothing tonight, sir?" she asked, doubtfully.

"Nothing at any time—nothing," he answered, firmly.

It would have been folly to have disbelieved the truthful look of his wondering face, and she turned away in amazement and confusion. There was a long pause.

"I hope, Mrs. Miller, you will not refuse any assistance I can render to your child," he said, at length.

She started, and replied, tremblingly and confusedly, "No, sir; we shall be grateful to you, if you can save her"—and went quickly, with a strange abstraction on her white face, into the inner room. He followed her at once, and, hardly glancing at Mrs. Flanagan, who sat there in stupefaction, with her apron over her head and face, he laid his hat on a table, went to the bedside of the little girl, and felt her head and pulse. He soon satisfied himself that the little sufferer was in no danger, under proper remedies, and now dashed down a prescription on a leaf from his pocketbook. Mrs. Flanagan, who had come out from the retirement of her apron, to stare stupidly at him during the examination, suddenly bobbed up on her legs, with enlightened alacrity, when he asked if there was any one that could go out to the apothecary's, and said, "sure I wull!" He had a little trouble to make her understand that the prescription, which she took by the corner, holding it away from her, as if it were going to explode presently, and staring at it upside down—was to be left—"*left,* mind you, Mrs. Flanagan—with the apothecary—Mr. Flint—at the nearest corner—and he will give you some things, which you are to bring here." But she had shuffled off at last with a confident, "yis, sur—aw, I knoo," her head nodding satisfied assent, and her big thumb covering the note on the margin, "charge to Dr. C. Renton, Bowdoin street," (which *I* know, could not keep it from the eyes of the angels!) and he sat down to await her return.

"Mrs. Miller," he said, kindly, "don't be alarmed about your child. She is doing well; and, after you have given her the medicine Mrs. Flanagan will bring, you'll find her much better, tomorrow. She must be kept cool and quiet, you know, and she'll be all right soon."

"Oh! Dr. Renton, I am very grateful," was the tremulous reply; "and we will follow all directions, sir. It is hard to keep her quiet, sir; we keep as still as we can, and the other children are very still; but the street is very noisy all the daytime and evening, sir, and—"

"I know it, Mrs. Miller. And I'm afraid those people downstairs disturb you somewhat."

"They make some stir in the evening, sir; and it's rather loud in the street sometimes, at night. The folks on the lower floors are troubled a good deal, they say."

Well they may be. Listen to the bawling outside, now, cold as it is. Hark! A hoarse group on the opposite sidewalk beginning a song. "Ro-o-l on, sil-ver mo-o-n"—. The silver moon ceases to roll in a sudden explosion of yells and laughter, sending up broken fragments of curses, ribald jeers, whoopings, and catcalls, high into the night air. "Ga-l-a-ng! Hi-hi! What ye-e-h *'bout!*"

"This is outrageous, Mrs. Miller. Where's the watchman?"

She smiled faintly. "He takes one of them off occasionally, sir; but he's afraid; they beat him sometimes." A long pause.

"Isn't your room rather cold, Mrs. Miller?" He glanced at the black stove, dimly seen in the outer room. "It is necessary to keep the rooms cool just now, but this air seems to me cold."

Receiving no answer, he looked at her, and saw the sad truth in her averted face.

"I beg your pardon," he said quickly, flushing to the roots of his hair. "I might have known, after what you said to me this evening."

"We had a little fire here today, sir," she said, struggling with the pride and shame of poverty; "but we have been out of firing for two or three days, and we owe the wharfman something now. The two boys picked up a few chips; but the poor children find it hard to get them, sir. Times are very hard with us, sir; indeed they are. We'd have got along better, if my husband's money had come, and your rent would have been paid—"

"Never mind the rent!—don't speak of that!" he broke in, with his face all aglow. "Mrs. Miller, I haven't done right by you—I know it. Be frank with me. Are you in want of—have you—need of—food?"

No need of answer to that faintly stammered question. The thin, rigid face was covered from his sight by the worn, wan hands, and all the pride and shame of poverty, and all the frigid truth of cold, hunger, anxiety, and sickened sorrow they had concealed, had given way at last in a rush of tears. He could not speak. With a smitten heart, he knew it all now. Ah! Dr. Renton, you know these people's tricks? you know their lying blazon of poverty, to gather sympathy?

"Mrs. Miller"—she had ceased weeping, and as he spoke, she looked at him, with the tearstains still on her agitated face, half ashamed that he had seen her—"Mrs. Miller, I am sorry. This shall be remedied. Don't tell me it shan't! Don't! I say it shall! Mrs. Miller, I'm—I'm ashamed of myself. I am, indeed."

"I am very grateful, sir, I'm sure," said she; "but we don't like to take charity though we need help; but we can get along now, sir—for, I suppose I must keep it, as you say you didn't send it, and use it for the children's sake, and thank God for his good mercy—since I don't know, and never shall, where it came from, now."

"Mrs. Miller," he said quickly, "you spoke in this way before; and I don't know what you refer to. What do you mean by—*it?*"

"Oh! I forgot sir: it puzzles me so. You see, sir, I was sitting here after I got home from your house, thinking what I should do, when Mrs. Flanagan came upstairs with a letter for me, that she said a strange man left at the door for Mrs. Miller; and Mrs. Flanagan couldn't describe him well, or understandingly; and it had no direction at all, only the man inquired who was the landlord, and if Mrs. Miller had a sick child, and then said the letter was for me; and there was no writing inside the letter, but there was fifty dollars. That's all, sir. It gave me a great shock, sir; and I couldn't think who sent it, only when you came tonight, I thought it was you; but you said it wasn't, and I never shall know who it was, now. It seems as if the hand of God was in it, sir, for it came when everything was darkest, and I was in despair."

"Why, Mrs. Miller," he slowly answered, "this is very mysterious. The man inquired if I was the owner of the house—oh! no—he only inquired who was—but then he knew I was the—oh! bother! I'm getting nowhere. Let's see. Why, it must be someone you know, or that knows your circumstances."

"But there's no one knows them but yourself; and I told you," she replied; "no one else but the people in the house. It must have been some rich person, for the letter was a gilt-edge sheet, and there was perfume in it, sir."

"Strange," he murmured. "Well, I give it up. All is, I advise you to keep it, and I'm very glad someone did his duty by you in your hour of need, though I'm sorry it was not myself. Here's Mrs. Flanagan."

There was a good deal done, and a great burden lifted off a humble heart—nay, two! before Dr. Renton thought of going home. There was a patient gained, likely to do Dr. Renton more good than any patient he had lost. There was a kettle singing on the stove, and blowing off a happier steam than any engine ever blew on that railroad, whose unmarketable stock had singed Dr. Renton's fingers. There was a yellow gleam flickering from the blazing fire on the sober binding of a good old Book upon a shelf with others, a rarer medical work than ever slipped at auction from Dr. Renton's hands, since it kept the sacred lore of Him who healed the sick, and fed the hungry, and comforted the poor, and who was also the Physician of souls.

And there were other offices performed, of lesser range than these, before he rose to go. There were cooling mixtures blended for the sick child; medicines arranged; directions given; and all the items of her tendance orderly foreseen, and put in pigeonholes of When and How, for service.

At last he rose to go. "And now, Mrs. Miller," he said, "I'll come here at ten in the morning, and see to our patient. She'll be nicely by that time. And—(listen to those brutes in the street!—twelve o'clock, too—ah! there's the bell),—as I was saying, my offense to you being occasioned by your debt to me, I feel my receipt for your debt should commence my reparation to you; and I'll bring it tomorrow. Mrs. Miller you don't quite come at me—what I mean is—you owe me, under a notice to quit, three months' rent. Consider that paid in full. I never will take a cent of it from you—not a copper. And I take back the notice. Stay in my house as long as you like; the longer the better. But, up to this date, your rent's paid. There. I hope you'll have as happy a Christmas as circumstances will allow, and I mean you shall."

A flush of astonishment—of indefinable emotion, overspread her face.

"Dr. Renton, stop, sir!" He was moving to the door. "Please, sir, *do* hear me! You are very good—but I can't allow you to—Dr. Renton, we are able to pay you the rent, and we *will,* and we *must*—here—now. Oh! sir, my gratefulness will never fail to you—but here—here—be fair with me, sir, and *do* take it!"

She had hurried to a chest of drawers, and came back with the letter which she had rustled apart with eager, trembling hands, and now, unfolding the single banknote it had contained, she thrust it into his fingers as they closed.

"Here, Mrs. Miller"—she had drawn back with her arms locked on her bosom, and he stepped forward—"no, no. This shan't be. Come, come, you must take it back. Good heavens!" he spoke low, but his eyes blazed in the red glow which broke out on his face, and the crisp note in his extended hand shook violently at her—"Sooner than take this money from you, I would perish in the street! What! Do you think I will rob you of the gift sent you by someone who had a human heart for the distresses I was aggravating? Sooner than—here, take it! O my God! what's this?"

The red glow on his face went out, with this exclamation, in a pallor like marble, and he jerked back the note to his starting eyes; Globe Bank—Boston—Fifty Dollars. For a minute he gazed at the motionless bill in his hand. Then, with his hueless lips compressed, he seized the blank letter from his astonished tenant, and looked at it, turning it over and over. Grained letter paper—gilt-edged—with a favorite perfume in it. Where's Mrs. Flanagan? Outside the door, sitting on the top of the stairs, with her apron over her head, crying. Mrs. Flanagan! Here! In she tumbled, her big feet kicking her skirts before her, and her eyes and face as red as a beet.

"Mrs. Flanagan, what kind of a looking man gave you this letter at the door tonight?"

"A-w, Docther Rinton, dawn't ax me!—Bother, an' all, an' sure an' I cudn't see him wud his fur-r hat, an' he a-ll boondled oop wud his co-at oop on his e-ars, an' his big han'kershuf smotherin' thuh mouth uv him, an' sorra a bit uv him tuh be looked at, sehvin' thuh poomple on thuh ind uv his naws."

"The *what* on the end of his nose?"

"Thuh poomple, sur."

"What does she mean, Mrs. Miller?" said the puzzled questioner, turning to his tenant.

"I don't know, sir, indeed," was the reply; "she said that to me, and I couldn't understand her."

"It's thuh poomple, docther. Dawn't ye knoo? Thuh big, flehmin poomple oop there." She indicated the locality, by flattening the rude tip of her own nose with her broad forefinger.

"Oh! the pimple! I have it." So he had. Netty, Netty!

He said nothing, but sat down in a chair, with his bold, white brow knitted, and the warm tears in his dark eyes.

"You know who sent it, sir, don't you?" asked his wondering tenant, catching the meaning of all this.

"Mrs. Miller, I do. But I cannot tell you. Take it, now, and use it. It is doubly yours. There. Thank you."

She had taken it with an emotion in her face that gave a quicker motion to his throbbing heart. He rose to his feet, hat in hand, and turned away. The noise of a passing group of roysterers in the street without, came strangely loud into the silence of that room.

"Good night, Mrs. Miller. I'll be here in the morning. Good night."

"Good night, sir. God bless you, sir!"

He turned around quickly. The warm tears in his dark eyes had flowed on his face, which was pale; and his firm lip quivered.

"I hope He will, Mrs. Miller—I hope He will. It should have been said oftener."

He was on the outer threshold. Mrs. Flanagan had, somehow, got there before him, with a lamp, and he followed her down through the dancing shadows, with blurred eyes. On the lower landing he stopped to hear the jar of some noisy wrangle, thick with oaths, from the barroom. He listened for a moment, and then turned to the staring stupor of Mrs. Flanagan's rugged visage.

"Sure, they're at ut, docther, wud a wull," she said, smiling.

"Yes. Mrs. Flanagan, you'll stay up with Mrs. Miller tonight, won't you?"

"Dade an' I wull, sur."

"That's right. Do. And make her try and sleep, for she must be tired. Keep up a fire—not too warm, you understand. There'll be wood and coal coming tomorrow, and she'll pay you back."

"A-w, docther, dawn't noo!"

"Well, well. And—look here; have you got anything to eat in the house? Yes; well; take it upstairs. Wake up those two boys, and give them something to eat. Don't let Mrs. Miller stop you. Make her eat something. Tell her I said she must. And, first of all, get your bonnet, and go to that apothecary's—Flint's—for a bottle of port wine, for Mrs. Miller. Hold on. There's the order." (He had a leaf out of his pocketbook in a minute, and wrote it down.) "Go with this, the first thing. Ring Flint's bell, and he'll wake up. And here's something for your own Christmas dinner, tomorrow." Out of the roll of bills, he drew one of the tens—Globe Bank—Boston—and gave it to Mrs. Flanagan.

"A-w, dawn't noo, docther."

"Bother! It's for yourself, mind. Take it. There. And now unlock the door. That's it. Good night, Mrs. Flanagan."

"An' meh thuh Hawly Vurgin hape blessn's on ye, Docther Rinton, wud a-ll thuh compliments uv thuh sehzin, for yur thuh—"

He lost the end of Mrs. Flanagan's parting benedictions in the moonlit street. He did not pause till he was at the door of the oyster room. He paused then, to make way for a tipsy company of four, who reeled out—the gaslight from the barroom on the edges of their sodden, distorted faces—giving three shouts and a yell, as they slammed the door behind them.

He pushed after a party that was just entering. They went at once for drink to the upper end of the room, where a rowdy crew, with cigars in their mouths, and liquor in their hands, stood before the bar, in a knotty wrangle concerning someone who was killed. Where is the keeper? Oh! there he is, mixing hot brandy punch for two. Here, you, sir, go up quietly, and tell Mr. Rollins Dr. Renton wants to see him. The waiter came back presently to say Mr. Rollins would be right along. Twenty-five minutes past twelve. Oyster trade nearly over. Gaudy-curtained booths on the left all empty but two. Oyster-openers and waiters—three of them in all—nearly done for the night, and two of them sparring and scuffling behind a pile of oysters on the trough, with the colored print of the great prize fight between Tom Hyer and Yankee Sullivan, in a veneered frame above them on the wall. Blower up from the fire opposite the bar, and stewpans and griddles empty and idle on the bench beside it, among the unwashed bowls and dishes. Oyster trade nearly over. Bar still busy.

Here comes Rollins in his shirt sleeves, with an apron on.

Thick-set, muscular man—frizzled head, low forehead, sharp, black eyes, flabby face, with a false, greasy smile on it now, oiling over a curious, stealthy expression of mingled surprise and inquiry, as he sees his landlord here at this unusual hour.

"Come in here, Mr. Rollins; I want to speak to you."

"Yes, sir. Jim" (to the waiter), "go and tend bar." They sat down in one of the booths, and lowered the curtain. Dr. Renton, at one side of the table within, looking at Rollins, sitting leaning on his folded arms, at the other side.

"Mr. Rollins, I am told the man who was stabbed here last night is dead. Is that so?"

"Well, he is, Dr. Renton. Died this afternoon."

"Mr. Rollins, this is a serious matter; what are you going to do about it?"

"Can't help it, sir. Who's a-going' to touch *me?* Called in a watchman. Whole mess of 'em had cut. Who knows 'em? Nobody knows 'em. Man that was stuck never see the fellers as stuck him in all his life till then. Didn't know which one of 'em did it. Didn't know nothing. Don't now, an' never will, 'nless he meets 'em in hell. That's all. Feller's dead, an' who's a-going' to touch *me?* Can't do it. Ca-n-'t do it."

"Mr. Rollins," said Dr. Renton, thoroughly disgusted with this man's brutal indifference, "your lease expires in three days."

"Well, it does. Hope to make a renewal with you, Dr. Renton. Trade's good here. Shouldn't mind more rent on, if you insist—hope you won't—if it's anything in reason. Promise sollum, I shan't have no more fightin' in here. Couldn't help this. Accidents *will* happen, yo' know."

"Mr. Rollins, the case is this: if you didn't sell liquor here, you'd have no murder done in your place—murder, sir. That man was murdered. It's your fault, and it's mine, too. I ought not to have let you the place for your business. It *is* a cursed traffic, and you and I ought to have found it out long ago. *I* have. I hope *you* will. Now, I advise you, as a friend, to give up selling rum for the future: you see what it comes to—don't you? At any rate, I will not be responsible for the outrages that are perpetrated in my building any more—I will not have liquor sold here. I refuse to renew your lease. In three days you must move."

"Dr. Renton, you hurt my feelin's. Now, how would you—"

"Mr. Rollins, I have spoken to you as a friend, and you have no cause for pain. You must quit these premises when your lease expires. I'm sorry I can't make you go before that. Make no appeals to me, if you please. I am fixed. Now, sir, good night."

The curtain was pulled up, and Rollins rolled over to his beloved bar, soothing his lacerated feelings by swearing like a pirate, while Dr. Renton strode to the door, and went into the street, homeward.

He walked fast through the magical moonlight, with a strange feeling of sternness, and tenderness, and weariness, in his mind. In this mood, the sensation of spiritual and physical fatigue gaining on him, but a quiet moonlight in all his reveries, he reached his house. He was just putting his latchkey in the door, when it was opened by James, who stared at him for a second, and then dropped his eyes, and put his hand before his nose. Dr. Renton compressed his lips on an involuntary smile.

"Ah! James, you're up late. It's near one."

"I sat up for Mrs. Renton and the young lady, sir. They're just come, and gone upstairs."

"All right, James. Take your lamp and come in here. I've got something to say to you." The man followed him into the library at once, with some wonder on his sleepy face.

"First, put some coal on that fire, and light the chandelier. I shall not go up stairs tonight." The man obeyed. "Now, James, sit down in that chair." He did so, beginning to look frightened at Dr. Renton's grave manner.

"James"—a long pause—"I want you to tell me the truth. Where did you go tonight? Come, I have found you out. Speak."

The man turned as white as a sheet, and looked wretched with the whites of his bulging eyes, and the great pimple on his nose awfully distinct in the livid hue of his features. He was a rather slavish fellow, and thought he was going to lose his situation. Please not to blame him, for he, too, was one of the poor.

"Oh! Dr. Renton, excuse me, sir; I didn't mean doing any harm."

"James, my daughter gave you an undirected letter this evening; you carried it to one of my houses in Hanover street. Is that true?"

"Ye-yes, sir. I couldn't help it. I only did what she told me, sir."

"James, if my daughter told you to set fire to this house, what would you do?"

"I wouldn't do it, sir," he stammered, after some hesitation.

"You wouldn't? James, if my daughter ever tells you to set fire to this house, do it, sir! Do it. At once. Do whatever she tells you. Promptly. And I'll back you."

The man stared wildly at him, as he received this astonishing command. Dr. Renton was perfectly grave, and had spoken slowly and seriously. The man was at his wits' end.

"You'll do it James—will you?"

"Ye-yes, sir, certainly."

"That's right. James, you're a good fellow. James, you've got a family—a wife and children—haven't you?"

"Yes, sir, I have; living in the country, sir. In Chelsea, over the ferry. For cheapness, sir."

"For cheapness, eh? Hard times, James? How is it?"

"Pretty hard, sir. Close, but toler'ble comfortable. Rub and go, sir."

"Rub and go. Ve-r-y well. Rub and go. James, I'm going to raise your wages—tomorrow. Generally, because you're a good servant. Principally, because you carried that letter tonight, when my daughter asked you. I shan't forget it. Tomorrow, mind. And if I can do anything for you, James, at any time, just tell me. That's all. Now, you'd better go to bed. And a happy Christmas to you!"

"Much obliged to you, sir. Same to you and many of 'em. Good night, sir." And with Dr. Renton's "good night" he stole up to bed, thoroughly happy, and determined to obey Miss

Renton's future instructions to the letter. The shower of golden light which had been raining for the last two hours, had fallen, even on him. It would fall all day tomorrow in many places, and the day after, and for long years to come. Would that it could broaden and increase to a general deluge, and submerge the world!

Now the whole house was still, and its master was weary. He sat there, quietly musing, feeling the sweet and tranquil presence near him. Now the fire was screened, the lights were out, save one dim glimmer, and he had lain down on the couch with the letter in his hand, and slept the dreamless sleep of a child.

He slept until the gray dawn of Christmas day stole into the room, and showed him the figure of his friend, a shape of glorious light, standing by his side, and gazing at him with large and tender eyes! He had no fear. All was deep, serene, and happy with the happiness of heaven. Looking up into that beautiful, wan face—so tranquil—so radiant; watching, with a childlike awe, the star-fire in those shadowy eyes; smiling faintly, with a great, unutterable love thrilling slowly through his frame, in answer to the smile of light that shone upon the phantom countenance; so he passed a space of time which seemed a calm eternity, till, at last, the communion of spirit with spirit—of mortal love with love immortal—was perfected, and the shining hands were laid on his forehead, as with a touch of air. Then the phantom smiled, and, as its shining hands were withdrawn, the thought of his daughter mingled in the vision. She was bending over him! The dawn—the room, were the same. But the ghost of Feval had gone out from earth, away to its own land!

"Father, dear father! Your eyes were open, and they did not look at me. There is a light on your face, and your features are changed! What is it—what have you seen?"

"Hush, darling: here—kneel by me, for a little while, and be still. I have seen the dead."

She knelt by him, burying her awestruck face in his bosom, and clung to him with all the fervor of her soul. He clasped her to his breast, and for minutes all was still.

"Dear child—good and dear child!"

The voice was tremulous and low. She lifted her fair, bright countenance, now convulsed with a secret trouble, and dimmed with streaming tears, to his, and gazed on him. His eyes were shining; but his pallid cheeks, like hers, were wet with tears. How still the room was! How like a thought of solemn tenderness, the pale gray dawn! The world was far away, and his soul still wandered in the peaceful awe of his dream. The world was coming back to him—but oh! how changed!—in the trouble of his daughter's face.

"Darling, what is it? Why are you here? Why are you weeping? Dear child, the friend of my better days—of the boyhood when I had noble aims, and life was beautiful before me—he has been here! I have seen him. He has been with me—oh! for a good I cannot tell!"

"Father, dear father!"—he had risen, and sat upon the couch, but she still knelt before him, weeping, and clasped his hands in hers—"I thought of you and of this letter, all the time. All last night till I slept, and then I dreamed you were tearing it to pieces, and trampling on it. I awoke, and lay thinking of you, and of——. And I thought I heard you come downstairs, and I came here to find you. But you were lying here so quietly, with your eyes open, and so strange a light on your face. And I knew—I knew you were dreaming of him, and that you saw him, for the letter lay beside you. O father! forgive me, but do hear me! In the name of this day—it's Christmas day, father—in the name of the time when we must both die—in the name of that time, father, hear me! That poor woman last night—O father! forgive me, but don't tear that letter in pieces and trample it under foot! You know what I mean—you know—you know. Don't tear it, and tread it under foot!"

She clung to him, sobbing violently, her face buried in his hands.

"Hush, hush! It's all well—it's all well. Here, sit by me. So. I have"—his voice failed him, and he paused. But sitting by him—clinging to him—her face hidden in his bosom—she heard the strong beating of his disenchanted heart!

"My child, I know your meaning. I will not tear the letter to pieces and trample it under foot. God forgive me my life's slight to those words. But I learned their value last night, in the house where your blank letter had entered before me."

She started, and looked into his face steadfastly, while a bright scarlet shot into her own.

"I know all, Netty—all. Your secret was well kept, but it is yours and mine now. It was well done, darling—well done. Oh! I have been through strange mysteries of thought and life since that starving woman sat here! Well—thank God!"

"Father, what have you done?" The flush had failed, but a glad color still brightened her face, while the tears stood trembling in her eyes.

"All that you wished yesterday," he answered. "And all that you ever could have wished, henceforth I will do."

"O father!"—She stopped. The bright scarlet shot again into her face, but with an April shower of tears, and the rainbow of a smile.

"Listen to me, Netty, and I will tell you, and only you, what I have done." Then, while she mutely listened, sitting by his side, and the dawn of Christmas broadened into Christmas day, he told her all.

And when he had told all, and emotion was stilled, they sat together in silence for a time, she with her innocent head drooped upon his shoulder, and her eyes closed, lost in tender and mystic reveries; and he musing with a contrite heart. Till at last, the stir of daily life began to waken in the quiet dwelling, and without, from steeples in the frosty air, there was a sound of bells.

They rose silently, and stood, clinging to each other, side by side.

"Love, we must part," he said, gravely and tenderly. "Read me, before we go, the closing lines of George Feval's letter. In the spirit of this let me strive to live. Let it be for me the lesson of the day. Let it also be the lesson of my life."

Her face was pale and lit with exaltation as she took the letter from his hand. There was a pause—and then upon the thrilling and tender silver of her voice, the words arose like solemn music:

Farewell—farewell! But, oh! take my counsel into memory on Christmas Day, and forever. Once again, the ancient prophecy of peace and good-will shines on a world of wars and wrongs and woes. Its soft ray shines into the darkness of a land wherein swarm slaves, poor laborers, social pariahs, weeping women, homeless exiles, hunted fugitives, despised aliens, drunkards, convicts, wicked children, and Magdalens unredeemed. These are but the ghastliest figures in that sad army of humanity which advances, by a dreadful road, to the Golden Age of the poets' dream. These are your sisters and your brothers. Love them all. Beware of wronging one of them by word or deed. O friend! strong in wealth for so much good—take my last counsel. In the name of the Saviour, I charge you, be true and tender to mankind! Come out from Babylon into manhood, and live and labor for the fallen, the neglected, the suffering, and the poor. Lover of arts, customs, laws, institutions, and forms of society, love these things only as they help mankind! With stern love, overturn them, or help to overturn them, when they become cruel to a single—the humblest—human being. In the world's scale, social position, influence, public power, the applause of majorities, heaps of funded gold, services rendered to creeds, codes, sects, parties, or federations—they weigh weight; but in God's scale—remember!—on the day of hope, remember!—your least service to Humanity, outweighs them all!

Sir Andrew Caldecott

CHRISTMAS REUNION

A ghost disguised as Santa Clause seeks vengeance.

Chapter I

"I cannot explain what exactly it is about him; but I don't like your Mr. Clarence Love, and I'm sorry that you ever asked him to stay."

Thus Richard Dreyton to his wife Elinor on the morning of Christmas Eve.

"But one must remember the children, Richard. You know what marvelous presents he gives them."

"Much too marvelous. He spoils them. Yet you'll have noticed that none of them likes him. Children have a wonderful intuition in regard to the character of grown-ups."

"What on earth are you hinting about his character? He's a very nice man."

Dreyton shuffled off his slippers in front of the study fire and began putting on his boots.

"I wonder, darling, whether you noticed his face just now, at breakfast, when he opened that letter with the Australian stamps on?"

"Yes; he did seem a bit upset: but not more so than you when you get my dressmaker's bill!"

Mrs. Dreyton accompanied this sally with a playful pat on her husband's back as he leant forward to do up his laces.

"Well, Elinor, all that I can say is that there's something very fishy about his antipodean history. At five-and-twenty, he left England a penniless young man and, heigh presto! he returns a stinking plutocrat at twenty-eight. And how? What he's told you doesn't altogether tally with what he's told me; but, cutting out the differences, his main story is that he duly contacted old Nelson Joy, his maternal uncle, whom he went out to join, and that they went off together, prospecting for gold. They struck it handsomely; and then the poor old uncle gets a heartstroke or paralysis, or something, in the bush, and bids Clarence leave him there to die and get out himself before the food gives out. Arrived back in Sydney, Clarence produces a will under which he is the sole beneficiary, gets the Court to presume old Joy's death, and bunks back here with the loot."

Mrs. Dreyton frowned. "I can see nothing wrong or suspicious about the story," she said, "but only in your telling of it."

"No! No! In *his* telling of it. He never gets the details quite the same twice running, and I'm certain that he gave a different topography to their prospecting expedition this year from what he did last. It's my belief that he did the uncle in, poor old chap!"

"Don't be so absurd, Richard; and please remember that he's our guest, and that we must be hospitable: especially at Christmas. Which reminds me: on your way to office, would you mind looking in at Harridge's and making sure that they haven't forgotten our order for their Santa Claus tomorrow? He's to be here at seven; then to go on to the Simpsons at seven-thirty, and to end up at the Joneses at eight. It's lucky our getting three households to share the expenses: Harridge's charge each of us only half their catalogued fee. If they could possibly send us the same Father Christmas as last year it would be splendid. The children adored him. Don't forget to say, too, that he will find all the crackers, hats, musical toys and presents inside the big chest in the hall. Just the same as last year. What should we do nowadays without the big stores? One goes to them for everything."

"We certainly do," Dreyton agreed; "and I can't see the modern child putting up with the amateur Father Christmas we used to suffer from. I shall never forget the annual exhibition Uncle Bertie used to make of himself, or the slippering I got when I stuck a darning-needle into his behind under pretense that I wanted to see if he was real! Well, so long, old girl: no, I won't forget to call in at Harridge's."

Chapter II

By the time the festive Christmas supper had reached the dessert stage, Mrs. Dreyton fully shared her husband's regret that she had ever asked Clarence Love to be of the party. The sinister change that had come over him on receipt of the letter from Australia became accentuated on the later arrival of a telegram which, he said, would necessitate his leaving towards the end of the evening to catch the eight-fifteen northbound express from King's Pancras. His valet had already gone ahead with the luggage and, as it had turned so foggy, he had announced his intention of following later by Underground, in order to avoid the possibility of being caught in a traffic jam.

It is strange how sometimes the human mind can harbor simultaneously two entirely contradictory emotions. Mrs. Dreyton was consumed with annoyance that any guest of hers should be so inconsiderate as to terminate his stay in the middle of a Christmas party; but was, at the same time, impatient to be rid of such a skeleton at the feast. One of the things that she had found attractive in Clarence Love had been an unfailing fund of small talk, which, if not brilliant, was at any rate bright and breezy. He possessed, also, a pleasant and frequent smile and, till now, had always been assiduous in his attention to her conversation. Since yesterday, however, he had turned silent, inattentive, and dour in expression. His presentation to her of a lovely emerald brooch had been unaccompanied by any greeting beyond an unflattering and perfunctory "Happy Christmas!" He had also proved unforgivably oblivious of the mistletoe, beneath which, with a careful carelessness, she stationed herself when she heard him coming down to breakfast. It was, indeed, quite mortifying; and, when her husband described the guest as a busted balloon, she had neither the mind nor the heart to gainsay him.

Happily for the mirth and merriment of the party Dreyton seemed to derive much exhilaration from the dumb discomfiture of his wife's friend, and Elinor had never seen or heard her husband in better form. He managed, too, to infect the children with his own ebullience; and even Miss Potterby (the governess) reciprocated his fun. Even before the entry of Father Christmas it had thus become a noisy, and almost rowdy, company.

Father Christmas's salutation, on arrival, was in rhymed verse and delivered in the manner appropriate to pantomime. His lines ran thus:

To Sons of Peace
Yule brings release
From worry at this tide;
But men of crime
This holy time
Their guilty heads need hide.

So never fear,
Ye children dear,

But innocent sing "Nowell";
For the Holy Rood
Shall save the good,
And the bad be burned in hell.

This is my carol
And Nowell my parole.

There was clapping of hands at this, for there is nothing children enjoy so much as mummery; especially if it be slightly mysterious. The only person who appeared to dislike the recitation was Love, who was seen to stop both ears with his fingers at the end of the first verse and to look ill. As soon as he had made an end of the prologue, Santa Claus went ahead with his distribution of gifts, and made many a merry quip and pun. He was quick in the uptake, too; for the children put to him many a poser, to which a witty reply was always ready. The minutes indeed slipped by all too quickly for all of them, except Love, who kept glancing uncomfortably at his wristwatch and was plainly in a hurry to go. Hearing him mutter that it was time for him to be off, Father Christmas walked to his side and bade him pull a farewell cracker. Having done so, resentfully it seemed, he was asked to pull out the motto and read it. His hands were now visibly shaking, and his voice seemed to have caught their infection. Very falteringly, he managed to stammer out the two lines of doggerel:

Reunited heart to heart
Love and joy shall never part.

"And now," said Father Christmas, "I must be making for the next chimney; and, on my way, sir, I will see you into the Underground."

So saying he took Clarence Love by the left arm and led him with mock ceremony to the door, where he turned and delivered this epilogue:

Ladies and Gentlemen, goodnight!
Let not darkness you affright.
Ought of evil here today
Santa Claus now bears away.

At this point, with sudden dramatic effect, he clicked off the electric-light switch by the door; and, by the time Dreyton had groped his way to it in the darkness and turned it on again, the parlor-maid (who was awaiting Love's departure in the hall) had let both him and Father Christmas out into the street.

"Excellent!" Mrs. Dreyton exclaimed, "quite excellent! One can always depend on Harridge's. It wasn't the same man as they sent last year; but quite as good, and more original, perhaps."

"I'm glad he's taken Mr. Love away," said young Harold.

"Yes," Dorothy chipped in; "he's been beastly all day, and yesterday, too: and his presents aren't nearly as expensive as last year."

"Shut up, you spoilt children!" the father interrupted. "I must admit, though, that the fellow was a wet blanket this evening. What was that nonsense he read out about reunion?"

Miss Potterby had developed a pedagogic habit of clearing her throat audibly, as a signal demanding her pupils' attention to some impending announcement. She did it now, and parents as well as children looked expectantly towards her.

"The motto as read by Mr. Love," she declared, "was so palpably inconsequent that I took the liberty of appropriating it when he laid the slip of paper back on the table. Here it is, and this is how it actually reads:

Be united heart to heart,
Love and joy shall never part.

That makes sense, if it doesn't make poetry. Mr. Love committed the error of reading "be united" as "reunited" and of not observing the comma between the two lines."

"Thank you, Miss Potterby; that, of course, explains it. How clever of you to have spotted the mistake and tracked it down!"

Thus encouraged, Miss Potterby proceeded to further corrective edification.

"You remarked just now, Mrs. Dreyton, that the gentleman impersonating Father Christmas had displayed originality. His prologue and epilogue, however, were neither of them original, but corrupted versions of passages which you will find in Professor Borleigh's *Synopsis of Nativity, Miracle and Morality Plays,* published two years ago. I happen to be familiar with the subject, as the author is a first cousin of mine, once removed."

"How interesting!" Dreyton here broke in; "and now, Miss Potterby, if you will most kindly preside at the piano, we will dance Sir Roger de Coverley. Come on, children, into the drawing room."

CHAPTER III

On Boxing Day there was no post and no paper. Meeting Mrs. Simpson in the Park that afternoon, Mrs. Dreyton was surprised to hear that Father Christmas had kept neither of his two other engagements. "It must have been that horrid fog," she suggested; "but what a shame! He was even better than last year:" by which intelligence Mrs. Simpson seemed little comforted.

Next morning—the second after Christmas—there were two letters on the Dreytons' breakfast table, and both were from Harridge's. The first conveyed that firm's deep regret that their representative should have been prevented from carrying out his engagements in Pentland Square on Christmas night owing to dislocation of traffic caused by the prevailing fog.

"But he kept ours all right," Mrs. Dreyton commented. "I feel so sorry for the Simpsons and the Joneses."

The second letter cancelled the first, "which had been written in unfortunate oversight of the cancellation of the order."

"What on earth does that mean?" Mrs. Dreyton ejaculated.

"Ask me another!" returned her husband. "Got their correspondence mixed up, I suppose."

In contrast to the paucity of letters, the morning newspapers seemed unusually voluminous and full of pictures. Mrs. Dreyton's choice of what to read in them was not that of a highbrow. The headline that attracted her first attention ran "XMAS ON UNDERGROUND," and, among other choice items, she learned how, at Pentland Street Station (their own nearest), a man dressed as Santa Claus had been seen to guide and support an invalid, or possibly tipsy, companion down the long escalator. The red coat, mask and beard were afterwards found discarded in a passage leading to the emergency staircase, so that even Santa's sobriety might be called into question. She was just about to retail this interesting intelligence to her husband when, laying down his own paper, he stared curiously at her and muttered "Good God!"

"What on earth's the matter, dear?"

"A very horrible thing, Elinor. Clarence Love has been killed! Listen;" here he resumed his paper and began to read aloud: " 'The body of the man who fell from the Pentland Street platform on Christmas night in front of an incoming train has been identified as that of Mr. Clarence Love, of II Playfair Mansions. There was a large crowd of passengers on the platform at the time, and it is conjectured that he fell backwards off it while turning to expostulate with persons exerting pressure at his back. Nobody, however, in the crush, could have seen the exact circumstances of the said fatality.' "

"Hush, dear! Here come the children. They mustn't know, of course. We can talk about it afterwards."

Dreyton, however, could not wait to talk about it afterwards. The whole of the amateur detective within him had been aroused, and, rising early from the breakfast-table, he journeyed by tube to Harridge's, where he was soon interviewing a departmental submanager. No: there was no possibility of one of their representatives having visited Pentland Square on Christmas evening. Our Mr. Droper had got hung up in the Shenton Street traffic-block until it was too late to keep his engagements there. He had come straight back to his rooms. In any case, he would not have called at Mr. Dreyton's residence in view of the cancellation of the order the previous day. Not canceled? But he took down the telephone message himself. Yes: here was the entry in the register. Then it must have been the work of some mischief maker; it was certainly a gentleman's, and not a lady's voice. Nobody except he and Mr. Droper knew of the engagement at their end, so the practical joker must have derived his knowledge of it from somebody in Mr. Dreyton's household.

This was obviously sound reasoning and, on his return home, Dreyton questioned Mrs. Timmins, the cook, in the matter. She was immediately helpful and forthcoming. One of them insurance gents had called on the morning before Christmas and had been told that none of us wanted no policies or such like. He had then turned conversational and asked what sort of goings-on there would be here for Christmas. Nothing, he was told, except old Father Christmas, as usual, out of Harridge's shop. Then he asked about visitors in the house, and was told as there were none except Mr. Love, who, judging by the tip what he had given Martha when he stayed last in the house, was a wealthy and openhanded gentleman. Little did she think when she spoke those words as Mr. Love would forget to give any tips or boxes at Christmas, when they were most natural and proper. But perhaps he would think better on it by the New Year and send a postal order. Dreyton thought it unlikely, but deemed it unnecessary at this juncture to inform Mrs. Timmins of the tragedy reported in the newspaper.

At luncheon Mrs. Dreyton found her husband unusually taciturn and preoccupied; but, by the time they had come to the cheese, he announced importantly that he had made up his mind to report immediately to the police certain information that had come into his possession. Miss Potterby and the children looked suitably impressed, but knew better than to court a snub by asking questions. Mrs. Dreyton took the cue admirably by replying: "Of course, Richard, you must do your duty!"

Chapter IV

The inspector listened intently and jotted down occasional notes. At the end of the narration, he complimented the informant by asking whether he had formed any theory regarding the facts he reported. Dreyton most certainly had. That was why he had been so silent and absent-minded at lunch. His solution, put much more briefly than he expounded it to the inspector, was as follows:

Clarence Love had abandoned his uncle and partner in the Australian bush. Having returned to civilization, got the Courts to presume the uncle's death, and taken probate of the will under which he was sole inheritor, Love returned to England a wealthy and still youngish man. The uncle, however (this was Dreyton's theory), did not die after his nephew's desertion, but was found and tended by bushmen. Having regained his power of locomotion, he trekked back to Sydney, where he discovered himself legally dead and his property appropriated by Love and removed to England. Believing his nephew to have compassed his death, he resolved to take revenge into his own hands. Having dispatched a cryptic letter to Love containing dark hints of impending doom, he sailed for the Old Country and ultimately tracked Love down to the Dreyton's abode. Then, having in the guise of a traveling insurance agent ascertained the family's program for Christmas day, he planned his impersonation of Santa Claus. That his true identity, revealed by voice and accent, did not escape his victim was evidenced by the latter's nervous misreading of the motto in the cracker. Whether Love's death in the Underground was due to actual murder or to suicide enforced by despair and remorse, Dreyton hazarded no guess: either was possible under his theory.

The inspector's reception of Dreyton's hypothesis was less enthusiastic than his wife's.

"If you'll excuse me, Mr. Dreyton," said the former, "you've built a mighty lot on dam' little. Still, it's ingenious and no mistake. I'll follow your ideas up and, if you'll call in a week's time, I may have something to tell you and one or two things, perhaps to ask."

"Why darling, how wonderful!" Mrs. Dreyton applauded. "Now that you've pieced the bits together so cleverly the thing's quite obvious, isn't it? What a horrible thing to have left poor old Mr. Joy to die all alone in the jungle! I never really liked Clarence, and am quite glad now that he's dead. But of course we mustn't tell the children!"

Inquiries of the Australian Police elicited the intelligence that the presumption of Mr. Joy's death had been long since confirmed by the discovery of his remains in an old prospecting pit. There were ugly rumors and suspicions against his nephew but no evidence on which to support them. On being thus informed by the inspector Dreyton amended his theory to the extent that the impersonator of Father Christmas must have been not Mr. Joy himself, as he was dead, but a bosom friend determined to avenge him. This substitution deprived the cracker episode, on which Dreyton had imagined his whole story, of all relevance; and the inspector was quite frank about his disinterest in the revised version.

Mrs. Dreyton also rejected it. Her husband's original theory seemed to her more obviously right and conclusive even than before. The only amendment required, and that on a mere matter of detail, was to substitute Mr. Joy's ghost for Mr. Joy: though of course one mustn't tell the children.

"But," her husband remonstrated, "you know that I don't believe in ghosts."

"No, but your aunt Cecilia *does;* and she is such a clever woman. By the way, she called in this morning and left you a book to look at."

"A book?"

"Yes, the collected ghost stories of M. R. James."

"But the stupid old dear knows that I have them all in the original editions."

"So she said: but she wants you to read the author's epilogue to the collection which, she says, is most entertaining. It's entitled "Stories I Have Tried to Write." She said that she'd sidelined a passage that might interest you. The book's on that table by you. No, not that: the one with the black cover."

Dreyton picked it up, found the marked passage and read it aloud.

There may be possibilities too in the Christmas cracker if the right people pull it and if the motto which they find inside has the right message on it. They will probably leave the party early, pleading indisposition; but very likely a previous engagement of long standing would be the more truthful excuse.

"There is certainly," Dreyton commented, "some resemblance between James's idea and our recent experience. But he could have made a perfectly good yarn out of that theme without introducing ghosts."

His wife's mood at that moment was for compromise rather than controversy.

"Well, darling," she temporized, "perhaps not exactly ghosts."

LEONARD KIP

THE GHOSTS AT GRANTLEY

A young man's engagement is impeded, then advanced, by two ghostly brothers.

CHAPTER I

THE London stagecoach dropped me at the gatelodge of Grantley Grange, and according to my usual custom I started up to the Hall on foot. It was such a pleasant Christmas morning as perhaps is not often seen, and might well have tempted to a longer walk than that short mile up the carefully trimmed avenue. There had been a slight fall of snow, a mere sprinkle indeed; but it was sufficient to clothe the brown turf with a dainty tint of pearl, and to make the dry leaves rattle crisp beneath the feet, and to project the great oaks in seemingly more ancient grandeur against the brightened background and generally to give an unusually cheery and exhilerating aspect to the whole scenery of the park.

When I had nearly reached the Hall, the church clock struck noon, and immediately all the bells began to ring out a merry Christmas peal. Up and down, hither and thither, now a snatch of tune and again a meaningless clashing of all the bells at once—single notes and double and triple concords, and, in fact, everything that well-disposed bells ever can or will do—so it ran on right cheerily. Now it was that I anticipated my Uncle Ruthven would hasten out to meet and welcome me. For I knew that he was fond of listening to the chimes; and when the changes were being sounded upon them he would not unfrequently sit at the open window, the better to enjoy them. And of course, as I could now plainly see the Hall through the leafless trees, he from his open window could as readily watch my approach. Somewhat to my momentary chagrin, however, he did not come forth or even meet me at the door, and I was suffered to enter unannounced. And passing through the main hall, I wandered into the library.

There I found my Uncle Ruthven standing in the middle of the floor, his head thrown back, his eyes fixed intently upon the opposite wall, one arm raised in front to the level of his face, the other hand thrown behind him, an expression of resolute determination impressed upon every feature, his whole appearance and position resembling that of the antique Quoit Thrower. Evidently he had been engaged in similar action; for, in a moment, he stepped to the other side of the room, picked up a short, fat book which had been thrown thither, and replaced it upon the table.

"*Anatomy of Melancholy,*" he remarked, turning to me with a little chuckling laugh. "The first person who for a long while has got the book all through him—eh, Geoffrey? Though, of course, we all relish a little of it, now and then. Hit him directly upon the breast, and it went through him as through a summer mist, dropping out behind between his shoulder blades. Of course he has vanished, taking the hint of not being longer wanted here."

"Who, Uncle Ruthven?" I asked.

"Why, the ghost, of course," was the answer.

I was a little startled at this. It is true that I had sometimes thought that the library at Grantley Grange might be just the place for ghosts. It was wainscoted heavily with carved oak darkened in tint with the seasoning of four centuries. Above, the walls were covered with hangings of Spanish leather, stamped in quaint pattern. The fireplace was deep set and broad—so deep and broad, indeed, that the great logs smoldering within appeared no larger than ordinary sticks. The windows were projected into oriels with heavy mullions and let in the light, encumbered with a thousand stray shadows. The tables and chairs and high bookcases seemed almost immovable with their sculptured massiveness, and as though designed for a race of giants. Queer lamps hung from the ceiling and grotesque candlesconces projected themselves from the walls, each with heavy metal shades that would shut in more light than they sent forth. Over the mantel and beside the doors were paintings blackened with age; a Salvator Rosa, turned by the grime of time into a mere confusion of different shadows, with only here and there a touch of faded light for contrast, and, on either hand, eight or ten old portraits in ruffs and crimson coats and armor, cracked and worm-eaten and sometimes almost undistinguishable in face, but serving in costume to show the different careers into which, in times past, the fates or inclinations of the originals had carried them. A gloomy old library, indeed, full of crevices that would not stay closed, and cobwebs that could not be got at, and drafts that came from no one knew where, and flickering shades that seemed to obey no philosophic law, but stole here and there across wall and ceiling as their fancy led them. So that not unnaturally it appeared at times as though the place could never have been made for man's enjoyment, but rather as a hall for witches' Sabbath or ghostly revels; and as I watched the subdued and hesitating flickering of an errant sunbeam across the tarnished gilt pattern of the Spanish leather, it was not difficult for queer fancies and imaginings to take hold of me. But, after all, they were mere idle conceits, and at the most I had not for an instant anticipated the actual presentment of unearthly visitants.

"The ghost, did you say?" I therefore repeated, in some amazement.

"Yes, the ghost. Has been here every Christmas for many a year. Always comes just as the chimes strike up at noon, as regularly as though they had waked him. If you had ever before this happened to spend a Christmas with us, you might have met him yourself. Assumes that he belongs to the house, and that therefore he has his vested rights in it. Frightened me a little at the first, but have become used to him now and do not care. Am rather disposed, indeed, to lord it over him with high hand; and he is such a patient ghost that it hardly seems to make much difference with him. Am sorry always, in fact, if I speak crossly to him. But, then, you know my temper, Geoffrey, and how little I can brook presumption. How, then, would you feel if a ghost were to come, implying that he was the master of the house and that you were merely a visitor? Gets just so far, indeed, and then vanishes without telling anything important."

I looked wonderingly at Uncle Ruthven thus calmly discoursing about the supernatural.

"But do you ever let him get further than that?" I suggested, my eyes wandering to the book upon the table.

"Perhaps not, Geoffrey—perhaps not. I suppose that if I were more patient he would talk a little better to the purpose. But then I am very quick tempered, and it is so exasperating, every Christmas to go through the very same thing. I always throw a book at him and am sorry for it afterward. It is certainly not the hospitable thing upon my part. But then to be so constantly beset, year after year, and not to know how many more there may be of them. For there is at least one other ghost somewhere about the house, Geoffrey. I have never seen him, but Bidgers the butler has, and he says it is as like this fellow as two peas. And if I am too polite to them, who knows but that they may be encouraged to come in swarms and make the house very uncomfortable? But let us leave all that for the present. You will be wanting to see your room, I suppose. The South Oriel, just past the second landing. Bidgers will carry up your portmanteau. Am sorry, by the way, that Lilian has not yet returned from the continent. She could, of course, make your stay much more pleasant for you than I can. But will do my best, Geoffrey. Luncheon at one, as usual."

Escorted by Bidgers, I proceeded upstairs to the South Oriel. It was a large apartment upon the south side of the house, with a broad octagonal window projection. If possible, the furniture was heavier and more antiquated than that of the library. There were quaint old tapestry hangings to the bedstead, so queer and faded that it seemed almost as though they might have been embroidered during the Crusades. The wardrobe was a marvel of size and solidity, and gave the impression that in troublous times, obnoxious owners of the estate might have safely been concealed in a false recess. Other articles of furniture were in similar style, and all together gave quite a gloomy aspect to an apartment that naturally, if left to itself, might have been well disposed to be cheerful. The effect was not diminished by a dingy picture over the mantelshelf, representing a funeral urn and drooping willow worked in hair, with an exceedingly numerous and mournfully dressed family coming two by two down a winding path to weep in concert around the tomb. While I gazed solemnly at this work of art, a ragged yew tree kept striving at every breath of wind to thrust one of its gnarled old branches in at the window; and putting all things together, the cheerfulness went out of me entirely, and the idea of ghosts came in quite as naturally as in the library. I tried to shake it off, remembering my late experience and not wishing to have my mind burdened with any further queer fancies of the kind; and after a moment or two, indeed, seemed to be succeeding very tolerably and became able to hum an operatic drinking song with comparative ease and correctness. Just then, however, happening to turn my head, I saw a strange figure standing near the foot of the bed and gazing at me with fixed but not unpleasing or unfriendly expression.

The figure of a pleasant young fellow; not, to all appearance, over twenty-two years of age, and exhibiting a lifelike rotundity and opacity that would have prevented any suspicion in my mind of the supernatural, if I had not had my uncle's word for it, or if I had discovered any way in which the stranger could have entered the room without my seeing him. A handsome young fellow, courtly in manner and dress, with coat of purple velvet, slashed and embroidered the whole length of the sleeves, a dainty little rapier swinging at his side and a plumed cap held in his hand. Hair falling in long curls over his broad lace collar, and the beard twisted into a point, while the small mustachios also twined into points turned up against the cheeks. A mild, responsive kind of face, with courteous smiles and replete with indications of gentle disposition.

"I am exceedingly happy to meet you," he remarked, playing with the gold-lace upon his sword hilt. "The more so that since I have been ill, so few persons come to visit me at all. I do not know that I have seen anybody of late, excepting the butler; and even he appears to be a new butler, most unaccountably put into possession by some other and pretended authority. I must inquire into it when I am completely restored."

"You say that you have been ill?"

"Yes; a faintness and much uneasy want of rest at night, principally arising from this lump in my chest; and that, in turn, coming from the attack upon me by my brother Harold. Would be glad to introduce him to you if it were not for that. But I put it to you now: after what has happened could I show him any such attention, or, indeed, associate with him at all? If cousin Beatrice were here, now—"

At this moment there came a rap at the door; and the ghost, shrinking a little toward one side, began to pale before me, and I saw that he was slowly fading away, beginning at the legs, and so the line of invisibility extending upward until gradually the whole figure had entirely vanished. Again I saw in its entirety the carved footboard which he had hitherto partially obscured; there was nothing left, indeed, to remind me of the strange visitant. And opening the door I saw only Bidgers, the butler.

"Luncheon is ready, Master Geoffrey," he said. "No fish

today, for the West stage is not in, but the mushrooms is particularly fine. Heard you talking to the ghost as I came along—the upstairs ghost, not Sir Ruthven's downstairs ghost. Sir Ruthven has only seen the downstairs one, but I've seen both. Saw this one last Christmas, about this time. He would not speak to me, however, it being that I am only the butler. They're very much alike, Master Geoffrey. There's a very nice haunch of venison for dinner today, let me recommend; and the kidneys is not to be despised, either."

Chapter II

After that, and during the remainder of my visit, nothing else happened especially worthy of mention. The Christmas festivities passed off as they generally do; and the next morning I returned to London, where my recollection of the ghosts soon began to die away. At first, indeed, as is natural, I could think of nothing else. But inasmuch as my Uncle Ruthven had taken the matter so coolly, I began to be impressed by a careful and more deliberate consideration of his manner, and to wonder whether I might not have imagined many of the most singular circumstances attending the incident; until, at last, I concluded that there could have been no ghost at all, but that I must have dreamed the whole story.

In addition, my time became so fully occupied that I had few occasions in which I might engage in desultory wandering of idle curiosity or speculation; for during the first eight months I was diligently employed reading for my admission to the Bar. After that, I was actively forgetting most of what I had learned, giving myself up as escort to my cousin Lilian. She had returned from her travels upon the continent, and with her father was stopping awhile in London before continuing on to the Grange. It was my pleasing duty to remain at Lilian's side most of the time, Sir Ruthven being glad to avoid the toil of active companionship. I was very much in love with Lilian, but would not for the world have prematurely told her of it—it would have made her so tyrannical. At last, of course, we quarreled. It was the day before Sir Ruthven and Lilian returned home; and she informed me that she was going on the 10.45 stagecoach, and that she would be seriously displeased if I attempted to see her off. This looked well for me upon the whole, I thought, and I started for the coach at once. As ill luck would have it, I missed it, a circumstance which really helped my cause; since Lilian, being thereby persuaded that I understood it to be a lasting quarrel, felt suitably piqued into anxiety and regret.

A little before Christmas, Sir Ruthven wrote me to run down to the Grange as usual. With his letter came a perfumed note from Lilian, stating that if she could, she would gladly be away at Christmas with her Aunt Eleanor; but since she could not, but was obliged to remain home, she would consider it a great insult if I presumed to visit the Grange before she could get away in some other direction. I was wonderfully encouraged at this, feeling that all was going on well; and packing my trunk at once, I went down by the earliest stage on Christmas morning.

Again the chimes happened to be ringing just as I alighted; and, as before, no one coming forth to meet me, I pressed on to the library, there to make my respects to Uncle Ruthven, feeling well assured that I should find him in his accustomed seat beside the fireplace. He was in the room, indeed, but not sitting down. He was standing beside the chair and bowing with great affection of cordiality to some one in the further corner of the room. Looking in that direction, I beheld a young fellow in court suit of two centuries ago, with hand upon his heart, bowing back to my uncle with still greater excess of old-fashioned courtesy and cordiality; and I did not for an instant doubt that I was looking upon the downstairs ghost. Almost the duplicate of the other one, indeed. Evidently about the same age, with equally agreeable, sunny, ingratiating expression. Like the other, he had thick curls falling over the collar, beard cultivated to a point, slashed velvet coat, laces, gold tassels, and a slim, daintily decorated rapier. The most notable differences consisted in his complexion and hair being a shade darker, and his coat being of a lively crimson. It was a pleasant thing to see these two persons salaaming cordially and ceremoniously to each other; my uncle bowing until he struck the table behind him, and the ghost bending over in responsive courtesy until the point of the scabbard of his sword tipping up, made a new scratch upon the worm-eaten picture of Salvator Rosa.

"You see, Geoffrey," my uncle whispered between his repeated genuflexions, "he has come again to the very minute. The very same time as last year, just as though the chimes waked him up. I remember that you then thought that perhaps I was accustomed to cut him short rather too suddenly. We will be more cautious now, and will not end until we get his whole story out of him." Then to the ghost: "I am rejoiced to see you once more, kind sir."

"It gives me equal and exceeding pleasure," responded the ghost. "And I know that my brother Arthur would be similarly gratified could he only know about your arrival. But, then, how is he to know? After his conduct toward me—the obloquy he has thrown around me, in fact—it certainly would be beneath my dignity to approach him, even for the sake of imparting information. I can, therefore, merely myself welcome you."

"Now, just listen to that!" muttered Uncle Ruthven, beginning to flush up angrily. "I have done my best; but is it possible to continue politeness with a person who insists upon treating me as his guest? I treat him with all the cordiality I can muster, and the only result of it is that he turns around and seems to patronize me."

It chanced that, moved by the first warmth of my uncle's courtesy, the ghost had advanced a little, as though to meet us, and thereby he now stood between us and the window. This change of position seemed to produce a marvelous alteration in his appearance. The face so fair and genial and prepossessing became at once a queer confusion of lines, every feature being obscured by what looked like converging cuts and wrinkles, making the whole expression of the countenance unintelligible.

It was only for an instant, however. The next moment, the ghost moving away from the window, his face became as before—clear, distinct, filled with amiable and courteous refinement and intelligence. It was not until afterward that the mystery explained itself. Now, indeed, the singular appearance had lasted for such a brief moment that it seemed scarcely worth while to seek an explanation. The only thing, in fact, that particularly struck me was a red line extending around the throat, as though the result of a forced compression. This was observable even after the ghost had passed from directly before the window, and until he had moved completely out of reach of the entire spread of sunlight.

"If Cousin Beatrice were here," remarked the ghost in continuation, "she would undoubtedly be very happy to take part in entertaining you. But where is she now? It is some days since I have seen her. Do you think it possible that Brother Arthur, in addition to the ignominy to which he has subjected me by his unjust suspicions, can have influenced her mind against me? If so, as long as I live, I will never—"

"Listen again to that! As long as he lives! How can anybody stand such drivel?" cried Uncle Ruthven. "I suppose, Geoffrey, you will now see that it is as well to put an end to this first as last?"

With that, as upon the previous Christmas, my uncle seized a large book and vindictively let fly at the stranger. If until that time I had had any doubts as to his unsubstantial nature, they were now relieved. Corporeal and opaque as he had seemed, it was none the less true that the volume, striking him in the stomach, passed completely through him as through a stratum of air, falling upon the floor behind, while the figure remained unblemished and uninjured; with this exception, however, that naturally he seemed scarcely pleased with the roughness of the reception, and a shadow of discontent flickered across his face. Then appearing to comprehend that possibly he might be unwelcome, he slowly faded away.

"Middleton's *Cicero,* this time," remarked my uncle, wiping his face and gazing toward the weapon he had just so successfully used. "And the fellow has digested that as well as the volume last year. At this rate he will get my whole library into him before long. I cannot help it, Geoffrey. You saw that I tried my best to be polite. But when a ghost acts as though he owned the house, and moreover talks as though he were alive, mortal man could not withstand the temptation to cut him down. Well, well, get ready for lunch, Geoffrey. The South Oriel, as last year."

Of course, being sent up to the same room and the old program seeming to begin being played, I expected once again to meet the purple-coated ghost. And as is natural, I went up with some little trepidation. For it is one thing to have a ghost appear to you, good natured and smiling from the first; and another thing deliberately to throw one's self in the way of a ghost who might not happen at the moment to be in a very pleasant humor, and might exert some supernatural power to make himself extremely disagreeable. All the time I was dressing, I looked uneasily over my shoulder, in search of apparitions. But inasmuch as we seldom find what we most surely expect to see, I was left entirely undisturbed, and finally began my descent to the dining room with feelings greatly relieved and composed.

Passing the drawing-room, I heard the subdued rustle of silk, and entering, found Cousin Lilian all arrayed for luncheon and smoothing herself out before the fire. Of course after what had passed in London, she swept me a stately courtesy, addressing me by my surname as though I were a stranger whom she had casually met the previous day; and of course I bowed in her presence with ceremonious reverence befitting the first presentation of Raleigh to Queen Elizabeth. Then Lilian, slightly lifting her eyebrows in spirit of wonderment at my intrusion, remarked that she believed Sir Ruthven was in the library. I replied that I had already seen Sir Ruthven and had found him busily engaged with a ghost; and that as this seemed to be their reception day and others might be expected by him, I would not intrude upon him for a while, but with her permission would prefer to remain where I was.

These preambles having been thus satisfactorily entered into, of course we began making up by throwing at each other little spiteful remarks of an epigrammatic nature; now and then spontaneous, but for the most part carefully manufactured weeks before and treasured up for the occasion. Snapping these off from side to side like torpedoes, and mutually rebounding them harmlessly from our casemated natures, we gradually composed our feelings and began getting along very well on the path to reconciliation. How long it might have taken under ordinary circumstances I cannot tell; but it happened all at once that Lilian was startled into an unexpectedly rapid advance. For of a sudden I felt her hand grasping my arm, and she called me by my first name in the old familiar manner; and turning, I saw her gaze fixed with a wondering but not altogether alarmed expression upon the opposite corner of the room.

"See, Geoffrey!" she whispered. "The upstairs ghost! How comes he in here?"

Chapter III

Turning, I saw the purple velvet ghost at last, bowing low to the floor, with a humble courtesy that disarmed wrath, though nonetheless did an explanation seem necessary.

"Really, my good sir," I therefore said, "this intrusion—"

"I must apologize for it, certainly," he remarked, again bowing low. "I was a little behindhand this morning in reaching the South Oriel. And passing through the hall, I saw a female figure inside this room. I entered, expecting to meet my Cousin Beatrice. I see that I am mistaken. Last night I slumbered more uneasily than usual—the lump in my chest causing me very great disturbance, and doubtless it has excited my nerves and made me easily deceived. It has all come from Brother Harold's outrage upon me, I suppose. Which being so, it only remains for me to take my leave, with apology for the intrusion."

"Stay yet a moment," I said. "This is my cousin Miss Lilian, who certainly will not fear you and will forgive your slight mistake. And—and I have so much to say to you."

In fact, I felt that this might be the last time I should see him; and that it would be no more than a charity to enlighten him as to his true condition. It was a very sad thing to see a bright, amiable young ghost going around century after century as though he were still alive, and I decided that it would be a kind action to correct his error. Moreover, it happened that just at this moment, chance threw a convincing explanation within my reach. For as the ghost stepped a little to one side preparatory to taking his departure, it came about that he stood between me and the window, just as the other ghost had done; and in like manner, every feature seemed obscured with a network of contrary lines and wrinkles. But as he chanced to remain there a little longer than the other one had done, the mystery became almost at once revealed. I saw that the singular appearance was caused by the strong sunlight showing through him, whereby his whole head appeared as a transparent object. It was exhibited as a mass of dim, lurid light, not entirely endowed with all the bright translucent qualities of glass, but rather as when a sheet of thin porcelain is held up to the light, so that its semicloudy transparency is revealed, and with it, any dark spots or imperfections in the surface are brought to notice. In like manner, our visitor's head now seemed transformed with the brightness of the sunlight behind it, so that its former opacity was gone and there was a light, cloudy appearance as of a dissolving mist, marked in every direction with straight and curved lines of greater or less intensity. At first, the features, excepting as they appeared in profile, seemed entirely to have vanished beneath a confusion of other lines; but a moment's observation assured me of the contrary. They were all still there—the sparkling eye, the delicate mouth, the well-shapen ear. With a little attention, I could still trace the sweep of their several outlines. It was merely that those outlines were now somewhat confused by the addition of other lines appearing from within the skull. These also, I found that with a little study, I could still make out. There was a broad, irregularly-curved mark showing the outline of the lobes of the brain. I could follow the whole ball of the eye beneath its socket and the fainter lines which connect the eye with the brain behind. The drum and the small bones of the ear, and the twisted passages from the nose to the ear were all now clearly defined. The palate, too, and the sides of the throat, until hidden at last beneath the laced collar of that courtly coat. In fine, under the influence of that bright sunlight behind it, the young fellow's head became something like one of the modern medical wax preparations, exhibiting every portion of its frame in exact position; except that, far superior to any work of art, it did not require to be taken apart for study, but could be examined in detail, just as it stood.

"How long," I said, myself moving a little one side so that he might not appear between me and the window; by which judicious movement he became at once like any other person, his features returning to their usual distinctness of outline, unclouded by any rival lines and curves from behind; "how long have you been thus ill and disturbed at night by pain within your chest?"

"A week, or even more, I think," he said.

"Pardon me," I responded; "here is where you have made a trifling mistake in your chronology—you, and the other, as well. This little episode which you believe has occupied a few days or so, has lasted, in reality, upward of two centuries. You have been thrown into a certain condition of mind in which you are unable to take due note of time. Why this is so, I cannot attempt to explain. The melancholy fact remains that you have already been wandering some two hundred years, and for all we know, may be destined to wander to all eternity. In proof of this, I might refer you to your costume, which is of the fashion of Charles the Second; while, in fact, we are living in the thirty-eighth of Victoria."

I paused for a moment here, thinking that he might wish to ask some question. But as he maintained a perplexed silence, I continued:

"You are in further error in believing that the only consequence of some injury you have received has been mere restlessness at night. Instead of which, you died and of course were suitably buried. And consequently, you are not now a man, but merely a ghost. It may be unpleasant to be told this, but it is as well that you should know it first as last. And, after all, there can be no harm in being a well-conducted, creditable ghost. As such, you are allowed to appear each Christmas day for a few minutes, at the expiration of which, doubtless, you return to your grave. There, I presume, you slumber until the next Christmas day, for you seem to have no definite knowledge of your whereabouts. At the least you must be comfortable, which perhaps is more than can be said of many ghosts. Even Hamlet's father seems to have suffered torments; though there is presumptive evidence that he was a very good man, and totally unlike his brother. You are incredulous about what I am now telling you? In proof of it, let me stand you directly in front of the window, so that the sunlight will strike full upon your person. Then let me hold this looking-glass before you. Now studying your reflection carefully, you will see that you are transparent; which, I take it, is the surest proof any man can enjoy of his being a ghost. You can trace out the passages of your ears, the convolutions of your brain, the course of your jugular vein. This line, which you might easily mistake for a nerve or cord, is merely a crack in the looking-glass. Should you feel disposed, hereafter, for your amusement, to study your internal anatomy more thoroughly, I would advise a new and more perfect mirror. But can you any longer doubt your condition?"

"I can no longer doubt, indeed," groaned the ghost. "But what, alas, can I now do?"

"A thousand things," I responded. "I take it that, inasmuch as men must not live idle lives, in like manner ghosts, also, may have their duties to perform. Surely, it can scarcely be intended, in the economy of the unseen world, that they should pass lives—or, rather, existences—of careless idleness. I know that, were I a ghost, I would do my best to find some useful employment. I think that I would endeavor to obtain some occupation that might be of benefit to the world I had left behind. Suppose, for instance, that you endeavored to retain some, even trifling, recollection of the nature of your abode in the unseen world, how you are associated, whither you are sent, and other facts of a kindred character, and were to impart them to the human race from time to time through myself. Do you not think that you would be doing great good, as well as entitling yourself to the gratitude of all living men?"

The ghost mutely shook his head. Evidently he did not care particularly about the gratitude of living men.

"Or suppose," I continued, struck with a new, and, in my estimation, better idea—for it happened that I had lately been interesting myself deeply in medical jurisprudence—"suppose that you were to apply yourself to the benefit of the human race in an anatomical or pathological capacity. There is on record the case of a man who had a hole in the side of his stomach through which processes of digestion could be watched, to the great service of medical science. Need I say that, for every purpose of interest or utility, you surpass him infinitely? I must assume, with tolerable certainty, that if your head is transparent, so, also, is your whole body; and that the workings of your inner system are simply hidden from sight by your clothing. Divested of that, you could easily unfold, in the strong light of the sun, the entire operations of your heart, your lungs and your stomach. Daily could you have your seances, and new discoveries could be noted down. There must be some thin, ghostly, almost impalpable fluid in your system answering the purpose of blood in the human frame, and of this physicians might succeed in watching the circulation and flow. There are vexed questions in medical science as to the real use of certain vessels and attachments—whether they are actually necessary in the human constitution, or whether they are mere rudimentary relics of a lower organization. These questions you might succeed in determining. In fact—"

I had reached thus far, becoming so transported with the increasing magnitude of my speculations that I no longer looked at the ghost, but with half-closed eyes gazed upward at the ceiling; when suddenly Lilian plucked me gently by the sleeve, and, with quiet movement of the eyes, called my attention more directly to our visitor. He was standing motionless beside the window; but I observed that the pleasant expression had faded from his face, an angry flush was mounting into every feature, grim, transporting rage was clouding every line. And, as I paused in natural hesitation, he turned roughly toward me.

"Have you done?" he cried, bursting out with an old-fashioned oath of the days of the royal Stuarts. "Have you come to the end of your base proposals? Have you reflected sufficiently what it is to dare to suggest to Sir Arthur Grantley, of the Court of Charles, that he should pass his time illustrating the labors and theories of leeches, quacks, and charlatans?"

Another old-fashioned oath, a half withdrawal of the slender rapier from its sheath, a driving it down again with impetuous, angry energy, and the ghost strode wildly out of the drawing room, and was no more seen. But for two or three moments we could hear him growling forth his queer old court oaths as he rattled away along the outside passage.

Chapter IV

Lilian and I gazed at each other in speechless wonderment. The bell rung for luncheon, and we passed toward the dining room; still with thoughts too deep for words.

"Can it be," I said at length, as we entered the other room, "that this person, whom we had supposed to be merely some retainer of the family, was in reality its head? That he could have been an ancestor of yours, Lilian?"

"Papa will know," she answered. "We will ask him at luncheon." Then, when the old gentleman sat eating his nuts and raisins and sipping his wine—before which time he disliked to be disturbed about anything excepting the occupation immediately in view—she began:

"Was there ever a Sir Arthur Grantley, papa?"

"Let me think," mumbled Uncle Ruthven. "Yes, there was a Sir Arthur about two centuries ago. And now the story begins to come to me. There were two brothers—twins; the oldest having the estate and title, and the youngest being a captain in the Royal Guard. One would have supposed that, being so nearly of an age and closely related, they would have kept the peace; but the contrary was the fact. They quarreled so that one of them murdered the other, and was suitably hanged for it."

"Is there record of the fact, Uncle Ruthven?"

"Nowhere, unless it may be in the State Trials. I have never looked there. You will find no allusion to it in Burke or Debrett. Those useful and accommodating compilers, out of regard for the family honor, I suppose, merely state that Harold Grantley died, aged twenty-two: a piece of reticence which, after all, was scarcely worthwhile, considering that it happened so long ago. Time is a great cleanser of family escutcheons. It would be unpleasant to have a murder attached to the reputation of one's father or grandfather; but carry it two centuries back, and no one seems to care. If it were not so, there is scarcely a royal family on earth which would not be hanging its head. I do not read that Her Most Gracious Majesty Victoria ever makes herself miserable about any suspicions attaching to the memory of Queen Mary of Scotland. In fact, rather a disreputable ancestry, if distinguished, is better than none at all. It is scarcely to be supposed, for instance, that any of us would take it much to heart at finding Guy Fawkes seated upon one of the limbs of the family tree. At any rate, we have no reason to complain of this little murder in the Grantley line, seeing that it finished up the direct descent in that quarter and sent down the entail to us through a collateral branch."

With that, having exhausted his knowledge upon the subject,

Uncle Ruthven went on sipping his wine and turned the subject upon the culture of turnips. But after luncheon Lilian and myself, feeling by no means contented, slipped up to the library again and took down one of the time-worn dusty volumes of the State Trials. The books had evidently not been moved out of place for years; but it was easy, having the reign, to find all that we wanted, and in a few minutes we opened at the case of *Rex* v. *Grantley.* The book was very heavy, and at the first we spread it upon the table. This proving inconveniently high we took to the sofa, where we let the volume rest on both our laps and read together. It was very pleasant, altogether. It was necessary for Lilian to lean over so that her curls brushed across my shoulder, and at times I could feel her breath warm upon my cheek. That she might have greater strength to hold her share of the book, I passed my arm sustainingly about her waist; a fact which she did not seem to realize, so intent was she upon the story of the murder. We have often read about young men and maidens looking upon the same book and in just such positions. In those narrations it is generally a book of poetry, or at least a novel that interests them. I question if very often a young lady sits with her lover absorbed in the story of a murder committed by one of her own family and reads it without any feeling except of curiosity about its mere incidents, and as coolly as though it were Jack Shepperd or Oliver Twist. But then, as Uncle Ruthven justly observed, it was so long ago.

It appeared, then, from the account in the State Trials, that Arthur and Harold Grantley were twin brothers of the age of twenty-two. As Uncle Ruthven had stated, Arthur was the oldest and in possession of the title and estate, while Harold held commission in the Palace Guard. Naturally the two brothers were thrown much together, and were supposed to be greatly attached to each other. Of course, they sometimes had their little disagreements; but, until the period of the murder, it was never supposed that there was any especial ill feelings between them. The trouble ensued about noon one Christmas day. Harold had obtained leave to visit his brother at the Grange; and after an early dinner—for they were alone and much form and ceremony was dispensed with—they sat at the table, conversing, eating filberts and drinking their wine. Possibly they had been drinking too much; but not so much, in fact, as to exhibit its effects upon them to any great extent. The most that could be said was, that it might have tended to make them quarrelsome; but as it turned out, this after all was the whole mischief in the case, and much worse in its results than downright and less harmful intoxication. It chanced that Sir Arthur had taken the opportunity of exhibiting to his brother a certain valuable heir-loom, known in the family as the great Lancaster diamond, having come into the line from a collateral Lancaster branch. It had lain concealed in a secret closet during the Cromwellian troubles, and had just been brought to light again. It is supposed that Sir Arthur, being attached to their cousin Beatrice and wishing marriage with her, had designed presenting her with the diamond; and that Harold, being equally in love with her and perhaps with no less prospect of success, had made objection; and that from this fact the quarrel had arisen. Be that as it may, their voices were heard in loud dispute; and suddenly Harold calling out for help, his brother was found lying upon his back lifeless and with every appearance about the throat of having been foully dealt with. Harold's account of the circumstance was to the effect that Sir Arthur all at once had thrown himself back in his chair and gasped and seemed to have been seized with a fit. On the other hand, it was argued that young men of his vigorous constitution did not readily die in fits—that the appearances of foul play by strangulation were too evident—that there had certainly been high words between them, a fact, indeed, which Harold was obliged to admit—that the known passion of both the young men for the same lady would have been sufficient of itself to produce fraternal hatred and strife—and furthermore, that Harold would have a supreme interest in his brother's death, by reason of the succession to the estate. And then again, the diamond had disappeared. If the death had been a natural one, the diamond would not have been disturbed; but inasmuch as it was the leading cause of the dissension, nothing was more natural than that the murderer should have made away with it, by throwing it out of the window, into the lake, most likely, so as to remove one great evidence of the crime. Altogether the feeling ran very high against the surviving brother, political prejudices that could scarcely now be explained intervened to increase the excitement, while certain favorites of the king, desiring promotion in the Guard by removal of one person of higher rank, prejudiced the royal mind against pity or pardon. In fine, after much agitation and a protracted trial, young Harold was found guilty and executed.

"And this explains," I said to Lilian, "many circumstances that hitherto have not been clear to me. The red line around the throat of the downstairs ghost; the pain in the chest of the upstairs ghost—a difficulty most naturally resulting from outside pressure—all these things now tell the story very clearly, and agree most wonderfully with the State trials account. Only—which at first seems strange—the murdered now does not seem to remember that he was put to death, nor the murderer that he was executed for it."

"That is, indeed, singular," said Lilian. "But, then, ghosts are so silly!"

"At first sight, it may seem strange," I answered; "but not after a moment's reflection. Violence endured by us in life is very often with difficulty afterward brought to our memory. One has a fall or is stricken down by a club and made senseless; he recovers after awhile, and knows that in some way he has been injured, but does not remember the actual fall or blow. And why should it be different if the injury leads to death? Looking upon it in this light, and with this philosophy, we see the young baronet awakening in the grave with no conception of ever having been killed, but merely with some indistinct idea of previous attack or vituperation. And, in the same manner, we find the younger brother awakening in the belief that he is still alive, and remembering not his execution at the hands of the law, but only the fact of having been charged with some outrage against the other, the nature of which he cannot comprehend, while the circumstance of any charge being made at all grievously offends and distresses him."

"All very plausible, indeed," responded Lilian. "But suppose that, after all, he was innocent?"

"A thing very hard to believe, with so much contrary evidence," I said. "All that is a mere woman's unreasoning supposition, with endeavor to wipe off a blemish from the family escutcheon."

"Pho! for the family escutcheon," responded Lilian, putting up her lips in pholike form. And as she spoke she looked so pretty that, having my arm still about her waist, I began seriously to consider whether I had not better improve the opportunity and now make my offer. So much was already understood between us, indeed; and everyone, even Lilian herself, knew very well that it was destined some day to come about, as a suitable family arrangement long foreseen and often talked about; and, therefore, what better moment than the present to unburden my heart?

"I think, Lilian," I said, "that it is about time I spoke a word or two to you about our future."

"Well, Geoffrey," she replied.

I saw the flush gather in her face, that she knew what must be coming, that she anticipated tender avowal with loving expression. In this last respect, at least, mindful of recent aggravations on her part, I determined that I would disappoint her.

"No," I said, "it is not probable that Harold was innocent. And therefore you must see for yourself, Lilian, that your family have been a most disreputable lot. But for all that, having unfortunately a strong personal prejudice in your favor, I am inclined to believe that I shall not be doing myself too great injustice in offering you my alliance."

"You are very kind, certainly, Geoffrey," she responded. "I cannot but feel intensely gratified at the preference. I suppose that every family must at some time or other meet its misfortune of a public execution or some similar disgrace. I consider it particularly fortunate that with us it has already happened. In your line of the family it is yet to come; and if I may judge by circumstances, it will probably take place during the present generation. And merely that I may legally enjoy the privilege of standing at your side and comforting you during that closing ordeal, I take pleasure in accepting your offer."

And this is how Lilian and I became engaged.

Chapter V

It was understood that the wedding would not take place immediately. Uncle Ruthven had some old-fashioned notions about matrimony, prominent among which was the idea that no young man should marry without having the means of support from his profession, so as to be independent of the fluctuations and liabilities to loss of private fortune. Upon this basis, it was determined that we should not wed until I had made a public and credible appearance at the Bar.

This came about in the following October. I had been engaged as third counsel in the great case of *Charity-boy* v. *Churchwarden,* for assault. Churchwarden had boxed the ears of Charity-boy for playing marbles on a tombstone; but unfortunately had not succeeded in catching him to do so until they were over the boundary-line of the graveyard. Upon this defect, want of jurisdiction as to place was alleged, and action brought. The suit had been running nearly five years, and therefore could now reasonably be moved for trial. The rector, curate, half the vestry and three of the bell-ringers had been subpoenaed to give evidence and stood ready. It was necessary to have, in addition, the testimony of the toy-maker who had sold the marbles; and he, it happened, was on his deathbed at the north of Scotland. A commission had been issued to take his testimony. The toy-maker lay delirious for the most part, having a lucid interval of about half an hour each day, during which he desired to make his will. He was constantly prevented from doing so, however, by the entrance of the commissioners demanding to take his testimony, which so confused him that he always went off wandering again. Pending the execution of the commission, of course an adjournment was desired.

Now it happened that, both the senior counsel being away, it devolved upon me to make the application for the adjournment, and with a little difficulty about the pitch of my voice, I succeeded in doing so. The judge said that if the other side were agreed, there could be no objection; and the other side having duly consented, the adjournment was ordered. Whereupon I wrote down to Sir Ruthven that I had made my first appearance. Sir Ruthven immediately wrote back, asking whether my speech would be reported in the Times. I replied that I did not suppose it would, as the papers were unusually interested in the Montenegro difficulty, to the exclusion of much other valuable news. Uncle Ruthven thereupon responded that he was satisfied, upon the whole, even if the Times was silent about me; and that now that I had resources for support independent of inherited estate, the wedding might come off immediately after Christmas. And he told me to run down the day before Christmas, so that we could have a pleasant little Christmas dinner by ourselves, before the invited visitors began to arrive.

Accordingly, I arrived at Grantley Grange upon the afternoon of the twenty-fourth, and was at once shown to my room by Bidgers, who not only lighted me up, but followed me in to assist in unpacking my wardrobe. And while doing so, naturally with the self-allowance of an old family servant he let his tongue run loose with the gossip and events of the day.

"A hamper just come in, Master Geoffrey, with a fine large salmon; but that is for tomorrow. You must praise it when you see it, for Sir Ruthven sets great store in having got it. There has been no ghosts seen since you was here last—perhaps they have all gone away for good. There is talk that the Earl of Kildare will be at the wedding next week; but any which way, he has sent a silver pitcher. Maybe, after all, the ghosts have all been locked up where they are. Miss Lilian's Aunt Eleanor has done better than the Earl of Kildare though. She cannot come, they say; but such diamond earrings as she has sent—almost as large as filberts, Mr. Geoffrey! As to the grapes today, I am fearful there's a little mold on some of them; but the oysters—"

"That will do—thank you, Bidgers," I said, tired of the running stream; and Bidgers, taking the hint, affected to blow a speck of dirt off the sleeve of my wedding coat, and gently glided out of the room. I was not so much tired, indeed, as that I felt I would like to be alone for thought. Something in Bidgers last remark had awakened an association of ideas in my mind; but of such intangible, confused character that I could not follow it up to any definite purpose. Diamonds as large as filberts—filberts and diamonds, so ran the words, through and through my mind like the strain of a tune; but out of it all I could not, with the utmost concentration of thought, gain any clue that I might follow up to a satisfactory certainty.

At night the same—I fell asleep with the old sequence of words running in my head, still like the strain of a tune, as sometimes we will set to meter the thumping of a railroad car. In the middle of the night I awoke; and then there flashed upon my mind a solution of the puzzle, but so wild and improbable, so idiotic and fantastic did it seem, that at once I discouraged it. Even then, when scarcely half aroused, and at an hour when the waking fancies run riot in premonition and alliance with hardly more fanciful dreams, did I laugh at the crude conception and try to beat it down, falling asleep again at last with mind apparently entirely relieved of the foolish notion. But when in the morning I awoke with the sun broadly shining in upon me, there again was the queer idea; and now, wonderful to relate, though I lay with the collectedness of thought appertaining to the open day, and with little chance of crude fancies any longer overwhelming me, the idea, though still as strange and ghostlike as before, no longer bore that first impress of the ridiculous, but was as something real and to be soberly and carefully considered. At least the experiment suggested by it might be tried, though secretly and cautiously, so as not to provoke ridicule in case it came to nothing.

Dressing myself, I stole softly downstairs. It was still very early, and there was no one stirring below, excepting a housemaid dusting the furniture. She merely looked up and then continued her task, my habit of morning walks being too well known to excite observation. I passed through the long window and came upon the bare winter-stained lawn. There was the gardener, muffling anew some plants in straw; but he too, merely touching his hat, said nothing. Then I followed a gravel path around the terrace to the rear of the house, and thence struck off to a little grove of pines a hundred yards or so away.

In the midst of these was the burial vault of the Grantley family. It was by no means a repulsive object, being merely a brick erection a few feet above the surface of the ground, and originally constructed with some pretense of architectural symmetry. Neither was it an object of superstitious or sentimental reverence. In fact, at the present time there were not more than twelve or fifteen of the family laid away in it. It had been built four centuries ago, and with accommodation for a hundred or so; but at the time of the rebellion a party of Cromwell's troops came sweeping down upon the house, and, being in want of material for bullets, turned all the dead Grantleys out of doors and took their leaden coffins to cast into ammunition. After that time the burials continued for only a few generations; since which, the yard around the village church had received the family dead. About ten years ago it had been found necessary to open the vault in order to get the date of some particular death for legal evidence. The long-closed door had stoutly resisted, and at length the lock was obliged to be broken. It was intended, of course, to restore the fastenings; but equally of course, and as happens so often with matters that can be done any day, the duty was postponed from time to time, and gradually came to be no longer remembered. The closed door then warped open a little of itself, and the gardeners leaned their tools against it, and after awhile pushed the door further back, and slipped their tools just inside out of the rain; and so, step by step, the almost empty vault became only used as a toolhouse. Vines were trained to grow over it, ferns gathered around its base, and a stranger would have taken it for a somewhat dilapidated ice-house.

I pushed the door open yet a little further and peeped within. The sunbeams, still low and shut out by the screen of trees, could not now enter; but enough light stole in to show a pile of rakes and hoes just inside, and a little further along, a row of empty recesses, built for coffins, but long since made vacant. Entering, I could see that the recesses ran in double rows for some distance in front of me, being at the further end shrouded in darkness. I drew out my cigar lighter and by the aid of repeated tapers proceeded to explore. Then I could see that at the further end, a few of the recesses were filled with coffins. These were in various stages of decay. In all cases, the dark coverings of cloth had moldered away and lay in fragments at the side or on the stone floor below. In some, the outer wooden shells were nearly whole; but in others, they had crumbled into dust and splinters. With a few of the recesses, the names and dates of the remains within were fastened at the lower edge upon brass plates; with others, the plates had entirely disappeared. There was one recess which contained a worm-eaten coffin of somewhat plain construction, but no name or date or even evidence that any such had ever been affixed. I could not resist the impression that here lay the unfortunate Harold Grantley; given, as matter of right, a place in this ancestral vault, but, through some charitable idea of letting his unhappy fate become forgotten, denied all record that could lead to future identification. Passing onward, with gathering assurance that my search would not prove unavailing, at each minute renewing my quickly expiring tapers, I carefully read every name, now and then rubbing the brass plates with my handkerchief before I could decipher the blurred old-fashioned letterings. Then, for a while, as the number of remaining niches one by one was lessened without rewarding my search, hope began to give way to disappointment. Only for a moment, however; for soon, to my abundant gratification, I read upon one of the plates, the words and characters, "Arthur Grantley, Obt. Dec. 25, 1663, Aet 22."

Here then, lay he whom I sought, and I scrutinized attentively all that remained. A moth-eaten, rat-torn pall, a nest of coffins, and that was all. Uneasily for the instant I turned my head, dreading lest the blithe young apparition with its purple and laced coat and dangling sword should arise and demand wherefore I was about to disturb him; but all remained quiet about me. I was alone with my own thoughts and purposes, and could prosecute my designs unquestioned and unimpeded.

I had feared lest I might be obliged to seek for assistance, but it was not so. Every thing, in fact, seemed made ready and convenient for me. The outer box was worm-eaten, warped and decayed, so that it could be broken and brushed away in places with a mere stroke of the hand; the leaden coffin inside had corroded, and the solder of the seams parted, so that the joints had spread apart, and, with no great effort, I was able to bend open the end; the mahogany coffin inside of all had suffered similar decay with the outer box, and readily parted. In a moment the outer end of all three coffins lay open, and I could easily insert my hand.

For a moment I hesitated. What if, as sometimes happens, the remains had not suffered corruption, and my touch were to encounter a solid form! Repressing this fear, I passed my hand stealthily within, finding no obstruction. Only a little dust at the bottom, hardly deep enough for a finger to write a name upon. This was all that was left of the gay young courtier, twelfth baronet of Grantley. Slowly I let my hand wander up along the bottom of the coffin, groping among the dust, until two-thirds up to the top; then I struck against a small, hard lump. My heart gave a loud thump of excitement. What could it be? Was it the prize that I had hoped for, or was it merely some fragment of unpulverized bone? Half wild with tremulous expectation, I grasped the little lump of substance firmly between thumb and forefinger, and hurried with it to the door of the vault. Even as I approached the dim, lurid light just within the half-opened entrance, I began to feel my assurances grow more sure; and when I emerged into the bright glow of day beyond, and held my prize up against the golden rays of the risen sun, I could no longer doubt that I had gained possession of the long lost Lancaster diamond.

Chapter VI

When I returned to the house, I said nothing about what I had been doing. It seemed as though the time for explanation would not come until toward evening. How, in that broad garish light of morning, could I venture to reveal that secret of dreams and darkness and rifled tombs? How, indeed, would my story be believed, unless with the glow of nightfall thrown around it to attune the listeners to credence?

Moreover, what if, during the day, the ghost were to appear, condemn my invasion of his sepulcher, demand his diamond, and possibly, by threats of supernatural force and terrors, obtain it? Certainly the accustomed hour for the ghosts was close at hand, and at any moment they might visit us. Already Sir Ruthven sat in the library awaiting his especial apparition. My uncle was, for the time, in no particularly friendly mood toward ghosts; and he now loudly declared that, whatever might before have been his courtesy, his forbearance had at last ceased, and he would not tolerate their coming. Certainly not now, he said, seeing that the house was preparing for a season of festivity, and had other things than the next world to think about. Accordingly he sat, watching, in his great elbow chair, with the heaviest volume of the *Encyclopaedia Brittanica* at his side, in readiness to crush out the first sign of ghost before even a word of salutation could be uttered.

But to the wonder of all and greatly to Sir Ruthven's disgust as well—seeing that, having made up his mind for action, he did not like to feel that his time had been thrown away—no ghost appeared, upstairs or down. Punctually at twelve, indeed, the chimes rang out the merriest peal we had enjoyed for years—the changes were sounded by the hundred with unusual exactness and celerity; yet all the time my uncle sat unmolested, with his *Encyclopaedia* lying idle beside him. At length the day wore itself out, the bell sounded for dinner, and we repaired to the dining room.

It was to be our last little dinner by ourselves; a very small Christmas party, indeed, but on the morrow the guests would begin to arrive and to break up our privacy, and then there could be no complaint about lack of excitement in the household. This last day Sir Ruthven had desired we should have for ourselves. But few as we were, no one had forgotten that it was the Christmas season and should be honored accordingly. Holly and mistletoe decked the room in every direction. A great yule log lay cosily esconced in the chimney-back and good humoredly tried to blaze up as merrily as the smaller branches that crackled around it; though being so unwieldy, it was not very successful in the attempt. But those smaller branches, invading the yule log's smoldering dignity with their blithe sport of gaiety, snapped and sputtered around it with uproarious mirthfulness; sending none but the prettiest colored smoke wreaths up the chimney, and casting out bright tongues of flames that lighted up every corner of the room and gave a ruddy glow to the time-faded portraits, and even brought out patches of cheerful sunlight upon an old cracked Rembrandt that no one had ever been able to decipher.

The table was set for us three only; but, in honor of the day, with as much ceremony as though there were to be twenty present. A tall branch wax-light, used only on occasions of great festivity, was brought out from its green baize covering and planted in the center. Treasures of antique silver, the very existence of which Sir Ruthven had nearly forgotten, were exhumed from their places of long concealment, and now once more, as in past centuries, pleasantly glimmered in the gentle gleam of wax-light. Flowers here and there unobtrusively exhaled sweet odors from tiny vases. There was to be a boar's head brought out and placed on the table at the proper time for each of us to look at and taste and pretend to enjoy. The plum-pudding was turning out a great success—the greatest for many years, as Bidgers whispered to me. All the circumstances of the scene around us were soft, harmonious and cheerful; certainly now was the time for me to tell my story.

With some little affectation of ceremony, perhaps, I drew forth the Lancaster diamond and placed it in Lilian's hand. I told her that I could make her no more valuable Christmas gift than to restore this rich family relic of the past. Lightly I touched upon the process whereby I had found it; rather elaborating, instead, the train of thought that had led me to suspect where it had lain hidden. I explained how the finding of the diamond gave new illustration to the record in the State Trials, proving that the younger brother had not been guilty of any murder at all—that during the agitation of a quarrel the older brother must have accidentally swallowed the diamond, mistaking it for one of the filberts that lay beside it near his plate, and which were of similar size—how that this unfortunate error had been sufficient of itself to cause his death by suffocation—how that thereby the discoloration around the neck of the deceased, as well as the disappearance of the diamond were properly accounted for—how that, most probably, it also gave an explanation of the unpleasant lump in the chest of the crimson-coated ghost.

"It is doubtless so," a soft voice thereat interrupted. We all looked up; and, at the further side of the table, we beheld both the ghosts. More alike now than ever before, it seemed to me; only with that single difference of color of the coats. The same bright engaging faces, the same gentle manner; as now, all heart burnings seemingly healed, they stood with their arms bound lovingly about each other in fraternal embrace.

"We have heard it all," continued the crimson ghost, "and thereby we find an explanation of some things that we never thought of before. Both Brother Arthur and myself now know that we are dead; and that it is fitting, therefore, that we should no longer haunt these scenes, to which indeed, we have no claim. I know that I have been hanged; a matter, however, which occasions me no concern, seeing that I deserved it not. I should at any rate have been dead long before this; and since my family can be satisfied of my innocence and I know that my Brother Arthur, in spite of a few harsh words, loves me still the same, I care not for others' opinions."

"And I," said the purple ghost, "cannot sufficiently thank you for the relief you have given me. Nightly have I lain in what I now perceive was my grave, unable to sleep by reason of the strange lump in my chest. This morning about eight, there came sudden relief; such sweet relief, indeed, that I overslept myself, and for the first time in many years have missed the chimes, and neglected at the appointed hour to make my usual Christmas visit. Even this bodily relief, perhaps, is not equal to what I feel at knowing that in reality I have suffered no wrong at the hands of Brother Harold. I think that if now we could only agree about the only subject which has ever estranged us—by which I refer to our mutual attachment to Cousin Beatrice we might—"

"I think I can easily make your mind easy about that matter," remarked Uncle Ruthven, coming forward. "If you will bear with me a minute, I will show you the lifelike picture of your Cousin Beatrice in after days."

He lifted one of the branch candlesticks from the table, and directed its light upon a painting on the wall. The portrait of Cousin Beatrice in more advanced life. A cracked, blackened and moth-eaten picture; but in which, by singular chance, the face had remained intact. The face of a woman who had long survived the natural freshness and graces of youth, and had gained in place of them none of those more matured and ennobling qualities that dignify age. The patched and painted and powdered face of a woman given up to all lightness and frivolity; a face in which there was nothing sweet or pleasant or kindly; in which all the art of Sir Godfrey Kneller had not succeeded in mingling with accurate likeness one spark of generous nature or blotting out the appearance of sordid vanity that pervaded it throughout all.

"The portrait of your Cousin Beatrice in her fiftieth year," remarked my Uncle Ruthven. "She never married, and was noted at Court for her skill in cheating at cards."

The two young ghosts gazed for a moment intently at the picture. As they did so, it seemed as though their embrace grew more intimate and fraternal. At last they turned again, as satisfied.

"I do not think that we shall ever quarrel again about Cousin Beatrice, even if at times we forget that we are all dead," the older ghost then said, with a sweet smile. "And now that all differences are so pleasantly made up, it remains for us only to bid you farewell. And since Brother Harold can now rest in his grave untroubled by any idea of wrong from me, and I can sleep, no longer annoyed by the lump that pained my chest, it is probable that we shall never be aroused to visit you again."

"But stay a moment," cried Uncle Ruthven, fairly touched at heart, and no longer remembering the *Encyclopaedia.* "You will not go so soon? At least you will take dinner with us?"

As he spoke the ghosts had already begun to vanish, the line of invisibility starting at the feet, as before, and working upward until they were half gone. Then, for a moment, the line trembled irresolutely, and so began to descend until again they stood entirely revealed. It was as though a person going out at a door had indeterminately held the handle for an instant and then returned.

"Moreover," continued my uncle, "I have apologies to make for many a past act of rudeness toward one of you."

"It is forgotten already," said the crimson ghost, bowing. "What do you say Brother Arthur, can we wait a little longer?"

"A very few minutes, Brother Harold, if only to give myself time to make amends for an act of impoliteness on my part toward this other gentleman only last year."

So they seated themselves at the table and the dinner began.

It was pleasant to watch the old-fashioned politeness with which they conducted themselves—the courtesy with which they bowed to Lilian at each word they addressed to her—the grace with which, wishing to cause no remark, they affected to eat and drink. Not able to do so, indeed, by reason of their incorporeal nature, but all the time lifting the full glasses and laden forks to their mouths and dropping them again untouched. It was delightful to listen to their conversation, marked here and there indeed, after the fashion of their time, with a light oath, but bright and sparkling throughout all, with vivacity and wit. At first, indeed; the time was somewhat occupied by Uncle Ruthven giving sketches of the late history of the family; but after that the ghosts were encouraged to talk, and pleasantly beguiled half an hour with hitherto unknown anecdotes of the Court of the Merry Monarch. As I listened my thoughts naturally strayed from the present back to the romantic past, and my imagination carried me, unresisting, into the olden days of the Stuarts. I was no longer in the prosaic nineteenth century, I was in the midst of a laughing, careless throng of king and courtiers, all busily making up for their enforced deprivations during the somber period of the Commonwealth. Hamilton and Nelly Gwynn, De Grammont and Villiers and Frances Stewart, these and others of those long dead disreputables, whose actions may not have been comely but whose names live vividly in story, and to whose memories some glamor of romance still kindly attaches us, now crowded around and made the past a reality and the present a mere unstable myth. In the hallucination of the moment even the portrait of the poor old card-cheating Beatrice Grantley seemed to invest itself with something of her long-departed youthfulness; and as the mingled gleam of wax-lights and yule log flickered upon it, it was as though some hitherto unnoted beauties of expression came to the surface, and the whole countenance became once more aglow with that youthful loveliness which, doubtless, in the time of it, and during her occasional visits to the Court, must have enticed Charles himself awhile from his more stable attachments in order to enjoy passing flirtation with her.

"A joyous Court, indeed; and sadly now coming to my memory as I feel that I can never mingle with it more," said the purple ghost. "A Court to which I know that my fair young kinswoman would have done ample honor, could she have been there," he added, bowing to Lilian; "even more abundantly, indeed, than Cousin Beatrice. Growing old with more grace and dignity than did Beatrice, I am very sure. And that she may live to grow old in such gentle manner, let her take heed and not make my sad mistake."

As he spoke, he pointed significantly to the Lancaster diamond which chanced at that moment to be beside her plate, and, by a singular coincidence, among a little pile of filberts.

"Yet I am sure," he added, still with the courtly manner of his period, "that such sweet lips could never make mistake about anything. Rather should the diamond, with its appropriate mate, be reserved to grace those beauteous ears."

"Its mate, do you say?" I remarked; not sure, for the moment, but that the young ghost had swallowed two diamonds, and that I had not carried my researches far enough.

"Yes, its mate," he said. "Surely you must know? Not so, indeed? Well, there were two of these great diamonds, the Lancaster and the York. They had come into possession of one family through union of adherents of those two rival parties, and thence into our own line, through subsequent alliance of that family with the Grantleys. In Cromwell's time, the diamonds were hidden in separate places to preserve them from confiscation, the knowledge of those places being handed down only by word of mouth, for greater security. At the Restoration, I alone knew the secret. At the time of my death I had already brought the Lancaster diamond to light, as you are well aware. The York still remains hidden. Permit us now, my brother and myself, to offer it to you as our joint Christmas present. You will find it in a little metal box close beside—"

At that very moment it chanced that a small bantam rooster outside the window set up a crow. It was a miserable little banty, scarcely half fledged. It had a drooping wing, and a twisted toe; and for these defects and others, perhaps, which we had not noticed, was constantly driven away from the general society of the poultry-yard. Even the hens were accustomed to pick at it. Its crow was weak, and piping, like a school-boy's first attempt at whistling. Nor was this the hour of midnight or early dawn, but merely seven in the evening. There seemed no reason why any ghost with self-respect should be moved by such a feeble crow from such a despicable source, and at such an early hour. And yet there may be a certain, inflexible rule for well-constituted ghosts; and perhaps, in cock-crowing, the line cannot easily be drawn between different styles. Be that as it may, at the very first pretense of sound from the little banty, the ghost stopped speaking, gazed inquiringly at his brother and received an answering nod; and then without another word they slowly faded away.

"Ghosts are so ridiculous!" said Lilian. But I thought that as she gazed at the Lancaster diamond and reflected how well the two Christmas gifts would have looked if worn together, she seemed sadly disappointed that the little banty had not put off his crowing for a minute longer.

NATHANIEL HAWTHORNE

THE CHRISTMAS BANQUET

The evil dead sit down to Christmas dinner.

"I HAVE here attempted," said Roderick, unfolding a few sheets of manuscript, as he sat with Rosina and the sculptor in the summerhouse—"I have attempted to seize hold of a personage who glides past me, occasionally, in my walk through life. My former sad experience, as you know, has gifted me with some degree of insight into the gloomy mysteries of the human heart, through which I have wandered like one astray in a dark cavern, with his torch fast flickering to extinction. But this man, this class of men, is a hopeless puzzle."

"Well, but propound him," said the sculptor. "Let us have an idea of him, to begin with."

"Why, indeed," replied Roderick, "he is such a being as I could conceive you to carve out of marble, and some yet unrealized perfection of human science to endow with an exquisite mockery of intellect; but still there lacks the last inestimable touch of a divine Creator. He looks like a man; and, perchance, like a better specimen of man than you ordinarily meet. You might esteem him wise; he is capable of cultivation and refinement, and has at least an external conscience; but the demands that spirit makes upon spirit are precisely those to which he cannot respond. When at last you come close to him you find him chill and unsubstantial—a mere vapor."

"I believe," said Rosina, "I have a glimmering idea of what you mean."

"Then be thankful," answered her husband, smiling; "but do not anticipate any further illumination from what I am about to read. I have here imagined such a man to be—what, probably, he never is—conscious of the deficiency in his spiritual organization. Methinks the result would be a sense of cold unreality wherewith he would go shivering through the world, longing to exchange his load of ice for any burden of real grief that fate could fling upon a human being."

Contenting himself with this preface, Roderick began to read.

In a certain old gentleman's last will and testament there appeared a bequest, which, as his final thought and deed, was singularly in keeping with a long life of melancholy eccentricity. He devised a considerable sum for establishing a fund, the interest of which was to be expended, annually, forever, in preparing a Christmas Banquet for ten of the most miserable persons that could be found. It seemed not to be the testator's purpose to make these half a score of sad hearts merry, but to provide that the stern or fierce expression of human discontent should not be drowned, even for that one holy and joyful day, amid the acclamations of festival gratitude which all Christendom sends up. And he desired, likewise, to perpetuate his own remonstrance against the earthly course of Providence, and his sad and sour dissent from those systems of religion or philosophy which either find sunshine in the world or draw it down from heaven.

The task of inviting the guests, or of selecting among such as might advance their claims to partake of this dismal hospitality, was confided to the two trustees or stewards of the fund. These gentlemen, like their deceased friend, were somber humorists, who made it their principal occupation to number the sable threads in the web of human life, and drop all the golden ones out of the reckoning. They performed their present office with integrity and judgment. The aspect of the assembled company, on the day of the first festival, might not, it is true, have satisfied every beholder that these were especially the individuals, chosen forth from all the world, whose griefs were worthy to stand as indicators of the mass of human suffering. Yet, after due consideration, it could not be disputed that here was a variety of hopeless discomfort, which, if it sometimes arose from causes apparently inadequate, was thereby only the shrewder imputation against the nature and mechanism of life.

The arrangements and decorations of the banquet were probably intended to signify that death in life which had been the testator's definition of existence. The hall, illuminated by torches, was hung round with curtains of deep and dusky purple, and adorned with branches of cypress and wreaths of artificial flowers, imitative of such as used to be strewn over the dead. A sprig of parsley was laid by every plate. The main reservoir of wine was a sepulchral urn of silver, whence the liquor was distributed around the table in small vases, accurately copied from those that held the tears of ancient mourners. Neither had the stewards—if it were their taste that arranged these details—forgotten the fantasy of the old Egyptians, who seated a skeleton at every festive board, and mocked their own merriment with the imperturbable grin of a death's head. Such a fearful guest, shrouded in a black mantle, sat now at the head of the table. It was whispered, I know not with what truth, that the testator himself had once walked the visible world with the machinery of that same skeleton, and that it was one of the stipulations of his will, that he should thus be permitted to sit, from year to year, at the banquet which he had instituted. If so, it was perhaps covertly implied that he had cherished no hopes of bliss beyond the grave to compensate for the evils which he felt or imagined here. And if, in their bewildered conjectures as to the purpose of earthly existence, the banqueters should throw aside the veil, and cast an inquiring glance at this figure of death, as seeking thence the solution otherwise unattainable, the only reply would be a stare of the vacant eye caverns and a grin of the skeleton jaws. Such was the response that the dead man had fancied himself to receive when he asked of Death to solve the riddle of his life; and it was his desire to repeat it when the guests of his dismal hospitality should find themselves perplexed with the same question.

"What means that wreath?" asked several of the company, while viewing the decorations of the table.

They alluded to a wreath of cypress, which was held on high by a skeleton arm, protruding from within the black mantle.

"It is a crown," said one of the stewards, "not for the worthiest, but for the woefullest, when he shall prove his claim to it."

The guest earliest bidden to the festival was a man of soft and gentle character, who had not energy to struggle against the heavy despondency to which his temperament rendered him liable; and therefore with nothing outwardly to excuse him from happiness, he had spent a life of quiet misery that made his blood torpid, and weighed upon his breath, and sat like a ponderous night fiend upon every throb of his unresisting heart. His wretchedness seemed as deep as his original nature, if not identical with it. It was the misfortune of a second guest to cherish within his bosom a diseased heart, which had become so wretchedly sore that the continual and unavoidable rubs of the world, the blow of an enemy, the careless jostle of a stranger, and even the faithful and loving touch of a friend, alike made ulcers in it. As is the habit of people thus afflicted, he found his chief employment in exhibiting these miserable sores to any who would give themselves the pain of viewing them. A third guest was a hypochondriac, whose imagination wrought necromancy in his outward and inward world, and caused him to see monstrous faces in the household fire, and dragons in the clouds of sunset, and fiends in the guise of beautiful women, and something ugly or wicked beneath all the pleasant surfaces of nature. His neighbor at table was one who, in his early youth, had trusted mankind too much, and hoped too highly in their behalf, and, in meeting with many disappointments, had become desperately soured. For several years back this misanthrope had employed himself in accumulating motives for hating and despising his race—such as murder, lust, treachery, ingratitude, faithlessness of trusted friends, instinctive vices of children, impurity of women, hidden guilt in men of saintlike aspect—and, in short, all manner of black realities that sought to decorate themselves with outward grace or glory. But at every atrocious fact that was added to his catalog, at every increase of the sad knowledge which he spent his life to collect, the native impulses of the poor man's loving and confiding heart made him groan with anguish. Next, with his heavy brown bent downward, there stole into the hall a man naturally earnest and impassioned, who, from his immemorial infancy, had felt the consciousness of a high message to the world; but essaying to deliver it, had found either no voice or form of speech, or else no ears to listen. Therefore his whole life was a bitter questioning of himself—"Why have not men acknowledged my mission? Am I not a self-deluding fool? What business have I on earth? Where is my grave?" Throughout the festival, he quaffed frequent draughts from the sepulchral urn of wine, hoping thus to quench the celestial fire that tortured his own breast and could not benefit his race.

Then there entered, having flung away a ticket for a ball, a gay gallant of yesterday, who had found four or five wrinkles in his brow, and more gray hairs than he could well number on his head. Endowed with sense and feeling, he had nevertheless spent his youth in folly, but had reached at last that dreary point in life where Folly quits us of her own accord, leaving us to make friends of Wisdom if we can. Thus, cold and desolate, he had come to seek Wisdom at the banquet, and wondered if the skeleton were she. To eke out the company, the stewards had invited a distressed poet from his home in the almshouse, and a melancholy idiot from the street corner. The latter had just the glimmering of sense that was sufficient to make him conscious of a vacancy, which the poor fellow, all his life long, had mistily sought to fill up with intelligence, wandering up and down the streets, and groaning miserably because his attempts were ineffectual. The only lady in the hall was one who had fallen short of absolute and perfect beauty, merely by the trifling defect of a slight cast in her left eye. But this blemish, minute as it was, so shocked the pure ideal of her soul, rather than her vanity, that she passed her life in solitude, and veiled her countenance even from her own gaze. So the skeleton sat shrouded at one end of the table and this poor lady at the other.

One other guest remains to be described. He was a young man of smooth brow, fair cheek, and fashionable mien. So far as his exterior developed him, he might much more suitably have found a place at some merry Christmas table, than have been numbered among the blighted, fate-stricken, fancy-tortured set of ill-starred banqueters. Murmurs arose among the guests as they noted the glance of general scrutiny which the intruder threw over his companions. What had he to do among them? Why did not the skeleton of the dead founder of the feast unbend its rattling joints, arise, and motion the unwelcome stranger from the board?

"Shameful!" said the morbid man, while a new ulcer broke out in his heart. "He comes to mock us!—we shall be the jest of his tavern friends!—he will make a farce of our miseries, and bring it out upon the stage!"

"O, never mind him!" said the hypochondriac, smiling sourly. "He shall feast from yonder tureen of viper soup; and if there is a fricassee of scorpions on the table, pray let him have his share of it. For the dessert, he shall taste the apples of Sodom. Then, if he likes our Christmas fare, let him return again next year!"

"Trouble him not," murmured the melancholy man, with

gentleness. "What matters it whether the consciousness of misery comes a few years sooner or later? If this youth deem himself happy now, yet let him sit with us for the sake of the wretchedness to come."

The poor idiot approached the young man with that mournful aspect of vacant inquiry which his face continually wore, and which caused people to say that he was always in search of his missing wits. After no little examination he touched the stranger's hand, but immediately drew back his own, shaking his head and shivering.

"Cold, cold, cold!" muttered the idiot.

The young man shivered too, and smiled.

"Gentlemen—and you, madam,"—said one of the stewards of the festival, "do not conceive so ill either of our caution or judgment, as to imagine that we have admitted this young stranger—Gervayse Hastings by name—without a full investigation and thoughtful balance of his claims. Trust me, not a guest at the table is better entitled to his seat."

The steward's guarantee was perforce satisfactory. The company, therefore, took their places, and addressed themselves to the serious business of the feast, but were soon disturbed by the hypochondriac, who thrust back his chair, complaining that a dish of stewed toads and vipers was set before him, and that there was green ditch water in his cup of wine. This mistake being amended, he quietly resumed his seat. The wine, as it flowed freely from the sepulchral urn, seemed to come imbued with all gloomy inspirations; so that its influence was not to cheer, but either to sink the revelers into a deeper melancholy, or elevate their spirits to an enthusiasm of wretchedness. The conversation was various. They told sad stories about people who might have been worthy guests at such a festival as the present. They talked of grisly incidents in human history; of strange crimes, which, if truly considered, were but convulsions of agony; of some lives that had been altogether wretched, and of others, which, wearing a general semblance of happiness, had yet been deformed, sooner or later, by misfortune, as by the intrusion of a grim face at a banquet; of death-bed scenes, and what dark intimations might be gathered from the words of dying men; of suicide, and whether the more eligible modes were by halter, knife, poison, drowning, gradual starvation, or the fumes of charcoal. The majority of the guests, as is the custom with people thoroughly and profoundly sick at heart, were anxious to make their own woes the theme of discussion, and prove themselves most excellent in anguish. The misanthropist went deep into the philosophy of evil, and wandered about in the darkness, with now and then a gleam of discolored light hovering on ghastly shapes and horrid scenery. Many a miserable thought, such as men have stumbled upon from age to age, did he now rake up again, and gloat over it as an inestimable gem, a diamond, a treasure far preferable to those bright, spiritual revelations of a better world, which are like precious stones from heaven's pavement. And then, amid his lore of wretchedness, he hid his face and wept.

It was a festival at which the woeful man of Uz might suitably have been a guest, together with all, in each succeeding age, who have tasted deepest of the bitterness of life. And be it said, too, that every son or daughter of woman, however favored with happy fortune, might, at one sad moment or another, have claimed the privilege of a stricken heart, to sit down at this table. But, throughout the feast, it was remarked that the young stranger, Gervayse Hastings, was unsuccessful in his attempts to catch its pervading spirit. At any deep, strong thought that found utterance, and which was torn out, as it were, from the saddest recesses of human consciousness, he looked mystified and bewildered; even more than the poor idiot, who seemed to grasp at such things with his earnest heart, and thus occasionally to comprehend them. The young man's conversation was of a colder and lighter kind, often brilliant, but lacking the powerful characteristics of a nature that had been developed by suffering.

"Sir," said the misanthropist bluntly, in reply to some observation by Gervayse Hastings, "pray do not address me again. We have no right to talk together. Our minds have nothing in common. By what claim you appear at this banquet I cannot guess; but methinks, to a man who could say what you have just now said, my companions and myself must seem no more than shadows flickering on the wall. And precisely such a shadow are you to us."

The young man smiled and bowed, but drawing himself back in his chair, he buttoned his coat over his breast, as if the banqueting hall were growing chill. Again the idiot fixed his melancholy stare upon the youth, and murmured, "Cold! cold! cold!"

The banquet drew to its conclusion, and the guests departed. Scarcely had they stepped across the threshold of the hall when the scene that had there passed seemed like the vision of a sick fancy, or an exhalation from a stagnant heart. Now and then, however, during the year that ensued, these melancholy people caught glimpses of one another, transient, indeed, but enough to prove that they walked the earth with the ordinary allotment of reality. Sometimes a pair of them came face to face while stealing through the evening twilight, enveloped in their sable cloaks. Sometimes they casually met in churchyards. Once, also, it happened that two of the dismal banqueters mutually started at recognizing each other in the noonday sunshine of a crowded street, stalking there like ghosts astray. Doubtless they wondered why the skeleton did not come abroad at noonday too.

But whenever the necessity of their affairs compelled these Christmas guests into the bustling world, they were sure to encounter the young man who had so unaccountably been admitted to the festival. They saw him among the gay and fortunate; they caught the sunny sparkle of his eye; they heard the light and careless tones of his voice, and muttered to themselves with such indignation as only the aristocracy of wretchedness could kindle—"The traitor! The vile imposter! Providence, in its own good time, may give him a right to feast among us!" But the young man's unabashed eye dwelt upon their gloomy figures as they passed him, seeming to say, perchance with somewhat of a sneer, "First, know my secret!—then measure your claims with mine!"

The step of Time stole onward, and soon brought merry Christmas round again, with glad and solemn worship in the churches, and sports, games, festivals, and everywhere the bright face of Joy beside the household fire. Again, likewise, the hall, with its curtains of dusky purple, was illuminated by the death torches gleaming on the sepulchral decorations of the banquet. The veiled skeleton sat in state, lifting the cypress wreath above its head, as the guerdon of some guest illustrious in the qualifications which there claimed precedence. As the stewards deemed the world inexhaustible in misery, and were desirous of recognizing it in all its forms, they had not seen fit to reassemble the company of the former year. New faces now threw their gloom across the table.

There was a man of nice conscience, who bore a blood stain in his heart—the death of a fellow-creature—which, for his more exquisite torture, had chanced with such a peculiarity of circumstances, that he could not absolutely determine whether his will had entered into the deed or not. Therefore, his whole life was spent in the agony of an inward trial for murder, with a continual sifting of the details of his terrible calamity, until his mind had no longer any thought, nor his soul any emotion, disconnected with it. There was a mother, too—a mother once, but a desolation now—who, many years before, had gone out on a pleasure party, and, returning, found her infant smothered in its little bed. And ever since she has been tortured with the fantasy that her buried baby lay smothering in its coffin. Then there was an aged lady, who had lived from time immemorial with a constant tremor quivering through her frame. It was terrible to discern her dark shadow tremulous upon the wall; her lips, likewise, were tremulous; and the expression of her eye seemed to indicate that her soul was trembling, too. Owing to the bewilderment and confusion which made almost a chaos of her intellect, it was impossible to discover what dire misfortune had thus shaken her nature to its depths; so that the stewards had admitted her to the table, not from any acquaintance with her history, but on the safe testimony of her miserable aspect. Some surprise was expressed at the presence of a bluff, red-faced gentleman, a certain Mr. Smith, who had evidently the fat of many a rich feast within him, and the habitual twinkle of whose eye betrayed a disposition to break forth into uproarious laughter for little cause or none. It turned out, however, that with the best possible flow of spirits, our poor friend was afflicted with a physical disease of the heart, which threatened instant death on the slightest cachinnatory indulgence, or even that titillation of the bodily frame produced by merry thoughts. In this dilemma he had sought admittance to the banquet, on the ostensible plea of his irksome and miserable state, but, in reality, with the hope of imbibing a life-preserving melancholy.

A married couple had been invited from a motive of bitter humor, it being well understood that they rendered each other unutterably miserable whenever they chanced to meet, and therefore must necessarily be fit associates at the festival. In contrast with these was another couple still unmarried, who had interchanged their hearts in early life, but had been divided by circumstances as unpalpable as morning mist, and kept apart so long that their spirits now found it impossible to meet. Therefore, yearning for communion, yet shrinking from one another and choosing none beside, they felt themselves companionless in life, and looked upon eternity as a boundless desert. Next to the skeleton sat a mere son of earth—a hunter of the Exchange—a gatherer of shining dust—a man whose life's record was in his ledger, and whose soul's prisonhouse the vaults of the bank where he kept his deposits. This person had been greatly perplexed at his invitation, deeming himself one of the most fortunate men in the city; but the stewards persisted in demanding his presence, assuring him that he had no conception how miserable he was.

And now appeared a figure which we must acknowledge as our acquaintance of the former festival. It was Gervayse Hastings, whose presence had then caused so much question and criticism, and who now took his place with the composure of one whose claims were satisfactory to himself, and must needs be allowed by others. Yet his easy and unruffled face betrayed no sorrow. The well-skilled beholders gazed a moment into his eyes and shook their heads, to miss the unuttered sympathy—the countersign, never to be falsified—of those whose hearts are cavern mouths, through which they descend into a region of illimitable woe, and recognize other wanderers there.

"Who is this youth?" asked the man with a blood stain on his conscience. "Surely he has never gone down into the depths! I know all the aspects of those who have passed through the dark valley. By what right is he among us?"

"Ah, it is a sinful thing to come hither without a sorrow," murmured the aged lady, in accents that partook of the eternal tremor which pervaded her whole being. "Depart, young man! Your soul has never been shaken; and, therefore, I tremble so much the more to look at you."

"His soul shaken! No; I'll answer for it," said bluff Mr. Smith, pressing his hand upon his heart, and making himself as melancholy as he could, for fear of a fatal explosion of laughter. "I know the lad well; he has as fair prospects as any young man about town, and has no more right among us miserable creatures than the child unborn. He never was miserable, and probably never will be!"

"Our honored guests," interposed the stewards, "pray have patience with us, and believe, at least, that our deep veneration for the sacredness of this solemnity would preclude any willful violation of it. Receive this young man to your table. It may not be too much to say that no guest here would exchange his own heart for the one that beats within that youthful bosom!"

"I'd call it a bargain, and gladly, too," muttered Mr. Smith, with a perplexing mixture of sadness and mirthful conceit. "A plague upon their nonsense! My own heart is the only really miserable one in the company; it will certainly be the death of me at last!"

Nevertheless, as on the former occasion, the judgment of the stewards being without appeal, the company sat down. The obnoxious guest made no more attempt to obtrude his conversation on those about him, but appeared to listen to the table talk with peculiar assiduity, as if some inestimable secret, otherwise beyond his reach, might be conveyed in a casual word. And in truth, to those who could understand and value it, there was rich matter in the upgushings and outpourings of these initiated souls to whom sorrow had been a talisman, admitting them into spiritual depths which no other spell can open. Sometimes out of the midst of densest gloom there flashed a momentary radiance, pure as crystal, bright as the flame of stars, and shedding such a glow upon the mysteries of life that the guests were ready to exclaim, "Surely the riddle is on the point of being solved!" At such illuminated intervals the saddest mourners felt it to be revealed that mortal griefs are but shadowy and external; no more than the sable robes voluminously shrouding a certain divine reality, and thus indicating what might otherwise be altogether invisible to mortal eye.

"Just now," remarked the trembling old woman, "I seemed to see beyond the outside. And then my everlasting tremor passed away!"

"Would that I could dwell always in these momentary gleams of light!" said the man of stricken conscience. "Then the bloodstain in my heart would be washed clean away."

This strain of conversation appeared so unintelligibly absurd to good Mr. Smith, that he burst into precisely the fit of laughter which his physicians had warned him against, as likely to prove instantaneously fatal. In effect, he fell back in his chair a corpse, with a broad grin upon his face, while his ghost, perchance, remained beside it bewildered at its unpremeditated exit. This catastrophe, of course, broke up the festival.

"How is this? You do not tremble?" observed the tremulous old woman to Gervayse Hastings, who was gazing at the dead man with singular intentness. "Is it now awful to see him so suddenly vanish out of the midst of life—this man of flesh and blood, whose earthly nature was so warm and strong? There is a never-ending tremor in my soul, but it trembles afresh at this! And you are calm!"

"Would that he could teach me somewhat!" said Gervayse Hastings, drawing a long breath. "Men pass before me like shadows on the wall; their actions, passions, feelings, are flickerings of the light, and then they vanish! Neither the corpse, nor yonder skeleton, nor this old woman's everlasting tremor, can give me what I seek."

And then the company departed.

We cannot linger to narrate, in such detail, more circumstances of these singular festivals, which, in accordance with the founder's will, continued to be kept with the regularity of an established institution. In process of time the stewards adopted the custom of inviting, from far and near, those individuals whose misfortunes were prominent above other men's, and whose mental and moral development might, therefore, be supposed to possess a corresponding interest. The exiled noble of the French Revolution, and the broken soldier of the Empire, were alike represented at the table. Fallen monarchs, wandering about the earth, have found places at that forlorn and miserable feast. The statesman, when his party flung him off, might, if he chose it, be once more a great man for the space of a single banquet. Aaron Burr's name appears on the record at a period when his ruin—the profoundest and most striking, with more of moral circumstance in it than that of almost any other man—was complete in his lonely age. Stephen Girard, when his wealth weighed upon him like a mountain, once sought admittance of his own accord. It is not probable, however, that these men had any lesson to teach in the lore of discontent and misery which might not equally well have been studied in the common walks of life. Illustrious unfortunates attract a wider sympathy, not because their griefs are more intense, but because, being set on lofty pedestals, they the better serve mankind as instances and bywords of calamity.

It concerns our present purpose to say that, at each successive festival, Gervayse Hastings showed his face, gradually changing from the smooth beauty of his youth to the thoughtful comeliness of manhood, and thence to the bald, impressive dignity of age. He was the only individual invariably present. Yet on every occasion there were murmurs, both from those who knew his character and position, and from them whose hearts shrank back as denying his companionship in their mystic fraternity.

"Who is this impassive man?" had been asked a hundred times. "Has he suffered? Has he sinned? There are no traces of either. Then wherefore is he here?"

"You must inquire of the stewards or of himself," was the constant reply. "We seem to know him well here in our city, and know nothing of him but what is creditable and fortunate. Yet hither he comes, year after year, to this gloomy banquet, and sits among the guests like a marble statue. Ask yonder skeleton, perhaps that may solve the riddle!"

It was in truth a wonder. The life of Gervayse Hastings was not merely a prosperous, but a brilliant one. Everything had gone well with him. He was wealthy, far beyond the expenditure that was required by habits of magnificence, a taste of rare purity and cultivation, a love of travel, a scholar's instinct to collect a splendid library, and, moreover, what seemed a magnificent liberality to the distressed. He had sought happiness, and not vainly, if a lovely and tender wife, and children of fair promise, could insure it. He had, besides, ascended above the limit which separates the obscure from the distinguished, and had won a stainless reputation in affairs of the widest public importance. Not that he was a popular character, or had within him the mysterious attributes which are essential to that species of success. To the public he was a cold abstraction, wholly destitute of those rich hues of personality, that living warmth, and the peculiar faculty of stamping his own heart's impression on a multitude of hearts by which the people recognize their favorites. And it must be owned that after his most intimate associates had done their best to know him thoroughly and love him warmly, they were startled to find how little hold he had upon their affections. They approved, they admired, but still in those moments when the human spirit most craves reality, they shrank back from Gervayse Hastings, as powerless to give them what they sought. It was the feeling of distrustful regret with which we should draw back the hand after extending it, in an illusive twilight, to grasp the hand of a shadow upon the wall.

As the superficial fervency of youth decayed, this peculiar effect of Gervayse Hastings's character grew more perceptible. His children, when he extended his arms, came coldly to his knees, but never climbed them of their own accord. His wife wept secretly, and almost adjudged herself a criminal because she shivered in the chill of his bosom. He, too, occasionally appeared not unconscious of the chillness of his moral atmosphere, and willing, if it might be so, to warm himself at a kindly fire. But age stole onward and benumbed him more and more. As the hoarfrost began to gather on him, his wife went to her grave, and was doubtless warmer there; his children either died or were scattered to different homes of their own; and old Gervayse Hastings, unscathed by grief—alone, but needing no companionship—continued his steady walk through life, and still on every Christmas day attended at the dismal banquet. His privilege as a guest had become prescriptive now. Had he claimed the head of the table, even the skeleton would have been ejected from its seat.

Finally, at the merry Christmas tide, when he had numbered fourscore years complete, this pale, high-browed, marble-featured old man once more entered the long-frequented hall, with the same impassive aspect that had called forth so much dissatisfied remark at his first attendance. Time, except in matters merely external, had done nothing for him, either of good or evil. As he took his place, he threw a calm, inquiring glance around the table, as if to ascertain whether any guest had yet appeared, after so many unsuccessful banquets, who might impart to him the mystery—the deep, warm secret—the life within the life—which, whether manifested in joy or sorrow, is what gives substance to a world of shadows.

"My friends," said Gervayse Hastings, assuming a position which his long conversance with the festival caused to appear natural, "you are welcome! I drink to you all in this cup of sepulchral wine."

The guests replied courteously, but still in a manner that proved them unable to receive the old man as a member of their sad fraternity. It may be well to give the reader an idea of the present company at the banquet.

One was formerly a clergyman, enthusiastic in his profession, and apparently of the genuine dynasty of those old puritan divines whose faith in their calling, and stern exercise of it, had placed them among the mighty of the earth. But yielding to the speculative tendency of the age, he had gone astray from the firm foundation of an ancient faith, and wandered into a cloud region, where everything was misty and deceptive, ever mocking him with a semblance of reality, but still dissolving when he flung himself upon it for support and rest. His instinct and early training demanded something steadfast; but, looking forward, he beheld vapors piled on vapors, and behind him an impassable gulf between the man of yesterday and today, on the borders of which he paced to and fro, sometimes wringing his hands in agony, and often making his own woe a theme of scornful merriment. This surely was a miserable man. Next, there was a theorist—one of a numerous tribe, although he deemed himself unique since the creation—a theorist who had conceived a plan by which all the wretchedness of earth, moral and physical, might be done away, and the bliss of the millennium at once accomplished. But the incredulity of mankind debaring him from action, he was smitten with as much grief as if the whole mass of woe which he was denied the opportunity to remedy were crowded into his own bosom. A plain old man in black attracted much of the company's notice, on the supposition that he was no other than Father Miller, who, it seemed, had given himself up to despair at the tedious delay of the final conflagration. Then there was a man distinguished for native pride and obstinacy, who, a little while before, had possessed immense wealth, and held the control of a vast moneyed interest which he had wielded in the same spirit as a despotic monarch would wield the power of his empire, carrying on a tremendous moral warfare, the roar and tremor of which was felt at every fireside in the land. At length came a crushing ruin—a total overthrow of fortune, power, and character—the effect of which on his imperious and, in many respects, noble and lofty nature, might have entitled him to a place, not merely at our festival, but among the peers of Pandemonium.

There was a modern philanthropist, who had become so deeply sensible of the calamities of thousands and millions of his fellow-creatures, and of the impracticableness of any general measures for their relief, that he had no heart to do what little good lay immediately within his power, but contented himself with being miserable for sympathy. Near him sat a gentleman in a predicament hitherto unprecedented, but of which the present epoch probably affords numerous examples. Ever since he was of capacity to read a newspaper, this person had prided himself on his consistent adherence to one political party, but, in the confusion of these latter days, had got bewildered and knew not whereabouts his party was. This wretched condition, so morally desolate and disheartening to a man who has long accustomed himself to merge his individuality in the mass of a great body, can only be conceived by such as have experienced it. His next companion was a popular orator who had lost his voice, and—as it was pretty much all that he had to lose—had fallen into a state of hopeless melancholy. The table was likewise graced by two of the gentler sex—one, a half-starved, consumptive seamstress, the representative of thousands just as wretched; the other, a woman of unemployed energy, who found herself in the world with nothing to achieve, nothing to enjoy, and nothing even to suffer. She had, therefore, driven herself to the verge of madness by dark broodings over the wrongs of her sex and its exclusion from a proper field of action. The roll of guests being thus complete, a side table had been set for three or four disappointed office seekers, with hearts as sick as death, whom the stewards had admitted partly because their calamities really entitled them to entrance here, and partly that they were in especial need of a good dinner. There was likewise a homeless dog, with his tail between his legs, licking up the crumbs and gnawing the fragments of the feast; such a melancholy air as one sometimes sees about the streets without a master, and willing to follow the first that will accept his service.

In their own way, these were as wretched a set of people as ever had assembled at the festival. There they sat, with the veiled skeleton of the founder holding aloft the cypress wreath, at one end of the table, and at the other, wrapped in furs, the withered figure of Gervayse Hastings, stately, calm, and cold, impressing the company with awe, yet so little interesting their sympathy that he might have vanished into thin air without their once exclaiming, "Whither is he gone?"

"Sir," said the philanthropist, addressing the old man, "you have been so long a guest at this annual festival, and have thus been conversant with so many varieties of human affliction, that, not improbably, you have thence derived some great and important lessons. How blessed were your lot could you reveal a secret by which all this mass of woe might be removed!"

"I know of but one misfortune," answered Gervayse Hastings, quietly, "and that is my own."

"Your own!" enjoined the philanthropist. "And, looking back on your serene and prosperous life, how can you claim to be the sole unfortunate of the human race?"

"You will not understand it," replied Gervayse Hastings, feebly, and with a singular inefficiency of pronunciation, and sometimes putting one word for another. "None have understood it—not even those who experience the like. It is a chillness—a want of earnestness—a feeling as if what should be my heart were a thing of vapor—a haunting perception of unreality! Thus seeming to possess all that other men have—all that men aim at—I have really possessed nothing, neither joy nor griefs. All things, all persons—as was truly said to me at this table long and long ago—have been like shadows flickering on the wall. It was so with my wife and children—with those who seemed my friends: it is so with yourselves, whom I see now before me. Neither have I myself any real existence, but am a shadow like the rest."

"And how is it with your views of a future life?" inquired the speculative clergyman.

"Worse than with you," said the old man, in a hollow and feeble tone; "for I cannot conceive it earnestly enough to feel either hope or fear. Mine—mine is the wretchedness! This cold heart—this unreal life! Ah! it grows colder still."

It so chanced that at this juncture the decayed ligaments of the skeleton gave way, and the dry bones fell together in a heap, thus causing the dusty wreath of cypress to drop upon the table. The attention of the company being thus diverted for a single instant from Gervayse Hastings, they perceived on turning again towards him that the old man had undergone a change. His shadow had ceased to flicker on the wall.

"Well, Rosina, what is your criticism?" asked Roderick, as he rolled up the manuscript.

"Frankly, your success is by no means complete," replied she. "It is true, I have an idea of the character you endeavor to describe; but it is rather by dint of my own thought than your expression."

"That is unavoidable," observed the sculptor, "because the characteristics are all negative. If Gervayse Hastings imbibed one human grief at the gloomy banquet, the task of describing him would have been infinitely easier. Of such persons—and we do meet with these moral monsters now and then—it is difficult to conceive how they came to exist here, or what there is in them capable of existence hereafter. They seem to be on the outside of everything; and nothing wearies the soul more than an attempt to comprehend them within its grasp."

MARJORIE BOWEN

THE CROWN DERBY PLATE

A china collector gets her wish . . . and wishes she hadn't.

MARTHA Pym said that she had never seen a ghost and that she would very much like to do so, "particularly at Christmas, for you can laugh as you like, that is the correct time to see a ghost."

"I don't suppose you ever will," replied her cousin Mabel comfortably, while her cousin Clara shuddered and said that she hoped they would change the subject for she disliked even to think of such things.

The three elderly, cheerful women sat round a big fire, cozy and content after a day of pleasant activities; Martha was the guest of the other two, who owned the handsome, convenient country house; she always came to spend her Christmas with the Wyntons and found the leisurely country life delightful after the bustling round of London, for Martha managed an antique shop of the better sort and worked extremely hard. She was, however, still full of zest for work or pleasure, though sixty years old, and looked backwards and forwards to a succession of delightful days.

The other two, Mabel and Clara, led quieter but nonetheless agreeable lives; they had more money and fewer interests, but nevertheless enjoyed themselves very well.

"Talking of ghosts," said Mabel, "I wonder how that old woman at 'Hartleys' is getting on, for 'Hartleys,' you know, is supposed to be haunted."

"Yes, I know," smiled Miss Pym, "but all the years that we have known of the place we have never heard anything definite, have we?"

"No," put in Clara; "but there *is* that persistent rumor that the house is uncanny, and for myself, *nothing* would induce me to live there!"

"It is certainly very lonely and dreary down there on the marshes," conceded Mabel. "But as for the ghost—you never hear *what* it is supposed to be even."

"Who has taken it?" asked Miss Pym, remembering "Hartleys" as very desolate indeed, and long shut up.

"A Miss Lefain, an eccentric old creature—I think you met her here once, two years ago—"

"I believe that I did, but I don't recall her at all."

"We have not seen her since, 'Hartleys' is so un-get-at-able and she didn't seem to want visitors. She collects china, Martha, so really you ought to go and see her and talk 'shop.' "

With the word "china" some curious associations came into the mind of Martha Pym; she was silent while she strove to put them together, and after a second or two they all fitted together into a very clear picture.

She remembered that thirty years ago—yes, it must be thirty years ago, when, as a young woman, she had put all her capital into the antique business, and had been staying with her cousins (her aunt had then been alive) that she had driven across the marsh to "Hartleys," where there was an auction sale; all the details of this she had completely forgotten, but she could recall quite clearly purchasing a set of gorgeous china which was still one of her proud delights, a perfect set of Crown Derby save that one plate was missing.

"How odd," she remarked, "that this Miss Lefain should collect china too, for it was at 'Hartleys' that I purchased my dear old Derby service—I've never been able to match that plate—"

"A plate was missing? I seem to remember," said Clara. "Didn't they say that it must be in the house somewhere and that it should be looked for?"

"I believe they did, but of course I never heard any more and that missing plate has annoyed me ever since. Who had 'Hartleys'?"

"An old connoisseur, Sir James Sewell; I believe he was some relation to this Miss Lefain, but I don't know—"

"I wonder if she has found the plate," mused Miss Pym. "I expect she has turned out and ransacked the whole place—"

"Why not trot over and ask?" suggested Mabel. "It's not much use to her, if she has found it, one odd plate."

"Don't be silly," said Clara. "Fancy going over the marshes, this weather, to ask about a plate missed all those years ago. I'm sure Martha wouldn't think of it—"

But Martha did think of it; she was rather fascinated by the idea; how queer and pleasant it would be if, after all these years, nearly a lifetime, she should find the Crown Derby plate, the loss of which had always irked her! And this hope did not seem so altogether fantastical, it was quite likely that old Miss Lefain, poking about in the ancient house, had found the missing piece.

And, of course, if she had, being a fellow-collector, she would be quite willing to part with it to complete the set.

Her cousin endeavored to dissuade her; Miss Lefain, she declared, was a recluse, an odd creature who might greatly resent such a visit and such a request.

"Well, if she does I can but come away again," smiled Miss

Pym. "I suppose she can't bite my head off, and I rather like meeting these curious types—we've got a love for old china in common, anyhow."

"It seems so silly to think of it—after all these years—a plate!"

"A Crown Derby plate," corrected Miss Pym. "It is certainly strange that I didn't think of it before, but now that I have got it into my head I can't get it out. Besides," she added hopefully, "I might see the ghost."

So full, however, were the days with pleasant local engagements that Miss Pym had no immediate chance of putting her scheme into practice; but she did not relinquish it, and she asked several different people what they knew about "Hartleys" and Miss Lefain.

And no one knew anything save that the house was supposed to be haunted and the owner "cracky."

"Is there a story?" asked Miss Pym, who associated ghosts with neat tales into which they fitted as exactly as nuts into shells.

But she was always told: "Oh, no, there isn't a story, no one knows anything about the place, don't know how the idea got about; old Sewell was half-crazy, I believe, he was buried in the garden and that gives a house a nasty name—"

"Very unpleasant," said Martha Pym, undisturbed.

This ghost seemed too elusive for her to track down; she would have to be content if she could recover the Crown Derby plate; for that at least she was determined to make a try and also to satisfy that faint tingling of curiosity roused in her by this talk about "Hartleys" and the remembrance of that day, so long ago, when she had gone to the auction sale at the lonely old house.

So the first free afternoon, while Mabel and Clara were comfortably taking their afternoon repose, Martha Pym, who was of a more lively habit, got out her little governess cart and dashed away across the Essex flats.

She had taken minute directions with her, but she had soon lost her way.

Under the wintry sky, which looked as gray and hard as metal, the marshes stretched bleakly to the horizon, the olive-brown broken reeds were harsh as scars on the saffron-tinted bogs, where the sluggish waters that rose so high in winter were filmed over with the first stillness of a frost; the air was cold but not keen, everything was damp; faintest of mists blurred the black outlines of trees that rose stark from the ridges above the stagnant dykes; the flooded fields were haunted by black birds and white birds, gulls and crows, whining above the long ditch grass and wintry wastes.

Miss Pym stopped the little horse and surveyed this spectral scene, which had a certain relish about it to one sure to return to a homely village, a cheerful house and good company.

A withered and bleached old man, in color like the dun landscape, came along the road between the sparse alders.

Miss Pym, buttoning up her coat, asked the way to "Hartley," as he passed her; he told her, straight on, and she proceeded, straight indeed across the road that went with undeviating length across the marshes.

"Of course," thought Miss Pym, "if you live in a place like this, you are bound to invent ghosts."

The house sprang up suddenly on a knoll ringed with rotting trees, encompassed by an old brick wall that the perpetual damp had overrun with lichen, blue, green, white colors of decay.

"Hartleys," no doubt, there was no other residence of human being in sight in all the wide expanse; besides, she could remember it, surely, after all this time, the sharp rising out of the marsh, the colony of tall trees, but then fields and trees had been green and bright—there had been no water on the flats, it had been summertime.

"She certainly," thought Miss Pym, "must be crazy to live here. And I rather doubt if I shall get my plate."

She fastened up the good little horse by the garden gate which stood negligently ajar and entered; the garden itself was so neglected that it was quite surprising to see a trim appearance in the house, curtains at the window and a polish on the brass door knocker, which must have been recently rubbed there, considering the taint in the sea damp which rusted and rotted everything.

It was a square-built, substantial house with "nothing wrong with it but the situation," Miss Pym decided, though it was not very attractive, being built of that drab plastered stone so popular a hundred years ago, with flat windows and door, while one side was gloomily shaded by a large evergreen tree of the cypress variety which gave a blackish tinge to that portion of the garden.

There was no pretense at flowerbeds nor any manner of cultivation in this garden where a few rank weeds and straggling bushes matted together above the dead grass; on the enclosing wall which appeared to have been built high as protection against the ceaseless winds that swung along the flats were the remains of fruit trees; their crucified branches, rotting under the great nails that held them up, looked like the skeletons of those who had died in torment.

Miss Pym took in these noxious details as she knocked firmly at the door; they did not depress her; she merely felt extremely sorry for anyone who could live in such a place.

She noticed, at the far end of the garden, in the corner of the wall, a headstone showing above the sodden colorless grass, and remembered what she had been told about the old antiquary being buried there, in the grounds of "Hartleys."

As the knock had no effect she stepped back and looked at the house; it was certainly inhabited—with those neat windows, white curtains and drab blinds all pulled to precisely the same level.

And when she brought her glance back to the door she saw that it had been opened and that someone, considerably obscured by the darkness of the passage, was looking at her intently.

"Good afternoon," said Miss Pym cheerfully. "I just thought that I would call to see Miss Lefain—it is Miss Lefain, isn't it?"

"It's my house," was the querulous reply.

Martha Pym had hardly expected to find any servants here, though the old lady must, she thought, work pretty hard to keep the house so clean and tidy as it appeared to be.

"Of course," she replied. "May I come in? I'm Martha Pym, staying with the Wyntons, I met you there—"

"Do come in," was the faint reply. "I get so few people to visit me, I'm really very lonely."

"I don't wonder," thought Miss Pym; but she had resolved to take no notice of any eccentricity on the part of her hostess, and so she entered the house with her usual agreeable candor and courtesy.

The passage was badly lit, but she was able to get a fair idea of Miss Lefain; her first impression was that this poor creature was most dreadfully old, older than any human being had the right to be, why, she felt young in comparison—so faded, feeble, and pallid was Miss Lefain.

She was also monstrously fat; her gross, flaccid figure was shapeless and she wore a badly cut, full dress of no color at all, but stained with earth and damp where Miss Pym supposed she had been doing futile gardening; this gown was doubtless designed to disguise her stoutness, but had been so carelessly pulled about that it only added to it, being rucked and rolled "all over the place" as Miss Pym put it to herself.

Another ridiculous touch about the appearance of the poor old lady was her short hair; decrepit as she was, and lonely as she lived she had actually had her scanty relics of white hair cropped round her shaking head.

"Dear me, dear me," she said in her thin treble voice. "How very kind of you to come. I suppose you prefer the parlor? I generally sit in the garden."

"The garden? But not in this weather?"

"I get used to the weather. You've no idea how used one gets to the weather."

"I suppose so," conceded Miss Pym doubtfully. "You don't live here quite alone, do you?"

"Quite alone, lately. I had a little company, but she was taken away, I'm sure I don't know where. I haven't been able to find a trace of her anywhere," replied the old lady peevishly.

"Some wretched companion that couldn't stick it, I suppose," thought Miss Pym. "Well, I don't wonder—but someone ought to be here to look after her."

They went into the parlor, which, the visitor was dismayed to see, was without a fire but otherwise well kept.

And there, on dozens of shelves was a choice array of china at which Martha Pym's eyes glistened.

"Aha!" cried Miss Lefain. "I see you've noticed my treasures! Don't you envy me? Don't you wish that you had some of those pieces?"

Martha Pym certainly did and she looked eagerly and greedily round the walls, tables, and cabinets while the old woman followed her with little thin squeals of pleasure.

It was a beautiful little collection, most choicely and elegantly arranged, and Martha thought it marvelous that this feeble ancient creature should be able to keep it in such precise order as well as doing her own housework.

"Do you really do everything yourself here and live quite alone?" she asked, and she shivered even in her thick coat and wished that Miss Lefain's energy had risen to a fire, but then probably she lived in the kitchen, as these lonely eccentrics often did.

"There was someone," answered Miss Lefain cunningly, "but I had to send her away. I told you she's gone, I can't find her, and I am so glad. Of course," she added wistfully, "it leaves me very lonely, but then I couldn't stand her impertinence any longer. She used to say that it was *her* house and her collection of china! Would you believe it? She used to try to chase me away from looking at my own things!"

"How very disagreeable," said Miss Pym, wondering which of the two women had been crazy. "But hadn't you better get someone else."

"Oh, no," was the jealous answer. "I would rather be alone with my things, I daren't leave the house for fear someone takes them away—there was a dreadful time once when an auction sale was held here—"

"Were you here then?" asked Miss Pym; but indeed she looked old enough to have been anywhere.

"Yes, of course," Miss Lefain replied rather peevishly and Miss Pym decided that she must be a relation of old Sir James Sewell. Clara and Mabel had been very foggy about it all. "I was very busy hiding all the china—but one set they got—a Crown Derby tea service—"

"With one plate missing!" cried Martha Pym. "I bought it, and do you know, I was wondering if you'd found it—"

"I hid it," piped Miss Lefain.

"Oh, you did, did you? Well, that's rather funny behavior. Why did you hide the stuff away instead of buying it?"

"How could I buy what was mine?"

"Old Sir James left it to you, then?" asked Martha Pym, feeling very muddled.

"*She* bought a lot more," squeaked Miss Lefain, but Martha Pym tried to keep her to the point.

"If you've got the plate," she insisted, "you might let me have it—I'll pay quite handsomely, it would be so pleasant to have it after all these years."

"Money is no use to me," said Miss Lefain mournfully. "Not a bit of use. I can't leave the house or the garden."

"Well, you have to live, I suppose," replied Martha Pym cheerfully. "And, do you know, I'm afraid you are getting rather morbid and dull, living here all alone—you really ought to have a fire—why, it's just on Christmas and very damp."

"I haven't felt the cold for a long time," replied the other; she seated herself with a sigh on one of the horsehair chairs and Miss Pym noticed with a start that her feet were covered only by a pair of white stockings; "one of those nasty health fiends," thought Miss Pym, "but she doesn't look too well for all that."

"So you don't think that you could let me have the plate?" she asked briskly, walking up and down, for the dark, neat, clean parlor was very cold indeed, and she thought that she couldn't stand this much longer; as there seemed no sign of tea or anything pleasant and comfortable she had really better go.

"I might let you have it," sighed Miss Lefain, "since you've been so kind as to pay me a visit. After all, one plate isn't much use, is it?"

"Of course not, I wonder you troubled to hide it—"

"I couldn't *bear,*" wailed the other, "to see the things going out of the house!"

Martha Pym couldn't stop to go into all this; it was quite clear that the old lady was very eccentric indeed and that nothing very much could be done with her; no wonder that she had "dropped out" of everything and that no one ever saw her or knew anything about her, though Miss Pym felt that some effort ought really to be made to save her from herself.

"Wouldn't you like a run in my little governess cart?" she suggested. "We might go to tea with the Wyntons on the way back, they'd be delighted to see you, and I really think that you do want taking out of yourself."

"I was taken out of myself some time ago," replied Miss Lefain. "I really was, and I couldn't leave my things—though," she added with pathetic gratitude, "it is very, very kind of you—"

"Your things would be quite safe, I'm sure," said Martha Pym, humoring her. "Who ever would come up here, this hour of a winter's day?"

"They do, oh, they do! And *she* might come back, prying and nosing and saying that it was all hers, all my beautiful china, hers!"

Miss Lefain squealed in her agitation and rising up, ran round the wall fingering with flaccid yellow hands the brilliant glossy pieces on the shelves.

"Well, then, I'm afraid that I must go, they'll be expecting me, and it's quite a long ride; perhaps some other time you'll come and see us?"

"Oh, must you go?" quavered Miss Lefain dolefully. "I do like a little company now and then and I trusted you from the first—the others, when they do come, are always after my things and I have to frighten them away!"

"Frighten them away!" replied Martha Pym. "However do you do that?"

"It doesn't seem difficult, people are so easily frightened, aren't they?"

Miss Pym suddenly remembered that "Hartleys" had the reputation of being haunted—perhaps the queer old thing played on that; the lonely house with the grave in the garden was dreary enough around which to create a legend.

"I suppose you've never seen a ghost?" she asked pleasantly. "I'd rather like to see one, you know—"

"There is no one here but myself," said Miss Lefain.

"So you've never seen anything? I thought it must be all nonsense. Still, I do think it rather melancholy for you to live here all alone—"

Miss Lefain sighed:

"Yes, it's very lonely. Do stay and talk to me a little longer." Her whistling voice dropped cunningly. "And I'll give you the Crown Derby plate!"

"Are you sure you've really got it?" Miss Pym asked.

"I'll show you."

Fat and waddling as she was, she seemed to move very lightly as she slipped in front of Miss Pym and conducted her from the room, going slowly up the stairs—such a gross odd figure in that clumsy dress with the fringe of white hair hanging on to her shoulders.

The upstairs of the house was as neat as the parlor, everything well in its place; but there was no sign of occupancy; the beds were covered with dust sheets, there were no lamps or fires set ready. "I suppose," said Miss Pym to herself, "she doesn't care to show me where she really lives."

But as they passed from one room to another, she could not help saying:

"Where *do* you live, Miss Lefain?"

"Mostly in the garden," said the other.

Miss Pym thought of those horrible health huts that some people indulged in.

"Well, sooner you than I," she replied cheerfully.

In the most distant room of all, a dark, tiny closet, Miss Lefain opened a deep cupboard and brought out a Crown Derby plate which her guest received with a spasm of joy, for it was actually that missing from her cherished set.

"It's very good of you," she said in delight. "Won't you take something for it, or let me do something for you?"

"You might come and see me again," replied Miss Lefain wistfully.

"Oh, yes, of course I should like to come and see you again."

But now that she had got what she had really come for, the plate, Martha Pym wanted to be gone; it was really very dismal and depressing in the house and she began to notice a fearful smell—the place had been shut up too long, there was something damp rotting somewhere, in this horrid little dark closet no doubt.

"I really must be going," she said hurriedly.

Miss Lefain turned as if to cling to her, but Martha Pym moved quickly away.

"Dear me," wailed the old lady. "Why are you in such haste?"

"There's—a smell," murmured Miss Pym rather faintly.

She found herself hastening down the stairs, with Miss Lefain complaining behind her.

"How peculiar people are—*she* used to talk of a smell—"

"Well, you must notice it yourself."

Miss Pym was in the hall; the old woman had not followed her, but stood in the semidarkness at the head of the stairs, a pale shapeless figure.

Martha Pym hated to be rude and ungrateful but she could not stay another moment; she hurried away and was in her cart in a moment—really—that smell—

"Good-bye!" she called out with false cheerfulness, "and thank you *so* much!"

There was no answer from the house.

Miss Pym drove on; she was rather upset and took another way than that by which she had come, a way that led past a little house raised above the marsh; she was glad to think that the poor old creature at "Hartleys" had such near neighbors, and she reined up the horse, dubious as to whether she should call someone and tell them that poor old Miss Lefain really wanted a little looking after, alone in a house like that, and plainly not quite right in her head.

A young woman, attracted by the sound of the governess cart, came to the door of the house and seeing Miss Pym called out, asking if she wanted the keys of the house?

"What house?" asked Miss Pym.

" 'Hartleys,' mum, they don't put a board out, as no one is likely to pass, but it's to be sold. Miss Lefain wants to sell or let it—"

"I've just been up to see her—"

"Oh, no, mum—she's been away a year, abroad somewhere, couldn't stand the place, it's been empty since then, I just run in every day and keep things tidy—"

Loquacious and curious the young woman had come to the fence; Miss Pym had stopped her horse.

"Miss Lefain is there now," she said. "She must have just come back—"

"She wasn't there this morning, mum, 'tisn't likely she'd come, either—fair scared she was, mum, fair chased away, didn't dare move her china. Can't say I've noticed anything myself, but I never stay long—and there's a smell—"

"Yes," murmured Martha Pym faintly, "there's a smell. What—what—chased her away?"

The young woman, even in that lonely place, lowered her voice.

"Well, as you aren't thinking of taking the place, she got an idea in her head that old Sir James—well, he couldn't bear to leave 'Hartleys,' mum, he's buried in the garden, and she thought he was after her, chasing round them bits of china—"

"Oh!" cried Miss Pym.

"Some of it used to be his, she found a lot stuffed away, he said they were to be left in 'Hartleys,' but Miss Lefain would have the things sold, I believe—that's years ago—"

"Yes, yes," said Miss Pym with a sick look. "You don't know what he was like, do you?"

"No, mum—but I've heard tell he was very stout and very old—I wonder who it was you saw up at 'Hartleys'?"

Miss Pym took a Crown Derby plate from her bag.

"You might take that back when you go," she whispered. "I shan't want it, after all—"

Before the astonished young woman could answer Miss Pym had darted off across the marsh; that short hair, that earth-stained robe, the white socks, "I generally live in the garden—"

Miss Pym drove away, breakneck speed, frantically resolving to mention to no one that she had paid a visit to "Hartleys," nor lightly again to bring up the subject of ghosts.

She shook and shuddered in the damp, trying to get out of her clothes and her nostrils—that indescribable smell.

Mrs. J.H. Riddell

A STRANGE CHRISTMAS GAME

A murder is reenacted by ghosts.

When, through the death of a distant relative, I, John Lester, succeeded to the Martingdale Estate, there could not have been found in the length and breadth of England a happier pair than myself and my only sister Clare.

We were not such utter hypocrites as to affect sorrow for the loss of our kinsman, Paul Lester, a man we had never seen, of whom we had heard but little, and that little unfavorable, at whose hands we had never received a single benefit—who was, in short, as great a stranger to us as the then Prime Minister, the Emperor of Russia, or any other human being utterly removed from our extremely humble sphere of life.

His loss was very certainly our gain. His death represented to us, not a dreary parting from one long loved and highly honored, but the accession of lands, houses, consideration, wealth, to myself—John Lester, Esquire, Martingdale, Bedfordshire: whilom, Jack Lester, artist and second-floor lodger at 32, Great Smith Street, Bloomsbury.

Not that Martingdale was much of an estate as county properties go. The Lesters who had succeeded to that domain from time to time during the course of a few hundred years, could by no stretch of courtesy have been called prudent men. In regard of their posterity they were, indeed, scarcely honest, for they parted with manors and farms, with common rights and advowsons, in a manner at once so baronial and so unbusinesslike, that Martingdale at length in the hands of Jeremy Lester, the last resident owner, melted to a mere little dot in the map of Bedfordshire.

Concerning this Jeremy Lester there was a mystery. No man could say what had become of him. He was in the oak parlor at Martingdale one Christmas eve, and before the next morning he had disappeared—to reappear in the flesh no more.

Over night, one Mr. Warley, a great friend and boon companion of Jeremy's, had sat playing cards with him until after twelve o'clock chimed, then he took leave of his host and rode home under the moonlight. After that, no person, as far as could be ascertained, ever saw Jeremy Lester alive.

His ways of life had not been either the most regular, or the most respectable, and it was not until a new year had come in without any tidings of his whereabouts reaching the house, that his servants became seriously alarmed concerning his absence.

Then inquiries were set on foot concerning him—inquiries which grew more urgent as weeks and months passed by without the slightest clue being obtained as to his whereabouts. Rewards were offered, advertisements inserted, but still Jeremy made no sign; and so in course of time the heir-at-law, Paul Lester, took possession of the house, and went down to spend the summer months at Martingdale with his rich wife, and her four children by a first husband. Paul Lester was a barrister—an overworked barrister, who, every one supposed would be glad enough to leave the bar and settle at Martingdale, where his wife's money and the fortune he had accumulated could not have failed to give him a good standing even among the neighboring county families; and perhaps it was with some such intention that he went down into Bedfordshire.

If this were so, however, he speedily changed his mind, for with the January snows he returned to London, let off the land surrounding the house, shut up the Hall, put in a caretaker, and never troubled himself further about his ancestral seat.

Time went on, and people began to say the house was haunted, that Paul Lester had "seen something," and so forth—all which stories were duly repeated for our benefit, when, forty-one years after the disappearance of Jeremy Lester, Clare and I went down to inspect our inheritance.

I say "our," because Clare had stuck bravely to me in poverty—grinding poverty, and prosperity was not going to part us now. What was mine was hers, and that she knew, God bless her, without my needing to tell her so.

The transition from rigid economy to comparative wealth, was in our case the more delightful also, because we had not in the least degree anticipated it. We never expected Paul Lester's shoes to come to us, and accordingly it was not upon our consciences that we had ever in our dreariest moods wished him dead.

Had he made a will, no doubt we never should have gone to Martingdale, and I, consequently, never written this story; but, luckily for us, he died intestate, and the Bedfordshire property came to me.

As for his fortune, he had spent it in traveling, and in giving great entertainments at his grand house in Portman Square. Concerning his effects, Mrs. Lester and I came to a very amicable arrangement, and she did me the honor of inviting me to call upon her occasionally, and, as I heard, spoke of me as a very worthy and presentable young man "for my station," which, of course, coming from so good an authority, was gratifying. Moreover, she asked me if I intended residing at Martingdale, and on my replying in the affirmative, hoped I should like it.

It struck me at the time that there was a certain significance in her tone, and when I went down to Martingdale and heard the absurd stories which were afloat concerning the house being haunted, I felt confident that if Mrs. Lester had hoped much, she feared more.

People said Mr. Jeremy "walked" at Martingdale. He had been seen, it was averred, by poachers, by gamekeepers, by children who had come to use the park as a near cut to school, by lovers who kept their tryst under the elms and beeches.

As for the caretaker and his wife, the third in residence since Jeremy Lester's disappearance, the man gravely shook his head when questioned, while the woman stated that wild horses, or even wealth untold, should not draw her into the red bedroom, nor into the oak parlor, after dark.

"I have heard my mother tell, sir—it was her as followed old Mrs. Reynolds, the first caretaker—how there were things went on in those self same rooms as might make any Christian's hair stand on end. Such stamping, and swearing, and knocking about of furniture; and then tramp, tramp, up the great staircase, and along the corridor and so into the red bedroom, and then bang, and tramp, tramp again. They do say, sir, Mr. Paul Lester met him once, and from that time the oak parlor has never been opened. I never was inside it myself."

Upon hearing which fact, the first thing I did was to proceed to the oak parlor, open the shutters, and let the August sun stream in upon the haunted chamber. It was an old-fashioned, plainly furnished apartment, with a large table in the center, a smaller in a recess by the fireplace, chairs ranged against the walls, and a dusty moth-eaten carpet on the floor. There were dogs on the hearth, broken and rusty; there was a brass fender, tarnished and battered; a picture of some sea-fight over the mantelpiece, while another work of art about equal in merit hung between the windows. Altogether, an utterly prosaic and yet not uncheerful apartment, from out of which the ghosts flitted as soon as daylight was let into it, and which I proposed, as soon as I "felt my feet," to redecorate, refurnish, and convert into a pleasant morning room. I was still under thirty, but I had learned prudence in that very good school, Necessity; and it was not my intention to spend much money until I ascertained for certain what were the actual revenues derivable from the lands still belonging to the Martingdale estates, and the charges upon them. In fact, I wanted to know what I was worth before committing myself to any great extravagance, and the place had for so long a time been neglected, that I experienced some difficulty in arriving at the state of my real income.

But in the meanwhile, Clare and I found great enjoyment in exploring every nook and corner of our domain, in turning over the contents of old chests and cupboards, in examining the faces of our ancestors looking down on us from the walls, in walking through the neglected gardens, full of weeds, overgrown with shrubs and birdweed, where the boxwood was eighteen inches high, and the shoots of the rose trees yards long. I have put the place in order since then, there is no grass on the paths, there are no trailing brambles over the ground, the hedges have been cut and trimmed, and the trees pruned, and the boxwood clipped; but I often say nowadays that spite of all my improvements, or rather in consequence of them, Martingdale does not look one half so pretty as it did in its pristine state of uncivilized picturesqueness.

Although I determined not to commence repairing and decorating the house till better informed concerning the rental of Martingdale, still the state of my finances was so far satisfactory that Clare and I decided on going abroad and take our long-talked-of holiday before the fine weather was past. We could not tell what a year might bring forth, as Clare sagely remarked; it was wise to take our pleasure while we could; and accordingly, before the end of August arrived we were wandering about the continent, loitering at Rouen, visiting the galleries in Paris, and talking of extending our one month of enjoyment to three. What decided me on this course was the circumstance of our becoming acquainted with an English family who intended wintering in Rome. We met accidentally, but discovering we were near neighbors in England—in fact, that Mr. Cronson's property lay close beside Martingdale—the slight acquaintance soon ripened into intimacy, and ere long we were traveling in company.

From the first, Clare did not much like this arrangement. There was "a little girl" in England she wanted me to marry, and Mr. Cronson had a daughter who certainly was both handsome and attractive. The little girl had not despised John Lester, artist, while Miss Cronson indisputably set her cap at John Lester of Martingdale, and would have turned away her pretty face from a poor man's admiring gaze—all this I can see plainly enough now, but I was blind then and should have proposed for Marybel—that was her name—before the winter was over, had news not suddenly arrived of the illness of Mrs. Cronson, senior. In a moment the program was changed; our pleasant days of foreign travel were at an end. The Cronsons packed up and departed, while Clare and I returned more slowly to England, a little out of humor, it must be confessed, with each other.

It was the middle of November when we arrived at Martingdale, and found the place anything but romantic or pleasant. The walks were wet and sodden, the trees were leafless, there were no flowers save a few late pink roses blooming in the garden.

It had been a wet season, and the place looked miserable. Clare would not ask Alice down to keep her company in the winter months, as she had intended; and for myself, the Cronsons were still absent in Norfolk, where they meant to spend Christmas with old Mrs. Cronson, now recovered.

Altogether, Martingdale seemed dreary enough, and the ghost stories we had laughed at while sunshine flooded the rooms, became less unreal, when we had nothing but blazing fires and wax candles to dispel the gloom. They became more real also when servant after servant left us to seek situations elsewhere; when "noises" grew frequent in the house; when we ourselves, Clare and I, with our own ears heard the tramp, tramp, the banging and the clattering which had been described to us.

My dear reader, you doubtless are utterly free from superstitious fancies. You pooh-pooh the existence of ghosts, and "only wish you could find a haunted house in which to spend a night," which is all very brave and praiseworthy, but wait till you are left in a dreary, desolate old country mansion, filled with the most unaccountable sounds, without a servant, with no one save an old caretaker and his wife, who, living at the extremest end of the building, heard nothing of the tramp, tramp, bang, bang, going on at all hours of the night.

At first I imagined the noises were produced by some evil-disposed persons, who wished, for purposes of their own, to keep the house uninhabited; but by degrees Clare and I came to the conclusion the visitation must be supernatural, and Martingdale by consequence untenantable. Still being practical people, and unlike our predecessors, not having money to live where and how we liked, we decided to watch and see whether we could trace any human influence in the matter. If not, it was agreed we were to pull down the right wing of the house and the principal staircase.

For nights and nights we sat up till two or three o'clock in the morning, Clare engaged in needlework, I reading, with a revolver lying on the table beside me; but nothing, neither sound nor appearance rewarded our vigil.

This confirmed my first idea that the sounds were not supernatural; but just to test the matter, I determined on Christmas eve, the anniversary of Mr. Jeremy Lester's disappearance, to keep watch by myself in the red bedchamber. Even to Clare I never mentioned my intention.

About ten, tired out with our previous vigils, we each retired to rest. Somewhat ostentatiously, perhaps, I noisily shut the door of my room, and when I opened it half an hour afterwards, no mouse could have pursued its way along the corridor with greater silence and caution than myself.

Quite in the dark I sat in the red room. For over an hour I might as well have been in my grave for anything I could see in the apartment; but at the end of that time the moon rose and cast strange lights across the floor and upon the wall of the haunted chamber.

Hitherto I had kept my watch opposite the window, now I changed my place to a corner near the door, where I was shaded from observation by the heavy hangings of the bed, and an antique wardrobe.

Still I sat on, but still no sound broke the silence. I was weary with many nights' watching, and tired of my solitary vigil, I dropped at last into a slumber from which I was awakened by hearing the door softly opened.

"John," said my sister, almost in a whisper; "John, are you here?"

"Yes, Clare," I answered; "but what are you doing up at this hour?"

"Come downstairs," she replied; "*they* are in the oak parlor."

I did not need any explanation as to whom she meant, but crept downstairs after her, warned by an uplifted hand of the necessity for silence and caution.

By the door—by the open door of the oak parlor, she paused, and we both looked in.

There was the room we left in darkness overnight, with a bright wood fire blazing on the hearth, candles on the chimney-piece, the small table pulled out from its accustomed corner, and two men seated beside it, playing at cribbage.

We could see the face of the younger player; it was that of a man of about five-and-twenty, of a man who had lived hard and wickedly; who had wasted his substance and his health; who had been while in the flesh Jeremy Lester. It would be difficult for me to say how I knew this, how in a moment I identified the features of the player with those of the man who had been missing for forty-one years—forty-one years that very night. He was dressed in the costume of a byegone period; his hair was powdered, and round his wrists there were ruffles of lace.

He looked like one who, having come from some great party, had sat down after his return home to play at cards with an intimate friend. On his little finger there sparkled a ring, in the front of his shirt there gleamed a valuable diamond. There were diamond buckles in his shoes, and, according to the fashion of his time, he wore knee-breeches and silk stockings, which showed off advantageously the shape of a remarkably good leg and ankle.

He sat opposite to the door, but never once lifted his eyes to it. His attention seemed concentrated on the cards.

For a time there was utter silence in the room, broken only by the momentous counting of the game.

In the doorway we stood, holding our breath, terrified and yet fascinated by the scene which was being acted before us.

The ashes dropped on the hearth softly and like the snow; we could hear the rustle of the cards as they were dealt out and fell upon the table; we listened to the count—fifteen-one, fifteen-two, and so forth—but there was no other word spoken till at length the player, whose face we could not see, exclaimed, "I win; the game is mine."

Then his opponent took up the cards, sorted them over negligently in his hand, put them close together, and flung the whole pack in his guest's face, exclaiming, "Cheat; liar; take that."

There was a bustle and confusion—a flinging over of chairs, and fierce gesticulation, and such a noise of passionate voices mingling, that we could not hear a sentence which was uttered.

All at once, however, Jeremy Lester strode out of the room in so great a hurry that he almost touched us where we stood; out of the room, and tramp, tramp up the staircase to the red room, whence he descended in a few minutes with a couple of rapiers under his arm.

When he reentered the room he gave, as it seemed to us, the other man his choice of the weapons, and then he flung open the window, and after ceremoniously giving place for his opponent to pass out first, he walked forth into the night air, Clare and I following.

We went through the garden and down a narrow winding walk to a smooth piece of turf sheltered from the north by a plantation of young fir trees. It was a bright moonlight night by this time, and we could distinctly see Jeremy Lester measuring off the ground.

"When you say 'three,'" he said at last to the man whose back was still towards us. They had drawn lots for the ground, and the lot had fallen against Mr. Lester. He stood thus with the moonbeams falling full upon him, and a handsomer fellow I would never desire to behold.

"One," began the other; "two," and before our kinsman had the slightest suspicion of his design, he was upon him, and his rapier through Jeremy Lester's breast. At the sight of that cowardly treachery, Clare screamed aloud. In a moment the combatants had disappeared, the moon was obscured behind a cloud, and we were standing in the shadow of the fir plantation, shivering with cold and terror.

But we knew at last what had become of the late owner of Martingdale, that he had fallen, not in fair fight, but foully murdered by a false friend.

When late on Christmas morning I awoke, it was to see a white world, to behold the ground, and trees, and shrubs all laden and covered with snow. There was snow everywhere, such snow as no person could remember having fallen for forty-one years.

"It was on just such a Christmas as this that Mr. Jeremy disappeared," remarked the old sexton to my sister who had insisted on dragging me through the snow to church, whereupon Clare fainted away and was carried into the vestry, where I made a full confession to the Vicar of all we had beheld the previous night.

At first that worthy individual rather inclined to treat the matter lightly, but when, a fortnight after, the snow melted away and the fir plantation came to be examined, he confessed there might be more things in heaven and earth than his limited philosophy had dreamed of.

In a little clear space just within the plantation, Jeremy Lester's body was found. We knew it by the ring and the diamond buckles, and the sparkling breast-pin; and Mr. Cronson, who in his capacity as magistrate came over to inspect these relics, was visibly perturbed at my narrative.

"Pray, Mr. Lester, did you in your dream see the face of—of the gentleman—your kinsman's opponent?"

"No," I answered, "he sat and stood with his back to us all the time."

"There is nothing more, of course, to be done in the matter," observed Mr. Cronson.

"Nothing," I replied; and there the affair would doubtless have terminated, but that a few days afterwards when we were dining at Cronson Park, Clare all of a sudden dropped the glass of water she was carrying to her lips, and exclaiming, "Look, John, there he is!" rose from her seat, and with a face as white as the tablecloth, pointed to a portrait hanging on the wall.

"I saw him for an instant when he turned his head towards the door as Jeremy Lester left it," she explained; "that is he."

Of what followed after this identification I have only the vaguest recollection. Servants rushed hither and thither; Mrs. Cronson dropped off her chair into hysterics; the young ladies gathered round their mamma; Mr. Cronson, trembling like one in an ague fit, attempted some kind of an explanation, while Clare kept praying to be taken away—only to be taken away.

I took her away, not merely from Cronson Park but from Martingdale. Before we left the latter place, however, I had an interview with Mr. Cronson, who said the portrait Clare had identified was that of his wife's father, the last person who saw Jeremy Lester alive.

"He is an old man now," finished Mr. Cronson, "a man of

over eighty, who has confessed everything to me. You won't bring further sorrow and disgrace upon us by making this matter public?"

I promised him I would keep silence, but the story gradually oozed out, and the Cronsons left the country.

My sister never returned to Martingdale; she married and is living in London. Though I assure her there are no strange noises now in my house, she will not visit Bedfordshire, where the "little girl" she wanted me so long ago to "think of seriously," is now my wife and the mother of my children.

RAMSEY CAMPBELL

CALLING CARD

Horrid Christmas cards from beyond the grave.

DOROTHY HARRIS stepped off the pavement and into her hall. As she stooped groaning to pick up the envelopes the front door opened, a yawn that wouldn't be suppressed. She wrestled it shut—she must ask Simon to see to it, though certainly not over Christmas—then she began to open the cards.

Here was Father Christmas, and here he was again, apparently after dieting. Here was a robin like a rosy apple with a beak, and here was an envelope whose handwriting staggered: Simon's and Margery's children, perhaps?

The card showed a church on a snowy hill. The hill was bare except for a smudge of ink. Though the card was unsigned, there was writing within. A Very Happy Christmas And A Prosperous New Year, the message should have said—but now it said

A Very Harried Christmas And No New Year. She turned back to the picture, her hands shaking. It wasn't just a smudge of ink; someone had drawn a smeary cross on the hill: a grave.

Though the name on the envelope was a watery blur, the address was certainly hers. Suddenly the house—the kitchen and living room, the two bedrooms with her memories stacked neatly against the walls—seemed far too large and dim. Without moving from the front door she phoned Margery.

"Is it Grandma?" Margery had to hush the children while she said, "You come as soon as you like, mummy."

Lark Lane was deserted. An unsold Christmas tree loitered in a shop doorway, a gargoyle craned out from the police station. Once Margery had moved away, the nearness of the police had been reassuring—not that Dorothy was nervous, like some of the old folk these days—but the police station was only a community center now.

The bus already sounded like a pub. She sat outside on the ferry, though the bench looked and felt like black ice. Lights fished in the Mersey, gulls drifted down like snowflakes from the muddy sky. A whitish object grabbed the rail, but of course it was only a gull. Nevertheless she was glad that Simon was waiting with the car at Woodside.

As soon as the children had been packed off to bed so that Father Christmas could get to work, she produced the card. It felt wet, almost slimy, though it hadn't before. Simon pointed out what she'd overlooked: the age of the stamp. "We weren't even living there then," Margery said. "You wouldn't think they would bother delivering it after sixty years."

"A touch of the Christmas spirit."

"I wish they hadn't bothered," Margery said. But her mother didn't mind now; the addressee must have died years ago. She turned the conversation to old times, to Margery's father. Later she gazed from her bedroom window, at the houses of Bebington sleeping in pairs. A man was creeping about the house, but it was only Simon, laden with presents.

In the morning the house was full of cries of delight, gleaming new toys, balls of wrapping paper big as cabbages. In the afternoon the adults, bulging with turkey and pudding, lolled in chairs. When Simon drove her home that night, Dorothy noticed that the unsold Christmas tree was still there, a scrawny glistening shape at the back of the shop doorway. As soon as Simon left, she found herself thinking about the unpleasant card. She tore it up, then went determinedly to bed.

Boxing Day was her busiest time, what with cooking the second version of Christmas dinner, and making sure the house was impeccable, and hiding small presents for the children to find. She wished she could see them more often, but they and their parents had their own lives to lead.

An insect clung to a tinsel globe on the tree. When she reached out to squash the insect it wasn't there, neither on the globe nor on the floor. Could it have been the reflection of someone thin outside the window? Nobody was there now.

She liked the house best when it was full of laughter, and it would be again soon: "We'll get a sitter," Margery promised, "and first-foot you on New Year's eve." She'd used to do that when she had lived at home—she'd waited outside at midnight of the Old Year so as to be the first to cross her mother's threshold. That reminded Dorothy to offer the children a holiday treat. Everything seemed fine, even when they went to the door to leave. "Grandma, someone's left you a present," little Denise cried.

Then she cried out, and dropped the package. Perhaps the wind had snatched it from her hands. As the package, which looked wet and moldy, struck the curb it broke open. Did its contents scuttle out and sidle away into the dark? Surely that was the play of the wind, which tumbled carton and wrapping away down the street.

Someone must have used her doorway for a wastebin, that was all. Dorothy lay in bed, listening to the wind which groped around the windowless side of the house, that faced onto the alley. She kept thinking she was on the ferry, backing away from the rail, forgetting that the rail was also behind her. Her nervousness annoyed her—she was acting like an old fogey—which was why, next afternoon, she walked to Otterspool promenade.

Gulls and planes sailed over the Mersey, which was deserted except for buoys. On the far bank, tiny towns and stalks of factory chimneys stood at the foot of an enormous frieze of clouds. Sunlight slipped through to Birkenhead and Wallasey, touching up the colors of microscopic streets; specks of windows glinted. She enjoyed none of this, for the slopping of water beneath the promenade seemed to be pacing her. Worse, she couldn't make herself go to the rail to prove that there was nothing.

Really, it was heartbreaking. One vicious card and she felt nervous in her own house. A blurred voice seemed to creep behind the carols on the radio, lowing out of tune. Next day she took her washing to Lark Lane, in search of distraction as much as anything.

The Westinghouse Laundromat was deserted. O O O, the washing machines said emptily. There was only herself, and her dervishes of clothes, and a black plastic bag almost as tall as she was. If someone had abandoned it, whatever its lumpy contents were, she could see why, for it was leaking; she smelled stagnant water. It must be a draft that made it twitch feebly. Nevertheless, if she had been able to turn off her machine she might have fled.

She mustn't grow neurotic. She still had friends to visit. The following day she went to a friend whose flat overlooked Wavertree Park. It was all very convivial—a rainstorm outside made the mince pies more warming, the chat flowed as easily as the whiskey—but she kept glancing at the thin figure who stood in the park, unmoved by the downpour. The trails of rain on the window must be lending him their color, for his skin looked like a snail's.

Eventually the 68 bus, meandering like a drunkard's monologue, took her home to Aigburth. No, the man in the park hadn't really looked as though his clothes and his body had merged into a single grayish mass. Tomorrow she was taking the children for their treat, and that would clear her mind.

She took them to the aquarium. Piranhas sank stonily, their sides glittering like Christmas cards. Toads were bubbling lumps of tar. Finny humbugs swam, and darting fish wired with light. Had one of the tanks cracked? There seemed to be a stagnant smell.

In the museum everything was under glass: shrunken heads like sewn leathery handbags, a watchmaker's workshop, buses passing as though the windows were silent films. Here was a slum street, walled in by photographs of despair, real flagstones underfoot, overhung by streetlamps on brackets. She halted between a grid and a drinking fountain; she was trapped in the dimness between blind corners, and couldn't see either way. Why couldn't she get rid of the stagnant smell? Gray forlorn faces, pressed like specimens, peered out of the walls. "Come on, quickly," she said, pretending that only the children were nervous.

She was glad of the packed crowds in Church Street, even though the children kept letting go of her hands. But the stagnant smell was trailing her, and once, when she grabbed for little Denise's hand, she clutched someone else's, which felt soft and wet. It must have been nervousness which made her fingers seem to sink into the hand.

That night she returned to the aquarium and found she was locked in. Except for the glow of the tanks, the narrow room was oppressively dark. In the nearest tank a large dead fish floated toward her, out of weeds. Now she was in the tank, her nails scrabbling at the glass, and she saw that it wasn't a fish but a snail-colored hand, which closed spongily on hers. When she woke, her scream made the house sound very empty.

At least it was New Year's eve. After tonight she could stop worrying. Why had she thought that? It only made her more nervous. Even when Margery phoned to confirm they would first-foot her, that reminded her how many hours she would be on her own. As the night seeped into the house, the emptiness grew.

A knock at the front door made her start, but it was only the

Harveys, inviting her next door for sherry and sandwiches. While she dodged a sudden rainstorm, Mr. Harvey dragged at her front door, one hand through the letter box, until the latch clicked.

After several sherries Dorothy remembered something she'd once heard. "The lady who lived next door before me—didn't she have trouble with her son?"

"He wasn't right in the head. He got so he'd go for anyone, even if he'd never met them before. She got so scared of him she locked him out one New Year's eve. They say he threw himself in the river, though they never found the body."

Dorothy wished she hadn't asked. She thought of the body, rotting in the depths. She must go home, in case Simon and Margery arrived. The Harveys were next door if she needed them.

The sherries had made her sleepy. Only the ticking of her clock, clipping away the seconds, kept her awake. Twenty past eleven. The splashing from the gutters sounded like wet footsteps pacing outside the window. She had never noticed she could smell the river in her house. She wished she had stayed longer with the Harveys; she would have been able to hear Simon's car.

Twenty to twelve. Surely they wouldn't wait until midnight. She switched on the radio for company. A master of ceremonies was making people laugh; a man was laughing thickly, sounding waterlogged. Was he a drunk in the street? He wasn't on the radio. She mustn't brood; why, she hadn't put out the sherry glasses; that was something to do, to distract her from the intolerably measured counting of the clock, the silenced radio, the emptiness displaying her sounds—

Though the knock seemed enormously loud, she didn't start. They were here at last, though she hadn't heard the car. It was New Year's day. She ran, and had reached the front door when the phone shrilled. That startled her so badly that she snatched the door open before lifting the receiver.

Nobody was outside—only a distant uproar of cheers and

bells and horns—and Margery was on the phone. "We've been held up, mummy. There was an accident in the tunnel. We'll be over as soon as we can."

Then who had knocked? It must have been a drunk; she heard him stumbling beside the house, thumping on her window. He'd better take himself off, or she would call Mr. Harvey to deal with him. But she was still inside the doorway when she saw the object on her step.

Good God, was it a rat? No, just a shoe, so ancient that it looked stuffed with mold. It wasn't mold, only a rotten old sock. There was something in the sock, something that smelled of stagnant water and worse. She stooped to peer at it, and then she was struggling to close the door, fighting to make the latch click, no breath to spare for a scream. She'd had her first foot, and now—hobbling doggedly alongside the house, its hands slithering over the wall—here came the rest of the body.

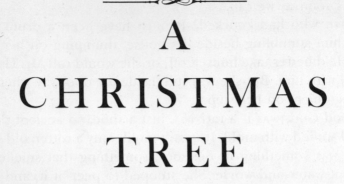

CHARLES DICKENS

A CHRISTMAS TREE

A vision of Christmas past and present, ghosts and all.

I HAVE been looking on, this evening, at a merry company of children assembled round that pretty German toy, a Christmas tree. The tree was planted in the middle of a great round table, and towered high above their heads. It was brilliantly lighted by a multitude of little tapers; and everywhere sparkled and glittered with bright objects. There were rosy-cheeked dolls, hiding behind the green leaves; there were real watches (with movable hands, at least, and an endless capacity of being wound up) dangling from innumerable twigs; there were French polished tables, chairs, bedsteads, wardrobes, eight-day clocks, and various other articles of domestic furniture (wonderfully made, in tin, at Wolverhampton), perched among the boughs, as if in preparation for some fairy housekeeping; there were jolly, broad-faced little men, much more agreeable in appearance than many real men—and no wonder, for their heads took off, and showed them to be full of sugarplums; there were fiddles and drums; there were tambourines, books, work-boxes, paint-boxes, sweetmeat-boxes, peep-show-boxes, all kinds of boxes; there were trinkets for the elder girls, far brighter than any grown-up gold and jewels; there were baskets and pincushions in all devices; there were guns, swords, and banners; there were witches standing in enchanted rings of pasteboard, to tell fortunes; there were teetotums, humming-tops, needle-cases, pen-wipers, smelling-bottles, conversation-cards, bouquet-holders; real fruit, made artificially dazzling with gold leaf; imitation apples, pears and walnuts, crammed with surprises; in short as a pretty child, before me, delightedly whispered to another pretty child, her bosom friend, "There was everything, and more." This motley collection of odd objects clustering on the tree like magic fruit, and flashing back the bright looks directed towards it from every side—some of the diamond-eyes admiring it were hardly on a level with the table, and a few were languishing in timid wonder on the bosoms of pretty mothers, aunts, and nurses—made a lively realization of the fancies of childhood; and set me thinking how all the trees that grow and all the things that come into existence on the earth, have their wild adornments at that well-remembered time.

Being now at home again, and alone, the only person in the house awake, my thoughts are drawn back, by a fascination which I do not care to resist, to my own childhood. I begin to consider, what do we all remember best upon the branches of the Christmas tree of our own young Christmas days, by which we climbed to real life.

Straight, in the middle of the room, cramped in the freedom of its growth by no encircling walls or soon-reached ceiling, a shadowy tree arises; and, looking up into the dreamy brightness of its top—for I observe, in this tree the singular property that it appears to grow downward toward the earth—I look into my youngest Christmas recollections!

All toys at first, I find. Up yonder among the green holly and red berries, is the Tumbler with his hands in his pockets, who wouldn't lie down, but whenever he was put upon the floor, persisted in rolling his fat body about, until he rolled himself still, and brought those lobster eyes of his to bear upon me—when I affected to laugh very much, but in my heart of hearts was extremely doubtful of him. Close beside him is that infernal snuffbox, out of which there sprang a demoniacal Counselor in a black gown, with an obnoxious head of hair, and a red cloth mouth, wide open, who was not to be endured on any terms, but could not be put away either; for he used suddenly, in a highly magnified state, to fly out of mammoth snuffboxes in dreams, when least expected. Nor is the frog with cobbler's wax on his tail, far off; for there was no knowing where he wouldn't jump; and when he flew over the candle, and came upon one's hand with that spotted back—red on a green ground—he was horrible. The cardboard lady in a blue silk skirt, who was stood up against the candlestick to dance, and whom I see on the same branch, was milder, and was beautiful; but I can't say as much for the larger cardboard man, who used to be hung against the wall and pulled by a string; there was a sinister expression in that nose of his; and when he got his legs round his neck (which he very often did), he was ghastly, and not a creature to be alone with.

When did that dreadful Mask first look at me? Who put it on, and why was I so frightened that the sight of it is an era in my life? It is not a hideous visage in itself; it is even meant to be droll; why then were its stolid features so intolerable? Surely not because it hid the wearer's face. An apron would have done as much; and though I should have preferred even the apron away, it would not have been absolutely insupportable, like the mask? Was it the immovability of the mask? The doll's face was immovable, but I was not afraid of *her*. Perhaps that fixed and set change coming over a real face, infused into my quickened heart some remote suggestion and dread of the universal change that is to come on every face, and make it still? Nothing reconciled me to it. No drummers, from whom proceeded a melancholy chirping on the turning of a handle; no regiment of soldiers, with a mute band, taken out of a box, and fitted, one by one, upon a stiff and lazy little set of lazy-tongs; no old woman, made of wires and a brown-paper composition, cutting up a pie for two small children; could give me a permanent comfort, for a long time. Nor was it any satisfaction to be shown the Mask, and see that it was made of paper, or to have it locked up and be assured that no one wore it. The mere recollection of that fixed face, the mere knowledge of its existence anywhere, was sufficient to awake me in the night all perspiration and horror, with, "Oh I know it's coming! Oh the mask!"

I never wondered what the dear old donkey with the panniers—there he is!—was made of, then! His hide was real to the touch, I recollect. And the great black horse with round red spots all over him—the horse that I could even get upon—I never wondered what had brought him to that strange condition, or thought that such a horse was not commonly seen at Newmarket. The four horses of no color, next to him, that went into the wagon of cheeses, and could be taken out and stabled under the piano, appear to have bits of fur-tippet for their tails, and other bits for their manes, and to stand on pegs instead of legs, but it was not so when they were brought home for a Christmas present. They were all right, then; neither was their harness unceremoniously nailed into their chests, as appears to be the case now. The tinkling works of the music-cart, I *did* find out, to be made of quill toothpicks and wire; and I always thought that little tumbler in his shirtsleeves, perpetually swarming up one side of a wooden frame, and coming down, head-foremost, on the other, rather a weakminded person—though good-natured; but the Jacob's Ladder, next him, made of little squares of red wood, that went flapping and clattering over one another, each developing a different picture, and the whole enlivened by small bells, was a mighty marvel and a great delight.

Ah! The Doll's house!—of which I was not proprietor, but where I visited. I don't admire the Houses of Parliament half so much as that stone-fronted mansion with real glass windows, and doorsteps, and a real balcony—greener that I ever see now, except at watering-places; and even they afford but a poor imitation. And though it *did* open all at once, the entire housefront (which was a blow, I admit, as canceling the fiction of a staircase), it was but to shut it up again, and I could believe. Even open, there were three distinct rooms in it: a sitting-room and bedroom, elegantly furnished, and, best of all, a kitchen, with uncommonly soft fire-irons, a plentiful assortment of diminutive utensils—oh, the warming-pan!—and a tin mancook in profile, who was always going to fry two fish. What Barmecide justice have I done to the noble feasts wherein the set of wooden platters figured, each with its own peculiar delicacy, as a ham or turkey, glued tight on to it, and garnished with something green, which I recollect as moss! Could all the Temperance Societies of these later days, united, give me such a tea-drinking as I have had through the means of yonder little set of blue crockery, which really would hold liquid (it ran out of the small wooden cask, I recollect, and tasted of matches), and which made tea, nectar. And if the two legs of the ineffectual little sugar tongs did tumble over one another, and want purpose, like Punch's hands, what does it matter? And if I did once shriek out, as a poisoned child, and strike the fashionable company with consternation, by reason of having drunk a little teaspoon, inadvertently dissolved in too hot tea, I was never the worse for it, except by a powder!

Upon the next branches of the tree, lower down, hard by the green roller and miniature gardening tools, how thick the books begin to hang. Thin books, in themselves, at first, but many of them, and with deliciously smooth covers of bright red or green. What fat black letters to begin with! "A was an archer, and shot at a frog." Of course he was. He was an apple-pie also, and there he is! He was a good many things in his time, was A, and so were most of his friends, except X, who had so little versatility, that I never knew him to get beyond Xerxes or Xantippe—like Y, who was always confined to a Yacht or a Yew Tree; and Z condemned forever to be a Zebra or a Zany. But, now, the very tree itself changes, and becomes a beanstalk—the marvelous beanstalk up which Jack climbed to the Giant's house! And now, those dreadfully interesting, double-headed giants, with their clubs over their shoulders, begin to stride along the boughs in a perfect throng, dragging knights and ladies home for dinner by the hair of their heads. And Jack—how noble, with his sword of sharpness, and his shoes of swiftness! Again those old meditations come upon me as I gaze up at him; and I debate within myself whether there was more than one Jack (which I am loath to believe possible), or only one genuine original admirable Jack, who achieved all the recorded exploits.

Good for Christmas time is the ruddy color of the cloak, in which—the tree making a forest of itself for her to trip through, with her basket—Little Red Riding Hood comes to me one Christmas eve to give me information of the cruelty and treachery of that dissembling Wolf who ate her grandmother, without making any impression on his appetite, and then ate her, after making that ferocious joke about his teeth. She was my first love. I felt that if I could have married Little Red Riding Hood, I should have known perfect bliss. But, it was not to be; and there was nothing for it but to look out the Wolf in the Noah's Ark there, and put him late in the procession on the table, as a monster who was to be degraded. Oh the wonderful Noah's Ark! It was not found seaworthy when put in a washing tub, and the animals were crammed in at the roof, and needed to have their legs well shaken down before they could be got in, even there—and then, ten to one but they began to tumble out at the door, which was but imperfectly fastened with a wire latch—but what was *that* against it! Consider the noble fly, a size or two smaller than the elephant; the ladybird, the butterfly—all triumphs of art! Consider the goose, whose feet were so small, and whose balance was so indifferent, that he usually tumbled forward, and knocked down all the animal creation. Consider Noah and his family, like idiotic tobacco-stoppers; and how the leopard stuck to warm little fingers; and how the tails of the larger animals used gradually to resolve themselves into frayed bits of string!

Hush! Again a forest, and somebody up in a tree—not Robin Hood, not Valentine, not the Yellow Dwarf (I have passed him and all Mother Bunch's wonders, without mention), but an Eastern King with a glittering cimeter and turban. By Allah! two Eastern Kings, for I see another, looking over his shoulder! Down upon the grass at the tree's foot, lies the full length of a coal-black Giant, stretched asleep, with his head in a lady's lap; and near them is a glass box, fastened with four locks of shining steel, in which he keeps the lady prisoner when he is awake. I see the four keys at his girdle now. The lady makes signs to the two kings in the tree, who softly descend. It is the setting-in of the bright Arabian Nights.

Oh, now all common things become uncommon and enchanted to me! All lamps are wonderful; all rings are talismans. Common flowerpots are full of treasure, with a little earth scattered on the top; trees are for Ali Baba to hide in; beefsteaks are to throw down into the Valley of Diamonds, that the precious stones may stick to them, and be carried by the eagles to their nests, whence the traders, with loud cries, will scare them. Tarts are made, according to the recipe of the Vizier's son of Bussorah, who turned pastry cook after he was set down in his drawers at the gate of Damascus; cobblers are all Mustaphas, and in the habit of sewing up people cut into four pieces, to whom they are taken blindfold.

Any iron ring let into stone is the entrance to a cave which only waits for the magician, and the little fire, and the necromancy, that will make the earth shake. All the dates imported come from the same tree as that unlucky date, with whose shell the merchant knocked out the eye of the genie's invisible son. All olives are of the stock of that fresh fruit, concerning which the Commander of the Faithful overheard the boy conduct the fictitious trial of the fraudulent olive merchant; all apples are akin to the apple purchased (with two others) from the Sultan's gardener for three sequins, and which the tall black slave stole from the child. All dogs are associated with the dog, really a transformed man, who jumped upon the baker's counter, and put his paw on the piece of bad money. All rice recalls the rice which the awful lady, who was a ghoul, could only peck by grains, because of her nightly feasts in the burial place. My very rocking horse—there he is, with his nostrils turned completely inside out, indicative of Blood!—should have a peg in his neck, by virtue thereof to fly away with me, as the wooden horse did with the Prince of Persia, in the sight of all his father's Court.

Yes, on every object that I recognize among those upper branches of my Christmas tree, I see this fairy light! When I wake in bed, at daybreak, on the cold dark winter mornings, the white snow dimly beheld, outside, through the frost on the windowpane, I hear Dinarzade. "Sister, sister, if you are yet awake, I pray you finish the history of the Young King of the Black Islands." Scheherazade replies, "If my lord the Sultan will suffer me to live another day, sister, I will not only finish that, but tell you a more wonderful story yet." Then, the gracious Sultan goes out, giving no orders for the execution, and we all three breathe again.

At this height of my tree I begin to see, cowering among the leaves—it may be born of turkey, or of pudding, or mince pie, or of these many fancies, jumbled with Robinson Crusoe on his desert island, Philip Quarll among the monkeys, Sandford and Merton with Mr. Barlow, Mother Bunch, and the Mask—or it may be the result of indigestion, assisted by imagination and overdoctoring—a prodigious nightmare. It is so exceedingly indistinct, that I don't know why it's frightful—but I know it is. I can only make out that it is an immense array of shapeless things, which appear to be planted on a vast exaggeration of the lazy tongs that used to bear the toy soldiers, and to be slowly coming close to my eyes, and receding to an immeasurable distance. When it comes closest, it is worst. In connection with it I descry remembrances of winter nights incredibly long; of being sent early to bed, as a punishment for some small offense, and waking in two hours, with a sensation of having been asleep two nights; of the laden hopelessness of morning ever dawning; and the oppression of a weight of remorse.

And now, I see a wonderful row of little lights rise smoothly out of the ground, before a vast green curtain. Now, a bell rings—a magic bell, which still sounds in my ears, unlike all other bells—and music plays, amidst a buzz of voices, and a fragrant smell of orange peel and oil. Anon, the magic bell commands the music to cease, and the great green curtain rolls itself up majestically, and The Play begins! The devoted dog of Montargis avenges the death of his master, foully murdered in the Forest of Bondy; and a humorous Peasant with a red nose and a very little hat, whom I take from this hour forth to my bosom as a friend (I think he was a Waiter or an Hostler at a village Inn, but many years have passed since he and I have met), remarks that the sassigassity of that dog is indeed surprising; and evermore this jocular conceit will live in my remembrance fresh and unfading, overtopping all possible jokes, unto the end of time. Or now, I learn with bitter tears how poor Jane Shore, dressed all in white, and with her brown hair hanging down, went starving through the streets; or how George Barnwell killed the worthiest uncle that ever man had, and was afterwards so sorry for it that he ought to have been let off. Comes swift to comfort me, the Pantomime—stupendous Phenomenon!—when Clowns are shot from loaded mortars into the great chandelier, bright constellation that it is; when Harlequins, covered all over with scales of pure gold, twist and sparkle, like amazing fish; when Pantaloon (whom I deem it no irreverence to compare in my own mind to my grandfather) puts red-hot pokers in his pocket, and cries "Here's somebody coming!" or taxes the Clown with petty larceny, by saying, "Now I sawed you do it!" when Everything is capable, with the greatest ease, of being changed into Anything; and "Nothing is, but thinking makes it so." Now, too, I perceive my first experience of the dreary sensation—often to return in after life—of being unable, next day, to get back to the dull settled world; of wanting to live forever in the bright atmosphere I have quitted; of doting on the little Fairy, with the wand like a celestial Barber's Pole, and pining for a Fairy immortality along with her. Ah she comes back, in many shapes, as my eye wanders down the branches of my Christmas tree, and goes as often, and has never yet stayed by me!

Out of this delight springs the toy theater—there it is, with its familiar proscenium, and ladies in feathers, in the boxes!—and all its attendant occupation with paste posing rows of trees seem to fall solemnly back on either side, to give us place. At intervals, all day, a frightened hare has shot across this whitened turf; or the distant clatter of a herd of deer trampling the hard frost, has, for the minute, crushed the silence too. Their watchful eyes beneath the fern may be shining now, if we could see them, like the icy dewdrops on the leaves; but they are still, and all is still. And so, the lights growing larger, and the trees falling back before us, and closing up again behind us, as if to forbid retreat, we come to the house.

There is probably a smell of roasted chestnuts and other good comfortable things all the time, for we are telling winter stories—ghost stories, or more shame for us—round the Christmas fire; and we have never stirred, except to draw a little nearer to it. But, no matter for that. We came to the house, and it is an old house, full of great chimneys where wood is burnt on ancient dogs upon the hearth, and grim portraits (some of them with grim legends, too) lower distrustfully from the oaken panels of the walls. We are a middle-aged nobleman, and we make a generous supper with our host and hostess and their guests—it being Christmas time, and the old house full of company—and then we go to bed. Our room is a very old room. It is hung with tapestry. We don't like the portrait of a cavalier in green, over the fireplace. There are great black beams in the ceiling, and there is a great black bedstead, supported at the foot by two great black figures, who seem to have come off a couple of tombs in the old baronial church in the park, for our particular accommodation. But, we are not a superstitious nobleman, and we don't mind. Well! we dismiss our servant, lock the door, and sit before the fire in our dressing gown, musing about a great many things. At length we go to bed. Well! we can't sleep. We toss and tumble, and can't sleep. The embers on the hearth burn fitfully and make the room look ghostly. We can't help peeping out over the counterpane, at the two black figures and the cavalier—that wicked-looking cavalier—in green. In the flickering light, they seem to advance and retire: which, though we are not by any means a superstitious nobleman, is not agreeable. Well! we get nervous—more and more nervous. We say "This is very foolish, but we can't stand this; we'll pretend to be ill, and knock up somebody." Well! we are just going to do it, when the locked door opens, and there comes in a young woman, deadly pale, and with long fair hair, who glides to the fire, and sits down in the chair we have left there, wringing her hands. Then, we notice that her clothes are wet. Our tongue cleaves to the roof of our mouth, and we can't speak; but, we observe her accurately. Her clothes are wet; her long hair is dabbled with moist mud; she is dressed in the fashion of two hundred years ago; and she has at her girdle a bunch of rusty keys.

Well! there she sits, and we can't even faint, we are in such a state about it. Presently she gets up, and tries all the locks in the room with the rusty keys, which won't fit one of them; then, she fixes her eyes on the portrait of the cavalier in green, and says, in a low, terrible voice, "The stags know it!" After that, she wrings her hands again, passes the bedside, and goes out at the door. We hurry on our dressing gown, seize our pistols (we always travel with pistols), and are following, when we find the door locked. We turn the key, look out into the dark gallery; no one there. We wander away, and try to find our servant. Can't be done. We pace the gallery till daybreak; then return to our deserted room, fall asleep, and are awakened by our servant (nothing ever haunts *him*) and the shining sun. Well! we make a wretched breakfast, and all the company say we look queer. After breakfast, we go over the house with our host, and then we take him to the portrait of the cavalier in green, and then it all comes out. He was false to a young housekeeper once attached to that family, and famous for her beauty, who drowned herself in a pond, and whose body was discovered, after a long time, because the stags refused to drink of the water. Since which, it has been whispered that she traverses the house at midnight (but goes especially to that room where the cavalier in green was wont to sleep), trying the old locks with the rusty keys. Well! We tell our host of what we have seen, and a shade comes over his features, and he begs it may be hushed up; and so it is. But, it's all true; and we said so, before we died (we are dead now) to many responsible people.

There is no end to the old houses, with resounding galleries, and dismal state bedchambers, and haunted wings shut up for many years, through which we may ramble, with an agreeable creeping up our back, and encounter any number of ghosts, but (it is worthy of remark perhaps) reducible to a very few general types and classes; for, ghosts have little originality, and "walk" in a beaten track. Thus, it comes to pass, that a certain room in a certain old hall, where a certain bad lord, baronet, knight, or gentleman, shot himself, has certain planks in the floor from which the blood *will not* be taken out. You may scrape and scrape, as the present owner has done, or plane and plane, as his father did, or scrub and scrub, as his grandfather did, or burn and burn with strong acids, as his great-grandfather did, but, there the blood will still be—no redder and no paler—no more and no less—always just the same. Thus, in such another house there is a haunted door, that never will keep open; or another door that never will keep shut; or a haunted sound of a spinning wheel, or a hammer, or a footstep, or a cry, or a sigh, or a horse's tramp, or the rattling of a chain. Or else, there is a turret clock, which, at the midnight hour, strikes thirteen when the head of the family is going to die; or a shadowy, immovable black carriage which at such a time is always seen by somebody, waiting near the great gates in the stable yard. Or thus, it came to pass how Lady Mary went to pay a visit at a large wild house in the

Scottish Highlands, and, being fatigued with her long journey, retired to bed early, and innocently said, next morning, at the breakfast table, "How odd, to have so late a party last night, in this remote place, and not to tell me of it, before I went to bed!" Then, every one asked Lady Mary what she meant? Then, Lady Mary replied, "Why, all night long, the carriages were driving round and round the terrace, underneath my window!" Then, the owner of the house turned pale, and so did his Lady, and Charles Macdoodle of Macdoodle signed to Lady Mary to say no more, and every one was silent. After breakfast, Charles Macdoodle told Lady Mary that it was a tradition in the family that those rumbling carriages on the terrace betokened death. And so it proved, for, two months afterwards, the Lady of the mansion died. And Lady Mary, who was a Maid of Honor at Court, often told this story to the old Queen Charlotte, by this token that the old King always said, "Eh, eh? What, what? Ghosts, ghosts? No such thing, no such thing!" And never left off saying so, until he went to bed.

Or, a friend of somebody's, whom most of us know, when he was a young man at college, had a particular friend, with whom he made the compact that, if it were possible for the Spirit to return to this earth after its separation from the body, he of the twain who first died, should reappear to the other. In course of time, this compact was forgotten by our friend; the two young men having progressed in life, and taken diverging paths that were wide asunder. But, one night, many years afterwards, our friend being in the north of England, and staying for the night in an inn, on the Yorkshire Moors, happened to look out of bed; and there, in the moonlight, leaning on a bureau near the window steadfastly regarding him, saw his old college friend! The appearance being solemnly addressed, replied, in a kind of whisper, but very audibly, "Do not come near me. I am dead. I am here to redeem my promise. I come from another world, but may not disclose its secrets!" Then, the whole form becoming paler, melted, as it were, into the moonlight, and faded away.

Or, there was the daughter of the first occupier of the picturesque Elizabethan house, so famous in our neighborhood. You have heard about her? No! Why. *She* went out one summer evening, at twilight, when she was a beautiful girl, just seventeen years of age, to gather flowers in the garden; and presently came running, terrified, into the hall to her father, saying, "Oh, dear father, I have met myself!" He took her in his arm, and told her it was fancy, but she said "Oh no! I met myself in the broad walk, and I was pale and gathering withered flowers, and I turned my head, and held them up!" And, that night, she died; and a picture of her story was begun, though never finished, and they say it is somewhere in the house to this day, with its face to the wall.

Or, the uncle of my brother's wife was riding home on horseback,one mellow evening at sunset, when, in a green lane close to his own house, he saw a man standing before him, in the very center of the narrow way. "Why does that man in the cloak stand there!" he thought. "Does he want me to ride over him?" But the figure never moved. He felt a strange sensation at seeing it so still, but slackened his trot and rode forward. When he was so close to it, as almost to touch it with his stirrup, his horse shied, and the figure glided up the bank, in a curious, unearthly manner—backward, and without seeming to use its feet—and was gone. The uncle of my brother's wife, exclaiming, "Good Heavens! It's my cousin Harry, from Bombay!" put spurs to his horse, which was suddenly in a profuse sweat, and, wondering at such strange behavior, dashed round to the front of his house. There he saw the same figure, just passing in at the long French window of the drawing room, opening on the ground. He threw his bridle to a servant, and hastened in after it. His sister was sitting there, alone. "Alice, where's my cousin Harry?" "Your cousin Harry, John?" "Yes. From Bombay. I met him in the lane just now, and saw him enter here, this instant." Not a creature had been seen by any one; and in that hour and minute, as it afterwards appeared, this cousin died in India.

Or, it was a certain sensible old maiden lady, who died at ninety-nine, and retained her faculties to the last, who really did see the Orphan Boy; a story which has often been incorrectly told, but, of which the real truth is this—because it is, in fact, a story belonging to our family—and she was a connection of our family. When she was about forty years of age, and still an uncommonly fine woman (her lover died young, which was the reason why she never married, though she had many offers), she went to stay at a place in Kent, which her brother, an Indian Merchant, had newly bought. There was a story that this place had once been held in trust, by the guardian of a young boy: who was himself the next heir, and who killed the young boy by harsh and cruel treatment. She knew nothing of that. It has been said that there was a cage in her bedroom in which the guardian used to put the boy. There was no such thing. There was only a closet. She went to bed, made no alarm whatever in the night, and in the morning said composedly to her maid when she came in, "Who is the pretty, forlorn-looking child who has been peeping out of that closet all night?" The maid replied by giving a loud scream, and instantly decamping. She was surprised; but she was a woman of remarkable strength of mind, and she dressed herself and went downstairs, and closeted herself with her brother. "Now, Walter," she said, "I have been disturbed all night by a pretty, forlorn-looking boy, who has been constantly peeping out of that closet in my room, which I can't open. This is some trick." "I am afraid not, Charlotte," said he, "for it is the legend of the house. It is the Orphan Boy. What did he do?" "He opened the door softly," said she, "and peeped out. Sometimes, he came a step or two into the room. Then, I called to him, to encourage him, and he shrank, and shuddered, and crept in again, and shut the door." "The closet has no communication, Charlotte," said her brother, "with any other part of the house, and it's nailed up." This was undeniably true, and it took two carpenters a whole forenoon to get it open, for examination. Then, she was satisfied that she had seen the Orphan Boy. But, the wild and terrible part of the story is, that he was also seen by three of her brother's sons, in succession, who all died young. On the occasion of each child being taken ill, he came home in a heat, twelve hours before, and said, Oh, Mamma, he had been playing under a particular oak tree, in a certain meadow, with a strange boy—a pretty, forlorn-looking boy, who was very timid, and made signs! From fatal experience, the parents came to know that this was the Orphan Boy, and that the course of that child whom he chose for his little playmate was surely run.

Legion is the name of the German castles, where we sit up alone to wait for the Specter—where we are shown into a room, made comparatively cheerful for our reception—where we glance round at the shadows, thrown on the blank walls by the crackling fire—where we feel very lonely when the village innkeeper and his pretty daughter have retired, after laying down a fresh store of wood upon the hearth, and setting forth on the small table such supper cheer as a cold roast capon, bread, grapes, and a flash of old Rhine wine—where the reverberating doors close on their retreat, one after another, like so many peals of sullen, thunder—and where, about the small hours of the night, we come into the knowledge of divers supernatural mysteries. Legion is the name of the haunted German students, in whose society we draw yet nearer to the fire, while the schoolboy in the corner opens his eyes wide and round, and flies off the footstool he has chosen for his seat, when the door accidentally blows open. Vast is the crop of such fruit, shining on our Christmas tree; in blossom, almost at the very top; ripening all down the boughs!

Among the later toys and fancies hanging there—as idle often and less pure—be the images once associated with the sweet old Waits, the softened music in the night, ever unalterable! Encircled by the social thoughts of Christmas time, still let the benignant figure of my childhood stand unchanged! In every cheerful image and suggestion that the season brings, may the bright star that rested above the poor roof, be the star of all the Christian world! A moment's pause, O vanishing tree, of which the lower boughs are dark to me as yet, and let me look once more! I know there are blank spaces on thy branches, where eyes that I have loved, have shone and smiled; from which they are departed. But, far above, I see the raiser of the dead girl, and the Widow's Son; and God is good! If Age be hiding for me in the unseen portion of thy downward growth, O may I, with a gray head, turn a child's heart to that figure yet, and a child's trustfulness and confidence!

Now, the tree is decorated with bright merriment, and song, and dance, and cheerfulness. And they are welcome. Innocent and welcome be they ever held, beneath the branches of the Christmas tree, which cast no gloomy shadow! But, as it sinks into the ground, I hear a whisper going through the leaves. "This, in commemoration of the law of love and kindness, mercy and compassion. This, in remembrance of Me!"